Comparative Tax Jurisprudence: Germany and Japan

Comparative Tax Jurisprudence: Germany and Japan

Takeshi Iizuka, Ph.D., J.D., C.P.A.
Chairman, The TKC National Federation
of Public Accountants

To Dr. Wilfried Dann
from Dr. Dr. Takeshi Iizuka

New York University Press
New York and London

NEW YORK UNIVERSITY PRESS
New York and London

Copyright © 1993 by New York University
All rights reserved

Library of Congress Cataloging-in-Publication Data
Iizuka, Takeshi, 1918–
    Comparative tax jurisprudence : Germany and Japan / Takeshi
Iizuka.
    p. cm.
    Includes bibliographical references and index.
    ISBN 0-8147-3755-2 (acid-free paper)
    1. Taxation—Law and legislation—Germany. 2. Taxation—Law and
legislation—Japan. I. Title.
K4460.4.I38   1993
343.4304—dc20   92-42207
[344.3034]   CIP

New York University Press books are printed on acid-free paper,
and their binding materials are chosen for strength and durability.

Manufactured in the United States of America

c 10 9 8 7 6 5 4 3 2 1

Contents

Preface   vii

Part One

1. The Essence of the Concept of the Principles of Regular Accounting   3

2. The Principles of Regular Accounting Viewed as Moral Obligations of a Positive Law   13

3. The Principle of "Timeliness"   29

4. The Principle of "Materiality" and Its Criticism   36

Part Two

5. Erroneous Theories of Dr. Kotaro Tanaka   51

6. Critical Review of the Opinions of Respectable Japanese Scholars: Part I   57

7. Critical Review of the Opinions of Respectable Japanese Scholars: Part II   73

8. Fair Accounting Practice in the Commercial Code of Japan   87

Part Three

9. Calculation Regulations in the Federal Republic of Germany: Part I   105

10. Calculation Regulations in the Federal Republic of Germany: Part II   122

11. Calculation Regulations in the Federal Republic of Germany: Part III   134

12. The Formation of an Especially Close Connection between Civil Law and the Tax Laws   152

13. The Calculation Regulations in the United States and England   180

Part Four

14. The Problems of the Fourth EC Guideline and the Seventh EC Guideline   197

15. Problems Relating to Union Européenne des Experts Comptables, Economiques et Financiers (U.E.C.)   228

16. The Problem of the "Declaration of Completeness"   240

17. Principles of Regular Bookkeeping and Electronic Data Processing   250

References   261

Index   271

Preface

The nucleus of this book was my previous monograph entitled: "Verifiable Bookkeeping Records," which was serialized in twenty-six parts over the course of three years (June 1979 to June 1982) in the Japan Society of Accounting's journal, *Accounting*, published in Tokyo by Moriyama Shoten. Since that time, I have added some material and done some rewriting, and the present book is the fruit of those labors.

I would like to acknowledge that the publication of the original monograph in *Accounting* was entirely dependent on the good offices, encouragement, and kind guidance of Dr. Kiyoshi Kurosawa, who holds a doctorate in Business Economics, has been an honorary professor at Yokohama National University, and has assumed the post of the Highest Adviser of the TKC National Federation of Public Accountants. Approaching Dr. Kurosawa was suggested to me by my respected teacher, the late Professor Tsunejiro Nakamura. He was a Doctor of Economics and a former professor at Fukushima Higher Commercial College and the University of Tokyo.

This monograph originated in December 1962, however, when I was ordered to write a doctoral thesis in tax jurisprudence by Masaaki Katsumoto, an honorary professor of Tohoku University, a former Dean of the Faculty of Jurisprudence of Senshu University, and a Doctor of Laws. Through the good offices of Dr. Katsumoto, in April 1963, I enrolled in the late Professor Katsujiro Tanaka's postgraduate lecture course. Dr. Tanaka was also a Doctor of Laws, a former professor of the Faculty of Jurisprudence, Senshu University, and a former law adviser to the National Tax Administration Agency. Although I continued to be enrolled in the course of law at the Faculty of Jurisprudence and Literature of the Tohoku Imperial University, I rarely attended the designated lecture classes and was one of the unworthy students. However, Dr. Katsumoto was kind enough to recommend me to an American lawyer named J. B. Anderson as an adviser on tax jurisprudence. Later, Dr. Katsumoto also recommended me for the position of adviser in charge of auditing for the American President Lines, which was then the largest shipping company in the world. If it were not for the good offices and kind guidance offered by the scholars mentioned above, this book would not have been written.

A human being has the essential qualities to live independently so long as he is left alone to do so. In the world of scholarship, however, one cannot progress until one absorbs and digests the work of previous scholars. Contrary to the expectations of Professors Nakamura and Katsumoto, I was irregular in attending lectures, not only at Fukushima Higher Commercial College but also at Tohoku Imperial University. The reason for this was that the pursuit of the principle of how to lead my life was the largest problem of my younger days. For a time, I had given myself up entirely to the ascetic practice of *Zazen* (sit-in meditation) under the cordial tutorial guidance of the Reverend Yoshio Ueki of the Ungenji Temple in Mt. Nasu and the Reverend Shoten Miura of the Zuiganji Temple in Matsushima.

In my personal reminiscences as the President of the TKC National Federation, which is composed of more than five thousand Certified Public Accountants and Licensed Tax Practitioners and is a nationwide organization due to its use of computerized accounting systems, I acknowledge that the source of my energy in completing this monograph, in the midst of the pressure of other work, can be found in the discipline given me by the Reverends Yoshio Ueki and Shoten Miura. Before writing this monograph, I planned to consult approximately five thousand volumes of foreign literature from Great Britain, the United States, Germany, France, and so forth. It was my hope to surpass the feat of Kukai Kobodaishi, who, 1650 years ago, wrote the spiritual book *Ju-Jyu-*

Shin-Ron at the age of sixty and after he had looked at over six hundred foreign references. I regret to say that I had to stop after consulting less than one-twentieth of the references I had intended to look at. I tried my best, but my achievement has fallen far short of that of Kukai Kobodaishi, who has no equal in history.

In this monograph, I was anxious to pose counterarguments to the opinions of several hundred noted scholars, not only in Japan, but also in Europe and America. The reason for this was that I have been greatly inspired by the words of Professor Gustav Radbruch, the professor of the Philosophy of Jurisprudence at the University of Berlin who said: "The personality is developed through selfless objectivity." At the same time, Zen requests the experience of conclusive evidence of the non-real existence of "ego" as the fixed real existence. There is a line of connection between these two theories, and they are the underpinnings of this monograph. I was pleased when Mr. Heinz Sebiger, one of the senior managing staff of the Tax Jurisprudence Learned Society in the Federal Republic of Germany, informed me in October 1982 that C. H. Beck Company, the largest publishing company in the Federal Republic of Germany, was going to publish my monograph.

Finally, I must remind my readers that tax jurisprudence has been emerging as more interdisciplinary, extending even to the study of administrative laws, the state, and the philosophy of jurisprudence, to say nothing of accounting, business economics, bookkeeping, and the study of commercial law.

For the completion of this book, I am greatly indebted to the assistance of Mr. Koume, the Editor-in-Chief, and Mr. Tsuchiya of Moriyama Shoten. Moreover, Mr. Eiichi Tanaka and Mr. Keisuke Matsumoto, who belong to the TKC International Division, were kind enough to compile the list of references and an index and to do all the proofreading. I would like to express my profound appreciation by citing, in particular, their names here.

                    TAKESHI IIZUKA
                    At a temporary abode in Shonan area

Part One

1

The Essence of the Concept of the Principles of Regular Accounting

It was in Prussia, in the eighteenth century, that the concept of "orderly books" was introduced into law for the first time in history. The concept of "regular accounting principles," however, came on stage in the form of a law for the first time as Article 38 of the German Commercial Code of 1897. It is over eighty years since the concept, which established the standard for a merchant's responsibility to keep accounts, appeared in history clad in today's attire. At this stage, however, it is necessary for us to ascertain the true character of this concept.

The reason is that Japan's Corporate Accounting Principles and the Enforcement Regulations for the Income Tax Law have used the German term just as it is, after translating it literally into Japanese. No problem will arise when the literally translated term is used in Japan, if the term has the same meaning as the term used in Germany. If this is not so, there is a serious problem. Needless to say, the civilization in any one country is the product of various international exchanges between that country and others. Therefore, to detail the characteristic culture of one country will occasionally reveal much that is of archaeological interest.[1]

The point is that one should have no objection to any imported concept at all. When an imported concept does not have the same meaning it had in its country of origin, however, it should be used only after a persuasive explanation of what was added to it. When

4 The Essence of the Concept

this is neglected, the result is similar to that of "to cry wine and sell vinegar," or "to cry beef and sell horse meat." What is the essence of "regular accounting principles"? I think it is proper to restrict the essence to the following attributes:

1. It is a collective concept that is the historic standard of the bookkeeping that should be performed by a merchant in a broad sense.
2. It is a concept whose limits have been clarified by a set of specified legal standards whenever the flow of history has been cut in a slice at a fixed point in time and its cross section reviewed.
3. It is the concept under which, when all its formal and substantial necessary conditions have been met, books of account display the function by which they are accepted as having evidential power to government and municipal tax offices.

In Japan at present, limiting the concept in this way may, I think, be taken as an uncommon and unprecedented conceptual regulation. As far as I have been able to ascertain, however, this is the concept of "the principles of regular bookkeeping" in the Federal Republic of Germany—a concept with a threefold structure.

First of all, there is the practical activity of bookkeeping that is conducted by a merchant. As it is an activity conducted in society, it is subject to various restrictions, such as economic and social conditions. This practical activity is a socially oriented one, so it can be said that it is also a historical one. The fact of the existence of such a practical activity can be formed into an idea by separating it from the law. Such a fact constitutes the very foundation of the law, and it occasionally goes ahead of the law historically.

When history is viewed macroscopically, it is natural for human beings to bring forth various principles as autonomous standards from such practical activities. At the same time, such a social phenomenon is naturally subjected to the participation of the law. In this way, "the principles of regular bookkeeping" become a legal concept.

Needless to say, the scope of these two principles is not the same. The former can be described as "various principles for orderly bookkeeping," while the latter may be defined as "various principles for prescribed regularity in bookkeeping." Essentially speaking, as an actual fact has a character that is the source of the law, "various principles for regular bookkeeping" can be grasped from two sides: actual fact and the law. The principles have come to include various standards and a group of principles with the passage of history.

For example, according to the theory of Dr. Ulrich Leffson, in "Principles of Documentation," there are the formal principles and the principle of completeness regarding accounting. In *The Principles of Regular Accounting*, the following principles have been included:

correctness

nonarbitrariness

clarity

completeness

classification of things according to time period

valuation under the assumption of the unlimited continuation of the business

classification by means of inventory valuation and cost and profit valuation

Walb's[2] rational profit and loss accounting

retail method of valuation, nonparity, verifiability, consistency, explaining inconsistencies, the elimination/segregation of abnormalities, caution etc.[3]

In the explanation of the principles of regular bookkeeping contained in the *Dictionary of German Tax Jurisprudence*, whose author, Dr. Klaus Bierle, is senior lecturer at the University of Saarland, Saarbrücken, the "principle of vouchers" is added to the principles above. Dr. Leffson of Münster University, however, did not include the principle of vouchers as a principle of regular bookkeeping in his own book. He is also the author of "Various Principles of Regular Bookkeeping," which is contained in the *Dictionary of Business Economics*. According to his explanation,

6   The Essence of the Concept

he divides the principles of documentation into five categories, and he cites the principle of vouchers as the fourth principle.[4]

The principles of documentation Dr. Leffson details in the *Dictionary of Business Economics* are:

a systematic set-up of accounting

verification of the completeness of the accounts

complete and comprehensible records

vouchers (no entry without a voucher)

verification of the dependability and the regularity of the accounting by means of an internal checking system

In his own book, especially in his explanation of the formal principles, he only touches lightly on the principle of vouchers.[5]

Dr. Leffson states, however: "The proof that any particular rule is a good accounting principle, can never depend upon laws, ordinances, or official guidelines." It is quite natural that he demonstrates that the regular accounting principles that originated from Article 38 of the German Commercial Code not only function as the source of the law but also, at the same time, have the character of a lawful standard that has the force of law.[6] It seems to me that his demonstration is worthy of special attention in Japan.

Dr. Heinrich Wilhelm Kruse, Privatdozent in Würzburg, who wrote a book with the same title as Dr. Leffson's and relied heavily on Dr. Leffson's work, wrote his *Principles of Regular Bookkeeping* from the standpoint of juridical methodology. In regard to Article 208 of the former *RAO* (Imperial Tax Code), he discusses the purpose of documentation, which is Section V of his concluding chapter: "Article 208 admitted the probative force of account books, the judicial evaluation of proof (records)" and it emphasized "the function of account books as evidence." A great deal of attention should be paid to this point of his argument.[7] In his attempt to define the principles of regular bookkeeping, Dr. Kruse also quotes the following sentence from the famous *Income Tax Law* (p. 653), which was written by Dr. Eberhard Littmann, the Director General of Germany's Federal Finance Court (BFH): "Good accounting principles contain an undetermined concept of law. They are legal propositions."[8]

I contend that an understanding that good accounting principles are legal propositions, as Dr. Littmann asserted and Dr. Kruse quotes, and an understanding of "the bookkeeping proof of books of account," which logically derives from the first concept, have generally been lacking in Japan. Through what I have written so far, I hope I have established that the principles of regular bookkeeping are also principles of positive law. The next question to be asked is what practical standard structure do the principles of regular bookkeeping require? That is to say, what type of practice does the law call for definitely regarding the bookkeeping of a merchant?

A Correction

Earlier, I wrote that it was in Article 38 of the German Commercial Code of 1897 that the "principles of regular accounting" appeared in the form of law for the first time. My reference on this matter was the original text of the German Commercial Code, which appeared in a book entitled *The Development of German Balance Sheet Law* (Vol. 1, p. 247), written by Dr. Kuno Barth of Tübingen University.[9]

I now must say, however, that as a practical businessman I find it hard to devote my life wholly to a scholastic work. I foolishly overlooked the contents of the Appendix in the second volume of this book. Volume 1 is devoted to commercial law, while Volume 2 is devoted to tax law. Dr. Barth traces the historical progress of the German laws on the balance sheet from the two viewpoints—commercial law and tax law.

In the Appendix to Volume 2 (p. 102), the full text of Paragraph 8 of Article 19 of the General Income Tax Law of the Hessian Provincial Government, enacted on June 25, 1895, appears. In this Hessian law can be found the phrase "according to regular accounting principles"; this was two years before the appearance of the German Commercial Code of 1897. The Hessian tax law had already been perfected and used this particular concept.

Consequently, the general understanding in Japan that, from a

8 The Essence of the Concept

historical viewpoint, the concept of the principles of regular bookkeeping originated in the German Commercial Code has been in error. The truth of the matter is that the concept originated in the Hessian Income Tax Law. With respect to my own error, I must apologize.[10]

The "principles of regular bookkeeping" can be looked at as a concept that has evolved; they reflect the historical progress of the standards of practice of tradespeople regarding bookkeeping. Another interesting subject is: What kind of development did bookkeeping go through in Germany before it became the contemporary system? Needless to say, this is not the main subject I am concerned with in this monograph. Some insight can be gained, however, by looking into the subject.

There are various viewpoints on this matter. For instance, there are books such as *The History of Accounting in Germany* by B. Penndorf and *Dictionary of German History of Law* by H. Kellenbenz of Cologne University. The latter book makes a point of describing German bookkeeping in terms of the history of law, and, moreover, it is brief and to the point. Kellenbenz states that "a western technique of accounting developed during the course of the Middle Ages, as written records came into use in commercial establishments."[11] He also reports that the "on document basis calculation" was already in existence in the commercial centers of the Mediterranean Sea in the tenth century and that various different kinds of approaches had been combined into a sort of integrated system of classification not later than 1400 A.D. Such being the case, "a Franciscan, Luca Paccioli, collected whatever had developed in practice and presented it for the first time in a theoretical work *(Summa di arithmetica, geometria, proportioni e proportionalitá)*, Venice 1494, as a textbook." It can safely be said that Shakespeare closely resembles Luca Paccioli in that one who has made an intensive compilation of traditional culture is greatly honored.

Mr. Kellenbenz further reports that "the development in Germany can be traced back to the last third of the thirteenth century," and that the oldest book of account preserved in southern Germany was "the debit ledger of the makers of wooden shoes of Nuremberg," which had been kept from 1304 to 1307 and had been written in Latin. It was around the end of the fourteenth century that the language of books of account changed from Latin to German. It is interesting to note that doctors in the present-day Federal Republic of Germany still make notations on charts in Latin.

The double-entry bookkeeping principle was already in use in northern Germany by the sixteenth century. Furthermore, in 1518, a resident of Nuremberg named Heinrich Schreiber published *Accountbook*, Chapter 1 of which was entitled "Bookkeeping by Journal 'Kaps,' and debit ledger by all businesses." In 1594, a book written by Passchier Goessen with the long title *Accounting summarized in brief and conceived in the method of the Italians* was published.

Also in the sixteenth century, the book *Exemplary Accounting* was distributed by a person named Mattäus Schwarz who was in charge of the books of account of a wealthy merchant firm, the Fugger Company. A double books of account system—a journal book and the original register of assets and liabilities, providing the side-by-side feature of a ledger—had been introduced. Emerging from a journal book and for the purpose of an individual entry, a separate entry for both credits and debits had been made. This era also saw the division of personnel accounts and inventory accounts, the separation of main books and subsidiary books, the emergence of cashbooks (in preparation for cash income and cash expenditures), the use of notebooks and memorandum books, bill ledgers, cartage books, journeymen's books for transactions of branch firms, fustian books, cooper books, silver books, and even black books and secretbooks.[12]

In 1741, a directory for single-entry bookkeeping was published by a person named Flügel. As far as the division of a ledger is concerned, meritorious business results were achieved by the following: a Frenchman named de la Porte in the latter part of the seventeenth century, a resident of Nuremberg named J. G. Schoapp at the beginning of the eighteenth century, the aforementioned Flügel, and, lastly, another Nuremberger named Johann Michael Leuchs at the beginning of the nineteenth century.

In 1804, the Frenchman Eduard Degrange introduced American accounting, through which a journal book and major books of account began to be combined. The same way of thinking resulted in the production of Mr. Philippson's work entitled *Letter Concerning Commercial Accounting* (1813). In 1832, a person named C. D. Fort in Dresden and, in 1974, a person named Schumacher in Mainz achieved good results in their respective new proposals for the simplification of the entry, in American bookkeeping. Their introduction of the revolving credit line became the most important feature of their respective new proposals.

In the twentieth century, bookkeeping in Germany was greatly affected by industrialization. At a time when the hitherto systematic classification had to face the necessity of refinement, Schmalenbach's *Charts of Accounts and Schedule of Accounts* made its appearance. As a result, continuous account books and index cards appeared, requiring transfer accounting and the technique of carbon copies. Finally, key punch card machines and electronic apparatus appeared. Mr. Kellenbenz writes: "This development made it necessary for the state to lay down provisions concerning accounting and auditing. In 1937 guidelines for the standardization of accounting were laid down for the entire economy."[13]

I think Kellenbenz's conclusion contains an error, however. I have no objection to the notion that bookkeeping and the preparation of balance sheets resulted in their being combined with positive law standards in the history of the law. But it was in 1919, not in 1937, as Mr. Kellenbenz states, that the demand for the unification of the bookkeeping system in the economy as a whole was legalized as the positive law. In 1927, Schmalenbach's *Charts of Accounts* came to the forefront. However, both Article 162 of the Imperial Tax Code, by which the law as a unified management standard was applied to the bookkeeping of all merchants in Germany, and Article 208, which acknowledged a decisive evidential value for income calculation in the books of account that were prepared according to the unified management standard, were included in the new Tax Code—the Fundamental Taxation Law *(AO)*, which was drafted by Enno Becker, a highly gifted scholar on the law of taxation, and was enacted in 1919.

This was eight years before the appearance of Schmalenbach's work. When *Charts of Accounts* was published, the nationwide unified standards for bookkeeping had already been enacted as law. It was nearly twenty years before the Enforcement Regulation appeared in 1937 as the authoritative explanatory regulation for Article 5 of the Hessian Income Tax Law. There may be no help for Mr. Kellenbenz, because his specialty is not tax jurisprudence.

Dr. Klaus Tipke of Cologne University, in his textbook on tax jurisprudence, discusses "the proof of accounts" in books of account by quoting the Commercial Code, Stock Law, German taxation law, and, especially, Article 158 of the new Tax Code in connection with German taxation law.[14] What happened to Mr. Kellenbenz? Did he not communicate with Dr. Tipke? The same is also applicable to Schmalenbach who was also a professor at Cologne University.

Mr. Schmalenbach, in his major work, *The Bases of Dynamic Accounting/Auditing Principles*, touched on "the principles of regular bookkeeping" six times and discussed "the principles for preparing a regular balance sheet" eight times. Nevertheless, he examined these principles only from the technical standpoint of bookkeeping. Moreover, from a historical viewpoint, he failed to point out that these concepts originated in the tax laws.[15] He also mistakenly asserted that when he wrote his book, the principles of regular bookkeeping had already been formed as a part of the German Positive Laws Standards System. In view of Mr. Schmalenbach's continued influence over junior scholars, his mistakes are not trifling.[16]

Notes

1. In my student days, I attended a lecture given by a foreign professor named E. V. Getenby, who emphasized the imitative peculiarity of the Japanese. I spoke up, saying: "All right. I will ask you a question. Is there anything in our civilization which is peculiar to the British?" After a long silence, the professor replied, blushing a bit, that "it might be only cricket and the Parliamentary System," His answer provoked a great deal of laughter among the students who were present.
2. He is the author of *Finanzwirtschaftliche Bilanz*.
3. Ulrich Leffson, *Die Grundsätze ordnungsmäßiger Buchführung*, 4 Auflage, 1976.
4. *Dictionary of Business Economics*, Vol. 1, p. 1014.
5. Ibid., p. 86.

12 The Essence of the Concept

6. Ibid., p. 12.
7. Dr. Heinrich Wilhelm Kruse, *Grundsätze ordnungsmäßiger Buchführung*, 3 Auflage, 1978, S. 199–200.
8. Ibid., p. 6.
9. In an Appendix, Dr. Barth reproduced the original texts of related laws in Germany, England, France, etc., ranging from *Vorschriften über Buchführung* to *Vorschriften über die Revision des Jahresabchlusses*, and classified by period, law, and country. Also included were the *Gutachten der Industrie- und Handelskammer Berlin* in General Provision, 1st Section, 1st Chapter, "Professional Section" of *Wirtschaftsprüfer—Handbuch* (1973), which was published by the Institute of Chartered Accountants in Germany; the full text of the opinion when the announcement of the first enactment was made; the full text of *Die Berichtigung des Gutachtens* in 1928; and the full text of *Die Ergänzung des Gutachtens*, the first made in 1929 and the second in 1930. This is an excellent reference book.
10. Dr. Kuno Barth, *The Development of German Audit Law, The Tax Law Volume*, App., p. 102.
11. Mr. H. Kellenbenz, in *Dictionary of German History of Law*, Vol. 1 (Erich Schmidt Verlag, 1971), p. 530.
12. After these developments in accounting in the course of the sixteenth century, no significant additions were made in Germany until the beginning of the nineteenth century (p. 532).
13. Kellenbenz, *Dictionary of German History of Law*, p. 534.
14. Dr. Klaus Tipke, *Tax Law: A Systematic Outline*, 6th ed., p. 198.
15. As stated earlier, the concept originated in Paragraph 8 of Article 19 of the Hessian Income Tax Law, which was enacted on June 25, 1895.
16. Refer to *The Bases of Dynamic Accounting/Auditing Principles*, 12th ed., trans. Masazo Doki (Moriyama Shoten), pp. 8, 13, 15, 150, 214, 233, 9, 84, 93, 150, 194, 199, 207, and 214.

2

The Principles of Regular Accounting Viewed as Moral Obligations of a Positive Law

In regard to the concept of the principles of regular accounting as moral obligations in positive laws, Dr. H. W. Kruse of Würzburg University wrote: "This principle was first codified in the empire by 162 II *AO* 1919/1931. However, it had already been considered valid for centuries."[1] This description, however, is not correct. The reason is that in Article 606 of the Prussian General Common Law of 1794 the following provision can be found: "This occurs specifically wherever the merchant has committed errors in bookkeeping, which are to his advantage."

In other words, the principle of "truthfulness" regarding accounting records, to the best of my knowledge, arose in Prussia in the eighteenth century. Furthermore, in Article 28 of the General German Commercial Law of 1861, the following substantive enactment appeared: "It is the duty of every merchant to keep accounts, in which his business transactions and the state of his assets can be seen completely." That is to say, the principle of the "completeness" of the entry in books of account was codified by this commercial code as a positive law.

As far as this matter is concerned, I must conclude that Professor Kruse's *Principles of Regular Bookkeeping* was incorrect. Article 162 of *Reichsabgabenordnung* (the Imperial Tax Code), enacted in 1919, dictates that in an entry in a book of account, a living language should be used. It is interesting to note that the term "a

13

living language" had already been used in the first part of Article 32 of the General Commercial Code, which was enacted in Germany in 1861, especially because this indicates that the tradition of the idea of positive laws and the terms regarding merchants' calculation system were already held in high esteem.

Early on, French tax laws permitted the use of foreign terms in accounting records.[2] However, the Fundamental Accounting Plan *(Plan Comptable Général),* which went into effect on April 4, 1946, immediately after World War II, mandated the use of the French language in accounting records.[3] Also in France, remarkable progress was made in 1958 when the French Supreme Court of Administrative Litigation delivered a decision that "in accounting records, a 'code number,' 'a symbol,' and 'a mark' that cannot be understood without the cooperation of taxpayers could not be acknowledged, because they had no value of verifiability in the determination of income."[4]

About ten years after I opened my first accounting office, I accepted a post as an adviser for an international trading company in Holland. One day the office was inspected by the Japanese Tax Administration Agency. Books of account in the French language were found and the inspection officials seemed extremely embarrassed. I lost no time clearing myself by saying that in Japan's Commercial Code and tax laws, there were no substantive enactments that prescribed the language to be used for accounting records. As a result, the inspection came to an uneventful end. It seems to me that specifying the language to be used in accounting records is reasonable and should be a legislative matter. I was also once informed by an executive officer of the Nuremberg Association of the Tax Practitioners in Germany that the living language that had been prescribed by Article 162 of the Imperial Tax Code should also include "ordinary Arabic numerals."

For a long time, I have been dissatisfied with such matters as the ambiguity of limiting the scope of a responsible person for making an entry in our Commercial Code, the lack of "comprehensiveness" of the calculation principle and its logical indigence, and the lack of a link between the calculation provisions in our commercial code and the tax and other laws, and so forth. I cannot help but wonder whether there is a person, or persons, who may have had the same apprehensions, among those governmental officials who are in charge of legislative matters in Japan.

Especially in regard to the Corporate Accounting Principles, I have long wondered why a radical reform has not been planned, leaving the errors in the fundamental theory of the Principles untouched for thirty years. For instance, in German legislation, the concept of the principles of regular bookkeeping in Article 38 of the German Commercial Code of 1897 has been quoted as also applicable to the Federal Banking Law, whose Article 26 substantively enacts that "the accounting of the Federal Bank must conform to the good principles of accounting."[5] That is to say, in the Federal Republic of Germany, the concept of the principles of regular accounting in Article 38 of the German Commercial Code, unlike the concept of "a fair habitual practice in accounting," which was prescribed by Article 32 of the Japanese Commercial Code, has been applied repeatedly to various laws, for example: in the Income Tax Law, to *5–(1) EstG*; in the Corporation Tax Law, to *7–(4) KStG*; in the Stock Law, to *149–(1), (2)-1 AktG*; in the Limited Company Law to *41 GmbHG*; in the Union Law, to *33 GenG*; and in the Fundamental Tax Law, to *141–(1) AO*.

As a consequence, this concept of principle functions, irrespective of the category and scale of the main constituent of a corporation, is an individual operational and official calculation principle that is the final unit of the national economy. This is one primary cause for the toughness in individual management that is the basis of the national economy in the Federal Republic of Germany. I regret that circumstances have brought it about that irrespective of the category and scale of the main constituent of a corporation, a comprehensive legalization of an official calculation system for individual management has never been realized in Japan, simply because the concept of the principles of regular bookkeeping were misinterpreted as a concept imported from Germany at the beginning of the enactment of the Corporate Accounting Principles in Japan.

At the present, what does my reader feel about the tax evasion that has become deeply rooted among the masses of the people in this country? One of the reasons this has happened is that we lack an ideology by which the calculation system of merchants should be positioned as the legal standard to be strictly followed by the nation as a whole, the principles that should be legislated in Japan and should be an important factor in the formation of the society of Japan.

Mr. Spangemacher, the presiding judge of the Federal Finance Court in the Federal Republic of Germany wrote in his book, *General Theory of Law*, that there is a tendency that "tax law follows its own path [is independent], wherever an attempt is made to evade taxation by abuse of possible interpretations of the law."[6] He also states: "There still exists a special internal connection between civil law and tax law. In 1918 Enno Becker had to solve the problem of defining (with the Imperial Tax Code among other things) the legal relationship between the state as the tax creditor and the citizen as the taxpayer."

As we have seen, the history of the formation of the internal associative relationship between civil law and the tax laws in the Federal Republic of Germany is not so old. Mr. Spangemacher was quite insightful to know of Enno Becker's historically meritorious deed in this point in particular. This may have been due to the fact that Spangemacher, like Becker, was a judge who specialized in the tax laws. It grieves me that the internal and associative relationship between civil law and the tax laws has not been established in this country. In other words, the internal and comprehensive relationship between these two law systems, compared with Germany's, may be said to have fallen behind by more than sixty years.

Through Enno Becker, the principles of regular bookkeeping had a profound effect on legislation as a whole in the Federal Republic of Germany. The articles that became its principal axes are Paragraph 1 of Article 160 of the former *AO* and Article 140 of the new *AO*. Spangemacher states that "according to 140 *AO*, accounting according to business law is also the duty of accounting for tax law with all the tax-related consequences which result therefrom."[7] According to his opinion, for instance, Article 158 of the new *AO*, which prescribes verifiable bookkeeping records of books of account, is a logical conclusion of Article 140. Article 140, to my surprise, contains so much related material that I would like to introduce it later on.

In any case, since I intend to reconsider fundamentally this country's accounting system and the tax law as positive law in my search for the concept of the principles of regular bookkeeping, I must inevitably ask, what is the law, what are its objectives, function, and limit?

Early Philosophy of Social Law

The German economist Werner Sombart wrote a voluminous study, six volumes in all, the title of which was *Modern Capitalism*. In the long run, however, he felt the need to return to his original point, the views that had formed the very basis of his learning. He also, therefore, wrote a book entitled *About People*, his study of the "mental, scientific human race," a close examination of the human views of a total of twenty-five philosophers, from Plato and Aristotle through Kant, Goethe, and Schopenhauer, to Nicolai Hartmann, and Al. Carrel. He reviewed their respective human views as well as studying the attitudes by which their views were formed.

Plato, who was an ancient Greek philosopher and who, it is said, laid the foundations for the system of constitutional government for ages to come, wrote in his later years a book entitled *Laws*, which is his final monumental work. Nowhere in this voluminous work, however, can be found a definition of the law. In "644D, Vol. 1," the following appears: "In the case when it is the 'common opinion' of a State, it is named 'Laws.' " The definition of "the law" was given by him in other books. There is one in *Minos* (314B): "After all, viewed collectively, the law is the thing which was decided upon by a State." The other definition is found only in *Definitions* (415B), which is presumed to have been taken down by Plato's nephew Speusippus, who became the second president of Plato's Academy: "Law, whose limit of time is none, is a political decision which is made by the masses."

As to the "objective" of the law, it is stated in *Laws:* "Some of the laws are intended for those good persons to instruct them how to associate with others mutually so that they are able to lead a life with the feeling of affection," and that "others of the law are made for those persons who had evaded education, namely for those persons who tend to plot evil of all kinds" (Vol. 9, 880E). Plato states that "the goal enacting the law is virtue" (*Laws*, Vol. 3, 688B). Regarding true laws, he concludes that "those laws which have not been enacted for the interests of the public in a state as a whole are not true laws" (*Laws*, Vol. 4, 715B). Moreover, he also states that "it is absolutely necessary for a human being to enact a law, under which we have to live in accordance with the law, otherwise there will be not a bit of difference between a human being and the most ferocious animals" (*Laws*, Vol. 9, 875A).

Although the above expression is an indirect one, he observes the function of the law therein. As to the limit of the law, he advocates that "it is the best of all to control by intellect," however, such a man of competence actually cannot be found. Therefore as "the next best" step, control by the law has to be selected (*Laws*, 875CD).

What drew my attention is as follows: "Any person found guilty of disobeying a legal regulation which provides that 'one must not render service in hopes of obtaining a present,' should be put to death" (*Laws*, Vol. 12, 955D). And as to a tax, Plato asserts that "each person's property should be properly assessed," and that "each person's amount of gains made in each year should be declared in writing to the local peace preservation officer concerned" (*Laws*, 955DE). It is indeed a very refreshing opinion. Furthermore, he states that the law should add the "persuasion and recommendation" in the form of a preamble to the text of the law (Vol. 4, 722B), and he asserts "the three-instances" system in justice and concludes that "in any state where a court is not established properly, it cannot be said at all to be a state in any sense" (Vol. 6, 766D). This conclusion is extremely striking. In general, Plato's opinions are creative and simple, which makes us feel that they are well founded.

In *The Metaphysics of Morals* Kant gives a definition of the law: "Therefore law is the quintessence of the conditions under which the arbitrariness of one person can be united with the arbitrariness of another according to a general law of freedom."[8] This definition has also been quoted by Jürgen Baumann, a Professor at the University of Tübingen, in his book *Introduction to Jurisprudence* (5th ed., Part I, General, p. 4). Rudolf Stammler (1856–

1938), who belonged to the New Kant school, clearly indicates the origin of his theory in Kant's *The Metaphysics of Morals*. His definition of the law is as follows: "Therefore the concept of law is a concept of unconditional universal validity."[9] Touching on it very briefly in the Introduction of his book, he discusses the concept of the law in forty-eight pages in *Book One: The Concept of Law*. As his discussion is too long to recount here, I will introduce only his description of the essence of the law:

Law means a special way to conduct human life together. Its essence must therefore be to elucidate by labeling the thought processes, in whose unity the unique composition of the judicial intention consists. Therefore, we must consider the possibility of exactly this standardization critically, if one is to determine the conceptual difference between law as opposed to other ways of the life of society.[10]

Stammler's description of the essence of the law is beyond my comprehension. The reason is that the term "judicial," which is the concept to be clarified, has also been included in his description. As to what is meant by the word "judicial," he states as follows: "The unconditional validity of the concept of law: The idea of 'judicial' signifies a stipulated way to determine certain behavior" (p. 24). He understands the concept of law as a concept that has originated in "unlimited fairness," instead of accepting it as one intellectual system of public order.

Mr. Radbruch criticized Stammler's philosophy of law, asserting that it was not "a building," even though it was a valuable "framework." A defense of Stammler depends on how to describe the principal problem of the philosophy of law. According to Stammler, the principal problem of the philosophy of law is how to clarify the concepts of the law and its idea.[11] From this viewpoint, I think Radbruch's criticism is simply a transcendental one from a different standpoint, and that it cannot be said to be an intrinsic one. Radbruch writes as follows:

The concept of law is a cultural concept, that is to say, the concept of a reality based on values, of a reality which intends to serve a value. Law is the reality, which intends [to serve?] the value of law, the idea of law. Therefore, the idea of law can only be that of justice. We are also entitled to consider justice to be an ultimate starting point, for what is "just" is an absolute, like Goodness, Truth, or Beauty, that is a value which can be derived from no other (value).[12]

Following Aristotle, Radbruch divides the concept of justice into two kinds: one is equalizing or compensatory justice, while the other is dispensed justice. The former, for instance, is the justice that exists between those persons having equal rights, such as between labor and wages, or between damage and compensation, while the latter is the justice, for instance, that governs "the taxation to be based on one's taxable capacity," or "the assistance to be given in proportion to one's level of poverty." He concludes that compensatory justice is the justice of private law, while dispensed justice is the justice of public law. He also concludes that dispensed justice is the basic form of justice. He states: "In this we have found the idea (essence) of justice toward which the concept law must be oriented."

Furthermore, in summarizing the essence of legal discipline, Radbruch writes: "We can summarize the essence of the judicial order by saying that it is of a positive and at the same time normative social and general nature, in this sense specify that law is the quintessence of the general direction for human corporate life (in community order)."[13] Radbruch, who was enriched in culture and had advocated this philosophy of law based on the relativism of value, has left his opinion only in his summarization of the legal discipline.

Sir Paul Gavrilovich Vinogradoff (1854–1925), a Russian-born jurist who later went to England where he became a Professor of Jurisprudence at Oxford University, wrote a work entitled *Common Sense in Law,* which is said to be a classic of English law. The second edition of this work was published in 1945 by Oxford University. In this book, Vinogradoff criticized one definition after another, such as the definition formulated by Ulpian, who was a jurist in Rome, and those of Hobbes, Austin, Kant, Jhering, and so forth. After that he states, as follows, his own definition of the concept of law: "Therefore law may be defined as a set of rules imposed and enforced by a society with regard to the attribution and exercise of power over persons and things."[14] He asserts that all laws, ranging from ancient times up to the present, must be taken account of in the definition, with no exceptions at all, and

The Principles of Regular Accounting 21

that the physical characteristic that all these definitions have in common is "the existence of a specified will that restricts others."

Opposed to Vinogradoff's opinion is a book written by George Whitecross Paton, entitled *A Textbook of Jurisprudence* (Oxford University Press, 2d ed., 1951). Paton concludes in Chapter 3 of Volume 1, under the subject "The Definition of Law," that "it is futile to attempt to be exhaustive, but an analysis of a few typical definitions is a useful approach to the problem." And he prescribes the concept of law in an Englishman-like style of expression of relativism, as follows: "Law may be defined firstly by its basis in nature, reason, religion, or ethics; secondly, by its source, in custom, precedent, or legislation; thirdly, by its effects on the life of society; fourthly, by the method of its formal expression or authoritative application; fifthly, by the ends that it seeks to achieve."[15]

My reader may think it strange that I have made my way into the sphere of the philosophy of law in this study, but it is not strange at all. Professor Erich Kosiol of Berlin University, who is ranked as one of the most authoritative scholars in present-day business economics circles in Germany, has written a voluminous book of more than a thousand pages, entitled *Pagatory Balance Sheet* (Berlin: Buncker & Humbolt, 1976), in which he has quoted twice (at pages 73 and 1013) from a book by Heinrich Nicklisch (1876–1946), *Business Administration* (7th ed., Stuttgart, 1932), a classic in German business economics. Professor Kosiol speaks very highly of Nicklisch's bringing up a problem of principle in business economics. It is well known that Nicklisch had absorbed a great deal of German idealistic philosophy before formulating his fundamental concepts of business economics.

Moreover, recently Dr. Klausjürgen Berger published *A Critical Analysis of Normative Elements in the Study of Business Administration*. On page 40 of this book, he quotes from Wittgenstein's Cambridge University work, *Tractatus logico-philosophicus* (1922), and under the subject of "The Relationship of Language, Reality, and the Transcendental in Wittgenstein's 'Tractatus,' " he first of all discusses the bases. It can be viewed as a good example that those who formulate fundamental theory in business economics seek the basis for organizing theory even in ontology in philosophy.

In this book, furthermore, I have frequently quoted various

22 The Principles of Regular Accounting

works like Hegel's *Phenomenology of the Spirit* (1807) and Kant's *Critique of Pure Reason*. This practice has also been observed by Professor R. K. Mautz of Illinois University. In *The Philosophy of Auditing* (American Accounting Association, 1961), he quotes approximately thirty works of philosophy, one of which is Kant's *Critique of Pure Reason*, translated into English by J. M. D. Meiklejohn. My copy of Kant's *Critique* was translated into English by Norman Kemp Smith of Edinburgh University. It is my opinion, however, that a translated book should not be used for exhaustive scholastic discussion, because of the nuances that may be lost in the process of translation. At any rate, I am sure my attitude is hardly a surprise.

The Moral Obligations of a Positive Law

In Chapter 9 of his fourteen-hundred-page collection of articles entitled *Paregra und Paralipomena*, Arthur Schopenhauer (1788–1860) discusses the concept of the law under the heading "Zu Rechtslehre und Politik." He states: "Whoever starts from the preconceived opinion that the concept of 'right' must be 'positive' and now undertakes to define it, will not make anything of it; for he is trying to grasp a shadow, pursues a ghost, and looks for a *nonens*. The concept of 'right,' like that of 'freedom,' is 'negative'; its content is a mere negation."[16]

Someone who has advocated a theory that is akin to Schopenhauer's is Karl Engisch (1899–), who is an authority in present-day circles of German jurisprudence. In Chapter 6 of his *Introduction to Judicial Thought* (7th ed., 1977), when he discusses the "legal right, concept of law which is impossible to be decided upon, standard concept, general condition, and free statement," he states: "By an 'indefinite' concept we understand a concept whose contents and range is largely uncertain. Absolutely defined concepts occur seldom within the realm of law."[17] And he lists, as follows, the names of those scholars and their works who have expressed opinions similar to his:

1. Wolff, *Administrative Law*, 8 Aufl., 31.
2. K. Larenz, *Study of Methods* (1960) p. 222; 2d ed., 1969, p. 268 f; 3d ed., 1975, p. 279 f.

3. Pietzonka, *The Indefinite Concept of Law in the Administrative Law* (1954), p. 1965.
4. Lukowsky, *Der unbestimmte Begriff usw.*, Verw. Arch. 53, 1962, S. 25 ff.
5. H. Müller-Tochtermann, *NJW 1962*, S. 1238 f.
6. G. Dahm, *German Law*, 2d ed., 1963, p. 63 ff.
7. K. Kuchinke, *Grenzen der Nachprüfbarkeit tatrichterlicher Würdigung*, 1964, S. 73 ff., 75 ff.
8. P. Seel, *Unbestimmte und normative Tatbestandsmerkmale usw.*, Munich, diss., 1965.
9. H. E. Henke, *Die Tatfrage. Der unbestimmte Begriff im Zivilrecht*, 1966, insbes. S. 54 ff.
10. H. Bogs, *Die verfassungskonforme Auslegung*, 1966, S. 137 ff.
11. O. Bachof, *Jura 1966*, S. 441 f.
12. M. Fellner, *Der unbestimmte Rechsbegriff usw.*, DVerBl. 1966, S. 161 ff.
13. F. Czermak, ibid., p. 366.
14. H. Schima, *Der unbestimmte Rechtsbegriff, Anz. österr. Akademie der wiss. Philosoph.-Histor. Kl. 1968*, S. 197 ff.
15. W. Hartz, *Gestzliche Generalklauseln und Richterrecht, Steuer, und Wirtschaft 1968*, S. 245 ff. unter II und V.
16. Th. Vogel, *Zur Praxis und Theorie der richterlichen Bindung an das Gesetz*, 1969, S. 32 ff.
17. D. C. Göldner, *Verfassungsprinzip u. Privatrechtsnorm*, 1969, S. 38 ff.
18. G. Kohlmann, *Der Begriff des Staatsgeheimnisses und das verfassungsrechtl. Gebot der Bestimmtheit von Strafvorschriften*, 1969, S. 149 ff.
19. H. P. Lemmel, *Unbestimmte Strafbarkeitsvoraussetzungen usw.*, 1970.
20. G. Patzig, *Sprache und Logik*, 1970, S. 27 f.
21. U. Schroth in A. Kaufmann (Hrsg.), *Rechtstheorie*, 1971, S. 108 f.
22. D. Leenen, *Typus u. Rechtsfindg.*, 1971, S. 34 ff.
23. K. O. Opp, *Soziol. im Recht*, 1973, S. 116 ff.
24. H. Soell, *a.a.o. (Anm, 115a)*, 1973, S. 163 ff.
25. H. Dubs, *Die Forderung der optimalen Bestimmtheit belastender Rechsnormen, 100 Jahre (schweizer.) Bundesverfassung*, 1974, S. 223 ff.

26. H. B. Grüber, *Zur Anwendung der Soziologie in der Jurisprudenz, Jurz 1974*, S. 665 ff.
27. H. J. Koch, *Der unbestimmte Begriff im Verwaltungsrecht*, in *Jurist. Methodenlehre usw.*, 1976, S. 186 ff.[18]

I must praise the intensity of Karl Engisch's scholarship, an intensity that manifests the tenacity of his purpose. Dr. Kyoji Funada, who was a jurist specializing in Roman law and formerly a Professor at Keio Imperial University, visited me about four or five years after the end of World War II. When our conversation touched upon the scholarship of Germans, he expressed his deep admiration for the breadth of German scholarship. Now, with Karl Engisch's book in front of me, I cannot help but recall the deep admiration Dr. Funada expressed over thirty years ago. Engisch's *Introduction to Judicial Thought* is 320 pages in all, however, the section containing his special articles extends to page 197, and the rest of the book—123 pages—contains notes on his references. Furthermore, the type size used for the notes is far smaller than that used for the articles. Thus the length of the article section and that of the notes are nearly the same. The book is a wonderful reference work. In this particular respect, it may be that my attitude has been too lenient indeed.

Hans Kelsen writes in *General Theory of the State* (1925), in Chapter 7 of Volume 3, *The Creation of the Order of the State*, under the heading "The Concepts of the Law: The General (Abstract) Norm":

> In using the word "law" one thinks only or at least primarily of general or abstract norms. And if one in essence identifies law making with the creation of law, then this is because one has conceived of law itself as a sum of general norms, because one has predicated the concept of law only in general abstract form. It will presently be demonstrated that this concept of law is clearly too narrow and therefore must lead to unsolvable contradictions.[19]

What he wanted to say was that abstract norms materialize through, and are shaped by, the decisions of justice. This can be understood by reviewing the argument that follows. Kelsen states: "By no means is this, as is commonly assumed, only given in the form of law, only in the stage of general norms. The 'law' is neither the only, nor the highest stage of the order of law."[20] His formulation of this early legal concept manifested the unique and intense characteristics of his *Pure Theory of Law* (1934), which was published ten years later.

In my possession are the first edition of this book, which was translated by Dr. Kisaburo Yokota, published by Iwanami Shoten, and first printed in April 1935, and the second edition, which was published by Franz Dueticke Press (Vienna) in 1960. Unhappily, I do not have the original German text of the first edition. Compared with my first edition, the second edition is more than twice the size. (The original text of the second edition has 444 pages, and the translated version of the first edition is 233 pages in length.) The second edition has expanded about 70 percent. Its fundamental assertion, however, remains essentially the same.

The structure of the theory of the law was clarified at the outset in Kelsen's Preface to the first edition. He states that he intends to "develop a pure judicial theory, i.e., cleansed of all political ideology and scientific elements, conscious of its unique properties due to observance of the laws inherent in its object." Therefore he asserts that the "object of law" exists only in "legal relationships as the object of a legal decision." In other words, he formulates that, as its "object," "law" is to search for something that is judicial and can be comprehended by a legal standard.[21] He compares the concept of justice as an absolute value to "the thing in itself," which had been discussed by Kant in *The Critique of Pure Reason*.[22] He also compares this concept to "the idea of the absolute Good," which Plato discussed in *Politeia*.[23] He asserts that the justice in these items cannot be absolutely attained by a rational perception. He concludes that as the material to be used for actual perception, only positive law has been given, and that in this particular instance, "justice" only indicates the relative value to be called "respectability," and that "to be righteous" is another phrase for "lawful." In this way, *The Pure Theory of Law*, which aims at becoming the science of law, parts from the concept of justice.

In the second edition of his book, Kelsen specifically provides a separate chapter at the end, entitled "The Problem of Justice," in which he spends about ninety pages in exhaustive discussion of this particular matter. He argues that whether it is as an absolute value, or a relative value, the concept of justice should be distinguished from law. This assertion, that "the science of a positive law should be distinguished from the philosophical principle of justice" has been evaluated as "perhaps the most important task of the 'pure' theory" by George C. Christie, Professor of Law at Duke University.[24] Presumably, as Kelsen himself says, the logic of placing law and justice in the same category justifies the given order of society just as it is. The given order of society, however, is a political one, not a scientific one. Consequently, as the result of withdrawing all heterogeneous things from the concept of law, Kelsen came to present the unparalleled proposition that "legal propositions are hypothetical judgments."[25] In this proposition, he mentioned that inherent laws, to which he had referred in the Introduction to his first edition, are included as a form by which laws and regulations combine the required condition of law with the effectiveness of law.

In regard to Radbruch's attitude toward Kelsen's doctrine, he quoted Kelsen's *General Theory of the State* as often as twelve times in *The Philosophy of Law*. As to Kelsen's *Pure Theory of Law* (1934), however, Radbruch did not touch on it at all. I must wonder why. Erik Wolf, the compiler and publisher of Radbruch's *Philosophy of Law*, wrote an Introduction on "the life and achievements of Gustav Radbruch" which extended to sixty pages at the beginning of Radbruch's book. At the same time, in the eighth edition of Radbruch's book, Mr. Wolf added fifteen pages of reference material at the end, under the heading "Notes and Comments." In this added reference material, Mr. Wolf describes Hans Kelsen: "Hans Kelsen (1881–1972), Professor in Vienna, Cologne, and Geneva, teacher of state law and the philosophy of law, developed the theory of the identity of the state and law in his work *The Sociological and Juristic Concept of the State* (2d ed., 1928), and in his *General Theory of the State*, 1925." Just as Radbruch did not touch on Kelsen's "pure theory of law," Mr. Wolf did not write even a single word on Kelsen's theory of law. These two scholars might have had opinions directly opposed to each other in regard to the relevant problem between law and justice.

Earlier I quoted Radbruch's statement: "The personality is developed [one becomes a person] by means of selfless objectivity." I think, however, that the fact that Radbruch made no mention at all of Kelsen's *Pure Theory of Law*, which holds views regarding the concept of justice that are opposed to Radbruch's, indicates the loss of Radbruch's objectivity. I also think it simply indicates Radbruch's negation of his own character.

Viewed from this particular point, I think the American Professor Christie is more unreserved and refreshing than these two scholars. Professor Christie devotes seventeen pages to Kelsen in his book *Jurisprudence: Text and Readings on the Philosophy of Law*. In the four pages in which he deals with *Pure Theory of Law*, Professor Christie not only introduces Kelsen's theory but also criticizes it. Space does not permit me to detail all the citicisms here, but I will cite one example. On page 631, Professor Christie writes as follows:

In the second edition of *The Pure Theory*, however, Kelsen clearly admits that, if one rejects the concept of a single absolute system of morals and accepts instead the relativity of morals, then the legal order, as a normative order, that is, as an order of ought propositions, is by that very fact a type of moral order. Under this view, a conflict between law and morality is no longer a conflict between the norms of two epistemologically distinct and noncomparable social orders but a conflict between the norms of two different moral orders.

Professor Christie points out that while Kelsen had tried to distinguish, strictly and analytically, between law and morality in the first edition of *Pure Theory of Law*, he had changed his way of thinking in the second edition.

What I have written so far is so rough that it cannot be said to constitute a general view. Regarding what is law, and how the concept of law is to be defined, there have been various theories divided in one way or another. These theories cannot be formulated with a single meaning. No one seems to dispute, however, that law is the order of norm that anticipates the specified actions of human beings. When one violates the law, a socially organized compelling power can be exercised upon one. We who are engaged in actual business practice must take an interest in how law is created and legislated. At this juncture, I must acknowledge the proposition Plato formulated in the work that is said to be his most important. In *Laws* (Vol. 4, 714B), Plato states: "Law which has not been enacted for the public benefit of the state as a whole is not a real law." This is simple, strong, and sturdy, and it hits the mark, although it has been roughly sketched. Contrary to our expectations, truth may lie concealed behind a simple expression.

Notes

1. Dr. Heinrich Wilhelm Kruse, *Grundsätze ordnungsmäβiger Buchführung*, 3 Auflage, 1978, S. 40.
2. *Code Général des Impôts*, 54.
3. Conseil National de la Comptabilité. *Plan Comptable Général*, 68.
4. *Conseil d'Etat 1958*, n. 36330.
5. Dr. Hans E. Büschgen, *Bankbetriebslehre* (Wiesbaden, 1972), S. 603.
6. Gerd Spangemacher, *Allgemeines Recht*, 5 Auflage, 1978, S. 50.
7. Ibid., p. 284.
8. *Immanuel Kants Werke, Band VII, Die Metaphysik der Sitten* (Hildesheim: Verlag Dr. H. A. Gerstenberg, 1973), S. 31.
9. *Lehrbuch der Rechtsphilosophie von Rudolf Stammler*, 3 Auflage (Berlin and Leipzig), S. 2.
10. Rudolf Stammler, *Erstes Buch, Der Begriff des Rechtes*, pp. 53–54.
11. Ibid., Sec. 9, p. 15.
12. *Rechtsphilosophie*, 1973, pp. 119–20.
13. Ibid., p. 124.
14. Sir Paul Gavrilovich Vinogradoff, *Common Sense in Law*, p. 44.
15. George Whitecross Paton, *A Textbook of Jurisprudence*, pp. 51–52.
16. Arthur Schopenhauer, *Sämtliche Werke, Band V: Paregra und Paralipomena II* (Cotta Insel-Verlag, 1965), S. 285.
17. Karl Engisch, *Einführung in das juristische Denken*, 7 Auflage, 1977, p. 108.
18. Ibid., pp. 257–58.
19. Hans Kelsen, *Allgemeine Staatslehre*, Vol. 3, *Drittes Buch. Die Erzeugung der Staatsordnung*, 1925, p. 232.
20. Ibid., p. 234.
21. Hans Kelsen, *Reine Rechtslehre*, 2d ed., 1960, p. 104.
22. Ibid., p. 72.
23. Ibid., p. 398.
24. George C. Christie, *Jurisprudence: Text and Readings on the Philosophy of Law*, 1973, p. 620.
25. Hans Kelsen, *Reine Rechtslehre*, p. 73.

3

The Principle of "Timeliness"

No one will deny the fact that the Corporate Accounting Principles and its explanatory notes have misplaced the principle of "timeliness" somewhere. Why have the scholars of Japan not advocated the establishment of the principle of "timeliness" in accounting records? For instance, the latter part of Paragraph 1 of Article 146 of *AO* (Tax Code) prescribes the following: "Cash receipts and disbursements must be recorded daily." This provision, in particular, was the outcome of the extensive revision undertaken in 1977, in which provisions were rearranged and the language of various provisions was modified. Before this revision, Paragraph 7 of Article 162 had the following stipulation: "Cash receipts and disbursements should be recorded at least daily during the conduct of business." Therefore, it is prescribed that, irrespective of the nonoccupational delivery and receipt of money, as far as business is concerned, monetary receipts and disbursement and, henceforth, a daily outstanding balance, are to be recorded, as a minimum demand, on a daily basis. The title of Article 162 of the former *AO* was "Accounting Regulations: Book and Business Audits." The title of Article 146 of the new *AO* is "Regulations of Order for Accounting for Record Keeping." Although the title has been changed, there is no noticeable change in what is said.

As mentioned earlier, however, the accumulation of judicial precedents has always existed in Germany, so that there are many facts under which the expressions of legal provisions have gradu-

30 The Principle of "Timeliness"

ally been modified. In his voluminous book *Income Tax Law* (12th ed.), Dr. Eberhard Littmann, who was adjunct presiding judge at the Federal Finance Court (BFH), lists five judicial precedents that have been set since 1967 and states: "According to this, the factual weight of the deficiency is decisive if there exists a deficiency in the inventory, the cash accounting, and the chronological posting."[1] Furthermore, as to the importance of bookkeeping regarding the record of receipts and disbursements of cash, he writes: "Proper (double entry) cash accounting is of the utmost importance for regularity in accounting. If there is no cash account book at all, then the entire accounting can no longer be considered proper."[2] Needless to say, the "accuracy" or "properness" of a cashbook, in this particular instance, hinges on "the timeliness" of the entry. In December 1978, Karl-Heinz Mittelsteiner, my friend and the president of the Association of Licensed Tax Practitioners in Hamburg, sent me a copy of his book. In it he expresses the same opinion: "The timely posting of cash receipts and disbursements is not sufficient. The required daily balancing of the cash on hand is only possible if cash receipts and disbursements are recorded daily."[3]

From a macroscopic viewpoint, what constitutes the very basis for the principles of regular bookkeeping is the principle regarding entries in a cashbook, and what constitutes the very essence of an entry is timeliness, together with the "perfectibility," "truthfulness," and "orderliness" of the record. Therefore, it is not enough that entries have been made sequentially; making entries on a daily basis has been demanded as the practical standard in the law.

Furthermore, if I may use the actual phrasing of a judicial decision of the German Federal Finance Court, just as it is: "Good accounting principles basically require the notation of every individual cash receipt and disbursement."[4] It must be said that it was a mistake for me to try to uncover problems only by examining sentences and terms in the Corporate Accounting Principles, to develop my study of related literature. As a scholar, there is no reason at all for me to limit the literature only to that of my own country. We cannot overlook the fact that misunderstandings and negligence on the part of scholars in Japan have been reflected in the tax laws, related laws, and regulations of the nation.

For instance, in Separate Sheet No. 20 of the Enforcement Regulations for the Corporation Tax Law, Item 1, "Matters relating to the receipt and disbursement of cash," directs that "the matters to be entered" should be the date of the transaction, the reason, the other party to whom receipts or disbursements were made, the sum, and the daily balance. At first sight, the expression "daily balance" seems to legalize the principle of "timeliness." The truth of this matter, however, is entirely different. The reason is that "daily balance," in this particular instance, indicates only that the entry of the cash balance into the books of account should be conducted sequentially, and it does not include the practical standard under which the mentioned items should be entered daily and realistically. Regarding this point, there are no indications that the Finance Ministry has given consideration to planning laws and regulations to establish a practical standard regarding "timeliness." It seems that none of our scholars have ever made an argument about this matter.

As a consequence, we who are out of office must follow, as our final line of defense, the judicial precedents regarding the meaning of "the entry of daily transactions" in our Commercial Code. Regarding this point, luckily or unluckily, the Court of Cessation in Japan handed down its decision in 1923: "It is not required to record daily transactions by following closely a calendar day." Therefore, it is judged that there has been no standard of the law under which the balance of daily cash transactions should be entered by sticking to the date on a calendar.

It seems to me that in pointing out the retrogressive character of the Finance Ministry authorities in the formation of laws and regulations, our scholars should try to provide a rational and constructive direction to the work that needs to be done by the staff of the Ministry of Finance. It seems to me that the "timeliness" of entries into books of account has never been stated or discussed in any literature in Japan concerning various accounting regulations, commercial law, tax jurisprudence, business economics, accounting, or the study of bookkeeping. The reason for this phenomenon may be the attitude of understanding of our scholastic circles and the Finance Ministry authorities, who may not care a bit whether or not the "entry" itself is made at one's convenience; that this is done is not a problem of any importance to them. I feel, however, that the truth of the matter may not be so; they may have conducted themselves on the tacit assumption that, after all, it would be desirable for the accounting record to be entered in a timely manner.

As far as Penal Code scholars are concerned, what one says passes to another subject. For instance, under the heading "Evidential Capability of Other Documents," Item No. 2 of Paragraph 1 of Article 323 of the Code of Criminal Procedure in Japan has an expressly stipulated enactment to the effect that "an account Book, a voyage log, and other documents prepared in the regular course of business may be used as evidence in criminal justice." This is the article that states that an account book and others in which timely entries have been made can possess evidential value in criminal justice. This article seems to acknowledge the logic of the recognition of "the proof of books" of such books of account in which the "timeliness of entry" has evidently been brought into focus. As a consequence, to tell the truth, it cannot be said that there is no legal standard at all in Japanese legislation that takes seriously the view of the "timeliness of entry." This country's scholars of accounting, bookkeeping, business administration, tax jurisprudence, and commercial law have failed, however, to notice the actual existence of the text of regulations that attach importance to the timeliness of entry into books of account and others in the total system of the legislative standard in Japan, provisions which, in turn, actually constitute one of the important elements of the principles of regular bookkeeping in the Federal Republic of Germany.

Testing for Tax-Advising Professions (11th ed., 1978), written by Professor Adolf Grass, is comprised of about a thousand pages and is divided into two sections: "Material for the Oral Exam" and "Material for the Written Exam." The book contains model questions and answers for each subject the two exams may cover. An outline of Section One follows:

The Principle of "Timeliness" 33

Subject	Number of questions
1. Tax Code, Tax Court Code	213
2. Income Tax	396
3. Corporation Tax	120
4. Sales Tax	260
5. Appraisal Law and Property Tax	229
6. Business Tax, License Tax	106
7. Professional Law	100
Total	1,424

Section Two, "Material for the Written Exam," is similar, but I will omit its contents here. In the first section under the subject "Income Tax," there is a model question and answer on the "timeliness of the accounting record" among a series of questions regarding the principles of regular bookkeeping.

Question 89: What is meant by "current/timely recording of business transactions"?
Answer: The timely recording of business transactions requires (in the case of cash transactions) daily notation in the register (journal). For practical reasons it is permissible to record credit transactions only periodically. Therefore it is not objectionable to record all the credit transactions of one month in the register before the end of the following month (Paragraph 29, Sec. 2, No. 2, *EStR*). However, one must take organizational precautions to insure that the accounting documents are not lost before being recorded.[5]

As it is a model answer, it is brief and to the point.

As we have seen, cash transactions should be entered on a daily basis is recommended by Paragraph 1 of Article 146 of the Tax Code. However, the timeliness of the entry of what we call "transfer transactions," or "credit transactions" under German law, is limited to less than one month from the time the said transactions occurred by Article 29 of the Enforcement Regulations for the Income Tax Law. The title of Article 29 is "Regular Accounting." It has already been stated that this Article 29 together with Article 162 of the former Tax Code are the main provisions prescribing the contents of "the principles of regular bookkeeping."

In evaluating the literature on tax jurisprudence in the Federal Republic of Germany, it seems to me that, as far as the Tax Code

34 The Principle of "Timeliness"

and Tax Court Code are concerned, the commentary by Hübschmann, Hepp, and Spitaler, *Commentary on the Tax Code and Tax Court Code* (7th ed., 1979), has the highest authority. It was compiled by a staff of writers who were chosen by the three well-known scholars. The writers are professors holding lectureships in tax jurisprudence in four German universities at Nuremberg, Damstadt, Würzburg, and Munich, and five justices in the Federal Finance Court. This book devotes thirty pages to an explanation of Articles 146 and 147 of the new Tax Code (presented in Vol. 2), which prescribe "the principles of regular bookkeeping."

In the section on Article 146, moreover, it is noted that "timeliness of entry" has been explained. Considering the text of this article, quoted above, it is self-evident that the principle of timeliness of entry, especially among "the principles of regular bookkeeping," has been given a great deal of importance by this commentary. It states: "All business transactions are to be posted in registers in a timely and orderly manner. The timely posting of business transactions—with the exception of cash transactions—does not require daily posting. However, there must exist a temporal relationship between the transactions and their posting in account books" (BFH VI 154/63 U. v. 5.3.65, *BStBl* III 1965, 285 = *StRK EstG* 10 d R.29).

Particular attention should be paid to the fact that the German word "sämtliche" is used in the phrase translated "all transactions," and that it has a stronger meaning than the English word "all." It should be understood that the word "sämtliche" means "all" in a strict sense under which no exceptions or omissions are allowed. It seems to me that the emphasis placed on "a temporal relationship" in the text of this taxation decision may have been the fundamental factor that caused the establishment of the explanatory standard for the limit that has been prescribed by Paragraph 2 of Article 29 of the Enforcement Regulations for the Income Tax Law: "The posting of credit transactions of one month takes place before the end of the following month." The reason is that the first part of Paragraph 2 of this article quotes the very text of the above Federal Finance Court decision itself, just as it is, and it indicates clearly the source by adopting the date on which the decision was made and even indicates the pages of the *Official Gazette* on which the decision was recorded.

It is interesting to note that in the Federal Republic of Germany, there have been a surprising number of instances in which the Enforcement Regulations concerning taxation laws have adopted a direct quotation from the text of a Federal Finance Court decision, even as to the date of the decision and the pages of the *Official Gazette* entering the decision in the text of the provisions. This writer has observed this German practice as the typical manifestation of the concept of the principle of lawful administration. It is my hope that the authorities of the Japanese Finance Ministry will make an effort to learn from Germany's example, in order to create a Japan that will win the respect of the world in the sphere of tax laws and also in the sphere of tax jurisprudence as Japan's system of social science.

Notes

1. Eberhard Littmann, *Einkommensteuerrecht*, 12 Auflage, 1978, p. 313.
2. Ibid., p. 320.
3. Karl-Heinz Mittelsteiner and Harald Schaumburg, *Abgabenordnung 1977, Materialen Zusammengestellt und bearbeitet von Karl-Heinz Mittelsteiner*, 2 Auflage, 1977, S. 240.
4. BFH-Urteil vom 12. 5. 1966 - *BStBl* III, S. 371.
5. Adolf Grass, *Die Prüfung der steuerberatenden Berufe*, 11 Auflage, 1978, p. 130.

4

The Principle of "Materiality" and Its Criticism

In Chapter 3, "System of the Principles of Regular Accounting," under the heading "Materiality," Ulrich Leffson writes as follows: "From the idea of accountability, to give information to those entitled to it as a basis for their decisions, one can derive the principle that is established as the principle of 'materiality' in American balance sheet discussions and is best called 'Prinzip der Wesentlichkeit' in German."[1]

In explaining this matter, he quotes from an article by S. M. Woolsey, "Objective Base for Making Materiality Decisions," in the bulletin *The Accountant,* which is issued by the Institute of Chartered Accountants in England and Wales (the I.C.A.): "Any item in between the two limits could be considered material or immaterial, depending upon the surrounding circumstances. An accountant would be expected to follow the recommended guidelines unless he could justify departure from them." He also quotes the following from James L. Dohr's article "Materiality—What Does It Mean in Accounting?," which was published in the *Journal of Accountancy* (the bulletin of the AICPA):

A statement, fact, or item is material, if giving full consideration to the surrounding circumstances, as they exist at the time, it is of such a nature that its disclosure, or the method of treating it, would be likely to influence or to "make a difference" in the judgment and conduct of a reasonable person. The same tests also apply to such words as "significant," "consequential," or "important."[2]

Originally, this principle was included in the concept of the principles of regular bookkeeping in Germany. It is worth noting that in the principle of "materiality," there is a difference between "quantitative materiality" and "qualitative materiality." For instance, when the possibility exists of the omission of mentioned items, it is regarded that there is a "material thing."[3] To the best of my knowledge the concept of "materiality" originated in Articles 11 and 24 of the U.S. Securities Act of 1933. Like the principles of regular bookkeeping in the Federal Republic of Germany, the concept of "materiality" is not a fixed one, but it evolves over time.

Moreover, although it may seem a trivial thing, I wish to correct one thing from the viewpoint of the pursuit of truth. In the "Postscript by the Editor" (pp. 192–93) of the September 1979 issue of *Accounting*, which was compiled by the Japan Society of Accounting and published by Moriyama Shoten, there is a critical article by Dr. Kurosawa, "The Principles of Regular Bookkeeping." Dr. Kurosawa is the most renowned accounting scholar in Japan and a "national treasure." He has been recognized as such by all. To criticize his article embarrasses me and prompts me to express my deep regrets to him.

We who live in this time, however, and have been brought up in an Eastern culture have to consider the teachings of Mencius in China who preached two thousand years ago that "if one gives one's credit to all the books, one is none the better than the one who has no book at all." In this sense, therefore, I sincerely wish the general reader to allow me to pass judgment on Dr. Kurosawa's criticism.

Dr. Kurosawa states in his critical sentence that "at the time Dr. Tanaka's *Logic of the Laws Concerning Balance Sheet* was written, there were no provisions concerning the principles of regular bookkeeping in the German Stock Law, except those in General Principle, Article 38." His statement, however, is in error. The target of his comment is a sentence on page 36 of the reprinted edition of Dr. Tanaka's book, issued in June 1946. On this page, Article 38 of the German Commercial Code and Article 129 of the German Stock Law and an explanation of these quoted laws actually appear. As Dr. Tanaka himself actually quoted from and discussed Article 129 of the German Stock Law, one cannot claim that at that time there was no such law.

The German Stock Law that served as the basis for Dr. Tanaka's quotation was the one that was revised in 1937. What was Article 129 at that time, however, became Article 149 of the German Stock Law when it was revised in 1965. Regarding the circumstances of this matter, please refer to page 306 of *Auditing* (1977 edition), written by Dr. Ulrich Leffson, Professor of Business Economics, Münster University, or to page 872 of Volume 1 of *Corporate Law* (4th edition, 1971), which was written by Freiherr von Godin in collaboration with Hans Wilhelmi. The former book explained, via negative proposition, that the change in the German Stock Law from Article 129 to Article 149 had not simply been of a declaration character. The latter explained, via positive proposition, that "the regulation corresponds to that of 129 *AktG*. Only the expansion of Section 1, Page 2 is new."[4] That is to say, the latter part of Paragraph 1 establishes and adds new standards on how to indicate the property and circumstances of the gains of a corporation.

In either case, it is a clear fact that both the former Article 129 and the new Article 149 include the expression "the principles of regular accounting." If we take a look at the text of Paragraph 2 of the new Article 149, this matter will be much clearer. Paragraph 2 states: "As long as nothing else is prescribed in the following regulations, the regulations of the fourth paragraph of the first book of the Commercial Law Book (Code) concerning business records are applicable." The reason is that Clause 4 of Volume 1 of the German Commercial Code is composed of a total of ten articles, one of which, Article 38, is the text that defines the principles of regular bookkeeping. As a consequence, this writer cannot help but state that it was a mistake on Dr. Kurosawa's part to say that only Article 38 of the General Principle was in existence. The text of the provisions that were included in Clause 4 of Volume 1 were not included in the General Principle.

Dr. Kurosawa also wrote that "Dr. Tanaka's theory, which was buttressed by Radbruch's *Philosophy of Law*, might have been justified in its own way at that time." It should be acknowledged that Dr. Radbruch was one of the greatest scholars of contempo-

The Principle of "Materiality" and Its Criticism 39

rary Germany. Dr. Heinrich Henkel, former Professor Emeritus of Salzburg University and currently Professor of the Faculty of Law, Hamburg University, has written a book of about 570 pages, *Introduction to the Philosophy of Law* (2d ed., 1977), and has quoted Radbruch's *Philosophy of Law* sixty-one times. I believe that Dr. Henkel acknowledges the authority of Professor Radbruch's theory and has, therefore, quoted *Philosophy of Law* so often in his own book.

At the beginning of Chapter 2, Radbruch declares: "In that case the philosophy of law would be the evaluative view of law, the . . . theory of correct justice." In Paragraph 7 of Chapter 3, "The Directions of the Philosophy of Law," Radbruch praises Rudolf Stammler highly: "The reestablishing of the philosophy of law, the restoration of the independence of the value of law, in addition to the exploration of judicial practice on the basis of the dualism of the methods of Kantian philosophy was Rudolf Stammler's great contribution." At the same time, however, Radbruch indicates the limit of the "theory of the right law" (Stammler) by concluding that "the theory of the right law neither tries to nor can develop a single judicial proposition, which could be proven to have universal validity." Furthermore, Radbruch gives Stammler the coup de grâce by saying: "It sacrifices the universality of its concepts in exchange for its purely formal character." Dr. Radbruch courageously cuts down Stammler's theory by stating that it is only "a logic of the philosophy of law" rather than "the philosophy of law," and that, therefore, "the theory of the right law" is, so to speak, the valuable " 'framework' of the philosophy of law," but not the " 'building' of the philosophy of law."[5]

Criticism of Professor Radbruch

I would like to speak very highly of Dr. Radbruch's farsightedness and courage. However, at this point, I cannot help but appeal to my reader. I must let you know that even Radbruch himself made a decisive error in the book I have just quoted. At the opening of Section 3 of Chapter 3 of *The Philosophy of Law*, by seizing on Hegel's famous expression "Whatever is rational, is actual, and what is actual is rational," Radbruch concluded that "Hegel has

40 The Principle of "Materiality" and Its Criticism

wrapped 'to be' and 'should be' into one" by putting together "the concept of reason in Hegel" and "the concept of 'Sollen' " (which means "moral obligation," or "what should be").[6]

This conclusion is a mistake, and it is a shallow and misdirected judgment. If I could speak to Professor Radbruch, I would say the following: "My dear Professor Radbruch: It is true that Hegel made frequent errors, but I wish to tell you that you must not make a fool of Hegel as a person who is poor in theory, and it is very impolite of you to do so." It is true that at the beginning of Section 5 of *Fundamentals of the Philosophy of Right* (Berlin, 1821), Hegel wrote what Radbruch quoted. However, I maintain that the true meaning of Hegel's expression cannot be understood unless one reads further. At the end of the first paragraph of Section 6, Hegel says: "Here is the rose, dance thou here" (trans. T. M. Knox, in Preface to *G. F. W. Hegel's Philosophy of Right* [London: Oxford, 1967], p. 11), and on the next page he writes: "To recognize Reason as the rose in the cross of the present" (ibid., p. 12).[7]

That is to say, in this particular work, Hegel describes human reason by comparing it to a rose. I would like to point out that the idea of depicting human reason figuratively as a rose was cultivated by Hegel for more than ten years. In the second sentence of Chapter 6, "The Spirit," of the second edition of his *Phenomenology of Spirit* (1807), written by Hegel when he was thirty-seven years of age, there had already appeared a description of reason as a rose. I must regretfully say that Radbruch failed to grasp the versatility and depth of Hegel's concept of reason.

Phenomenology of Spirit is Hegel's most important work. He became so attached to it that he was busily engaged in minor revisions of it for several weeks prior to his death. The latest edition of this book, which I keep at my elbow, is the fifty-sixth (Hamburg: Verlag von Felix Meiner, 1952). In Chapter 5, "Reason," Hegel devoted 138 pages to a discussion of reason. In other chapters, Hegel also energetically discussed reason from various viewpoints. He wrote, for example: "Self-consciousness is Reason."[8] At another time, he stated: "Reason is the certainty of consciousness that it is all reality" (G. W. F. Hegel, *Phenomenology of Spirit*, trans. A. V. Miller [Oxford: Clarendon Press, 1977], S. 233, p. 140), or "Reason is the conscious certainty of being all reality" (G. W. F. Hegel, *The Phenomenology of Mind*, trans. J. B. Baille [N.Y.: Macmillan, 1931], p. 273), and so forth.[9] He made various statements of this sort.

To sum up, Hegel never thought of human reason only in terms of its function. Together with Schopenhauer, Hegel, who was strongly influenced by the Upanishad philosophy of ancient India, held a basic belief that reason as a rose, namely, "the absolute Essence"[10] could be perceived in such a thing that could be called "Actual Cross" or "Real Life" in "Seven Flowers & Eight Shattered Pieces" (which is a term in Buddhism that implies that a thing is shattered into fine pieces). It seems to me that Hegel compared his concept of reason with the concept of "the World Will" that was used by Schopenhauer in his representative work, *The World As Will and Imagination*. Hegel often called reason "the World reason," and positioned the concept of reason as *an arena* in which a man tries to comprehend, with deep understanding, "the absolute Essence" through "pure insight."[11] In this particular instance, however, "to be" should not be considered identical with "what should be," but the concept of "reason" is grasped and constructed as *an arena* where "the absolute Essence" is perceived in "to be." Therefore, Radbruch made an irredeemable error when he took Hegel's concept of "reason" as "what should be."

I have a high regard for Radbruch's skill at literary embellishments, which should be called his work of art. As to the rigor of his intellect, however, I cannot help but say that he is not yet an expert. (The expression "special expert" is found in the *Analects* of Confucius.) However, I also cannot help but ask myself whether the remnants of our admiration of Western Europe in the sphere of social science are not responsible for remarks like "Tanaka's theory was buttressed by Radbruch's *Philosophy of Law*." Furthermore, in regard to criticisms like "Tanaka's theory might have had justification in its own way at that time," or "It may not necessarily be appropriate to attack it simply from the standpoint of judgment at present in defiance of history," I think such criticism may be considered the first-rate criticism of those scholars who would not break their respective sonorous attitudes.

If my reader has been kind enough to follow the thrust of my argument, composedly and strictly, I am sure he will understand that there is not a trace of "reproach" in it, and that there exists only one indication that an error in Dr. Tanaka's method as a scholar in social science has caused the mistake in his conclusion. I hope the reader fathoms that, in the past when the restoration of "direct imperial rule" was established in the period of Kemmu (133–1335), a Japanese samurai named Masashige Kusunoki clearly expressed that "when one cuts off a forked thought of doubt at the same time, one is able to enjoy looking at a sword sparkling and piercing in mid-air." I am sure the reader will be able to comprehend his frame of mind at that time.

I am only a believer in the Zen sect, however, and a man of business who seeks neither fame nor wealth. I would like to add here that the basis for writing earlier that "Hegel was strongly influenced by the Upanishad philosophy of ancient India" was the book *The Thirteen Principal Upanishads Translated from the Sanskrit*, by Robert Ernest Hume (Oxford University Press, 2d rev. ed., 1931), p. 70.

Criticism of Professor Schmalenbach

I audaciously wrote earlier that "Schmalenbach's mistakes are not trifling," a statement based on my knowledge of the book *Dynamic Balance Sheet* (12th ed.), translated by Masazo Doki. It was not the fifth edition of Schmalenbach's book, which was referred to by Dr. Tanaka. Through a German bookseller, I placed an order for both the fifth and the twelfth editions of Schmalenbach's book, but I was informed that both were unavailable, because they were out of print. Through the good offices of Mr. Shiro Yoshikawa, the Executive Director of Fujitsu, Ltd., with whom I have been on intimate terms for a long time, via Fujitsu's Resident Office in Germany, I was able to obtain copies of the fifth edition of Schmalenbach's book and the second edition of Enno Becker's exegesis of the Imperial Tax Code of December 13, 1919, both of which were owned by Munich University. The fifth edition of Schmalenbach's *Dynamic Balance Sheet* ran 376 pages, and its contents and many of its details were considerably different from those of the twelfth edition. Enno Becker, who had drafted the Imperial Tax Code, had written a voluminous book of 731 pages.

The Principle of "Materiality" and Its Criticism 43

The fifth edition of Schmalenbach's *Dynamic Balance Sheet* was published in 1931, twelve years after the enactment of the Imperial Tax Code. The first edition of *Dynamic Balance Sheet* was published early in 1919, so this book was also twelve years old. Among the works published during those years, the following are quoted by Schmalenbach in his Introduction to the fifth edition.

1. Schmalenbach, *Basics of Cost Accounting and Pricing Policy* (3d ed., Leipzig, 1926), p. 4.
2. Walb, "The Profit and Loss Statement of Cameralistics," *Journal for Commercial Research*, Vol. 19, 1925, p. 17.
3. Weber, A., "Cost Estimation in Agriculture," *Journal for Commercial Research*, Vol. 18, 1924, p. 51.
4. Prof. Krieger, "Necessity and Essence of Forestry Accounting in 'Waldheil,' " *Almanac for German Foresters and Hunters*, 1926, p. 53.
5. Hausendorf, R., "The Success of the Forestry Industry?" (Berlin, 1926), p. 54.
6. Leonhard, A., *The Historical Development of Dynamic Balance Sheets* (1921), p. 62.
7. Ferner, A., "The Development of Bookkeeping and Balance Statements during the Sixteenth Century," *The Enterprise*, Vol. 1, 1921/22, p. 62.
8. Walb, "The Theory of Profit and Loss Accounting," *Journal of Commercial Research*, Vol. 17 (1923), p. 71.
9. Lehmann, *On the Theory of Industrial Cost Accounting*, 1920, p. 73.
10. Schmidt, Prof. F., *Die organische Bilanz im Rahmen der Wirtschaft. Betriebs- und finanzwirtschaftliche Forschungen.* Leipzig, 1921, 1922, S. 80.
11. Bauckner, *Der privatwirtschaftliche Einkommensbegriff.* 1921, S. 86.
12. Schanz, *Der Einkommensbegriff und die Einkommensteuergesetze.* Finanzarchiv. 13. Jahrg, 1920, S. 87.
13. Strutz, "The Income Tax," *Handbook of the Imperial Tax Law* (Berlin, 1924), p. 88.
14. Lüpke, *Journal of Commercial Research*, Vol. 18 (1924), p. 112.

15. Morgenroth, W., *"Indexziffern" im Handwörterbuch der Staatswissenschaften*, 1923, S. 221.
16. *Business and Statistics*, 1922, 1923, p. 228 (no author's name was given; this is a magazine—au.).
17. *Statistical Yearbook for the German Empire*, Vol. 44, 1924–25, p. 231.
18. Dr. Hermann, *Die Ausschaltung von saisonmäßigen und säkularen Schwankungen aus Wirtschaftskurven, Vierteljahrshefte zur Konjunkturforschung, herausgegeben vom Institut für Konjunkturforschung*, 1. Jahrgang, 1926, Ergänzungshet 1, S. 295.
19. Stern, *Buchhaltungslexikon*, 2 Aufl., Leipzig, 1923, S. 309.

These are the materials I overlooked at the beginning. This was because the year of publication was lacking in each case in the annotation of the quoted literature.

In addition to the above, there were more quotations from several kinds of magazines, such as *Commercial Research*, but their respective publication years are not known. In the literature whose year of publication is unknown, there are more quotations to page 355 of Volume 1 of Lutz, Anlagenbank, and Ehrenberg, *Handbook of . . . Commercial Law*. The list above is an approximation of the literature so quoted.

I think Schmalenbach's achievements in the broad sphere of business economics were highly admirable, especially in regard to the balance sheet, which he positioned as an auxiliary step for profit and loss accounting. By overturning long-standing general opinion with his *Dynamic Balance Sheet*, he established, for the first time in history, modern accounting thought. The *Dictionary of Business Economics* quotes Schmalenbach's name and his theory 165 times in its four volumes. The only scholars quoted more often are: E. Kosiol (216 times), E. Gutenberg (199 times), and E. Grochla (198 times). His record allows us to see how great his achievements in this field were. In my personal opinion, however, this work by Schmalenbach also had a momentous defect.

In the first place, the positive law standard that had special particulars regarding the principles of regular bookkeeping was enacted in Germany when his work was published, namely in 1919. Despite the passage of twelve years since the first publication of this book, not a single word referring to the existence of the

Imperial Tax Code appears anywhere in the 376 pages of the fifth edition. This is a conspicuous defect in the work of a scholar who must render every possible service to truth.

Secondly, it was in May 1931 when the fifth edition of this book was published. During the whole period from the publication of the first edition to the publication of the fifth, however, the Federal Finance Court (BFH) handed down judicial decisions, which bridged the gap between business economics and tax jurisprudence, in a total of twenty-nine cases from *BFH vom 13. 1. 1920. 1 A 232/19 to BFH vom 24. 3. 1931. 1 A 235/30.*[12] The fifth edition, however, did not quote even one case from the above twenty-nine cases, and Schmalenbach discontinued his further examination of the judicial precedents that were handed down up to 1918. I cannot help but conclude, therefore, that Schmalenbach's scholastic attitude is extremely irresponsible, irrespective of the reasons for the above interruption.

Among the twenty-nine precedents, it has been noted that the following seven juridical precedents, set by the Federal Finance Court, are considered the ones that restrict legally and directly the meaning of the principles of regular bookkeeping:

1. *11. 11. 1925—VIA 491/25—amtl. Slg. Bd. 17, S.332:* Concerning the posting of pending transactions.
2. *16. 4. 1930—W.A 339/30—StW 1930/601:* Concerning the amount of depreciation when a machine is to be used in its remaining life only as a backup.
3. *6. 5. 1930—1 e A 888/29—StW 30/677.*
4. *21. 3. 1930—III A 224/29—StW 30/678.*
5. *27. 3. 1930—III A 444/29—StW 30/679:* Concerning the undervaluation of a mortgage claim with low interest rates and other reasons for an undervaluation.
6. *11. 3. 1931—VI A 118/31—StW 1931/440:* Concerning the estimation of the amount of reserves according to the merchant's subjective expectations.
7. *17. 3. 1931—IA 479/30—StW 1931/517: Erwartete Forderungsausfälk können nicht unberücksichtigt bleiben.*[13]

In this connection, I wish to recall Radbruch's words in Chapter 7, "The Purpose of Law," of his *Philosophy of Law*: *"Personlichkeit auf wissenschaftlichen Gebiet hat nur der, der rein der Sache dient."*[14]

He also said: *"Zur Persönlichkeit wird man durch selbstvergessene Sachlichkeit."*[15] I believe that those engaged in the study of learning who render service to truth without discarding their "ego," are really those persons who have lost their respective originality of character.

Thirdly, it is of great importance that Schmalenbach made the following statement:

These rules, resulting from expert opinion, are not purely artistic rules without juristic meaning. Rather, the law tries to apply these very artistic laws universally; they are a legal requirement. An accounting statement that does not conform to expert opinion is not only unprofessional, it is also legally wrong, *since that which is professionally correct is the legal norm.*[16]

I must ask you whether or not the passage above suggests to you the existence of a detailed and special treatise on legal provisions, namely the Imperial Tax Code, regarding the principles of regular bookkeeping? Dr. Tanaka was at a loss here, especially in the last passage. For Dr. Tanaka, who did not notice that this indirect description suggested the existence of the Imperial Tax Code as a positive law, this description was the source of the perplexity that caused his misunderstanding.[17]

Is it possible to say that, as a scholar in Japan, Dr. Tanaka's misunderstanding could not be helped? I firmly believe, however, that this very misunderstanding brought about a chain reaction of further misunderstanding among scholars of commercial law and accounting in Japan. This intentionally oblique description, or this unscholarly description, constituted the basic reason for the national misunderstanding that resulted in a serious intellectual loss, which lasted for several decades in this country's circles of accountants, even a serious defect in this country's accounting system, which was not confined only to the loss of accountants. Can you now understand the reason for my assertion that Schmalenbach's mistakes are not trifling?

Notes

1. Ulrich Leffson, *Principles of Regular Accounting*, 4th ed., 1976.
2. James L. Doer, *Journal of Accountancy* (July 1950), p. 60.

3. Lee J. Seidler and D. R. Carmichael, *Accountants' Handbook* (6th ed., 1981), Vol. 1, pp. 10 and 34.

4. "The regulation" means Article 149, while "page 2" refers to the latter part.

5. Gustav Radbruch, *The Philosophy of Law*, 8th ed., 1973, pp. 112 ff.

6. Ibid., p. 197.

7. Hegel, *Rechtsphilosophie*, Edition Ilting 2 (Stuttgart-Bad Constatt: Friedrich Frommann Verlag Gunther Holzboog KG, 1974), S. 70 ff.

8. Hegel, *Phanomenologie des Geistes*, p. 175.

9. Ibid., p. 176.

10. Ibid., p. 413.

11. The same view as that of this writer on this particular point can be found in line 3 of an annotation at p. 271 of the completely translated book published in 1931, *Phanomenologie des Geistes*, 1841 ed., trans. J. B. Baillie (Leeds: The University).

12. Gunter Wohe, Professor of Business Administration at the University of Saarland, *Tax Theory for Business Administration*, Vol. 1, 5th ed., p. 797.

13. Leffson, *Principles of Regular Accounting*, 4th ed., p. 17.

14. Radbruch, *Philosophy of Law*, p. 144

15. Ibid., p. 149.

16. Schmalenbach, *Dynamic Balance Sheet*, 12th ed., p. 362; emphasis mine.

17. Tanaka, *Logic of the Laws Concerning Balance Sheet*, p. 61, n. 23.

Part Two

5

Erroneous Theories of Dr. Kotaro Tanaka

Referring to the concept of "the principles of regular bookkeeping" for the first time in *Logic of the Laws Concerning Balance Sheet,* Dr. Tanaka writes that the German law prescribes that the adjustment of books of account should follow regular accounting principles, namely, "the principles of regular bookkeeping" (Article 38 of the German Commercial Code and Article 129 of the German Stock Law).[1] It is extremely unclear what the phrase "the principles of regular bookkeeping" means. After all, legislators should acknowledge that there has been a principle for practical business that has generally been practiced by businessmen, and aside from the case when the law itself prescribes regulations for specific occurrences, the law itself only establishes the "provision on a clean slate," the details of which have been entrusted by the law to customary practice in business. In this case, in particular, the author states that the contents of the entrusted practical business is to have a legal character. Furthermore, under Section 2: "Relationship between Law and the Principles of Regular Bookkeeping," the author comments as follows: "The law considered it a wiser measure to accept regular accounting techniques so as to take it into law itself comprehensively, and to entrust the determination of its details to the practice and the commonsense judgment of the enterpriser in each instance."[2]

In the Commercial Code in Japan, the legislators, unlike those in Germany, have not prepared such provisions "on a clean slate," either in the revised law or prior to the revision. As a consequence, the actual business regarding the preparation of balance sheets is to be totally incorporated into the legal system of this country, the result of which is that the actual business is to have, naturally, a legal force. From the viewpoint of our legal system, however, the above action should not be acknowledged. As a result, it is questionable whether the actual business has to remain as a mere technique that will have no legal restrictive power over businessmen in general.

It is very appropriate for our legislative policy to acknowledge the existence of one article of the general regulations like those in German law. Even from the viewpoint of our current laws, however, it is unthinkable that the same conclusion as that in German law cannot be acknowledged from an interpretative viewpoint. As a matter of fact, in Japan's Commercial Code—and especially so in the new revised law—when the regulations regarding merchants in general and those regarding incorporated companies are considered comprehensively, each concept and the regulation in each provision cannot be understood unless the existence of systematic bookkeeping and accounting techniques are acknowledged as underlying these fragmentary regulations. It should thus be acknowledged that even in our Commercial Code, "the principles of regular bookkeeping" have been incorporated into the legal system in this country.

I admit that my discussion of this point has been rather lengthy, however, I must state frankly that the reason Japan's present-day scholars in tax jurisprudence, its authors of books on accounting for taxation, and its scholars in accounting or the Commercial Code have committed errors originates in Dr. Tanaka's logic. When we immerse ourselves in this logic, the following applies. In the first place, the principles of regular bookkeeping that have been prescribed by Article 38 of the German Commercial Code are only regulations "on a clean slate" that have entrusted their details to the customary practice of actual business. Secondly, even in the case of the Commercial Code in Japan, it should be acknowledged that the principles of regular bookkeeping have been incorporated into the system of the law in Japan. To be sure, when we adopt a clear-cut attitude to the principles of regular bookkeeping that have been prescribed by Article 38 of the German Commercial

Code as the regulations on a clean slate, it can be acknowledged that the principles of regular bookkeeping have been incorporated into the legal system of our Commercial Code; the German Commercial Code can be viewed as "the mother law" for the Commercial Code of this country.[3]

The grounds of Dr. Tanaka's argument are as follows: "For instance, in our Commercial Code, there is no direct provision that prescribes that the sum of capital shall be stated in the column 'Liability of Balance Sheet' of a corporation. This particular matter cannot be brought forth from Articles 33 and 34 regarding merchants in general.[4] This fact shows that this particular matter is brought forth from the principles of regular bookkeeping in general."[5] It is doubtful that we can say that this subjective inevitability in the organization of Dr. Tanaka's theory assumes objective universality at the same time. However, as this point digresses from the subject of this chapter, and as I am not a scholar of the Commercial Code, I will refrain from further reference to this point.

What is problematic is Dr. Tanaka's "theory of a provision on a clean slate" and his "theory of commitment to actual business practices." Where do these two theories come from? The answer to this question can be found by reviewing in detail the literature on which Dr. Tanaka based his discussion of the general character of the balance sheet in Chapter 2. I think that there is a goodwill error in the scope of Dr. Tanaka's research. The quoted literature is as follows:

1. Schmalenbach, *Dynamic Balance Sheet*, 5 Aufl., 1931.
2. Adler-Penndorf, in *Dictionary of Political Science*, Vol. III.
3. Max Weber, *History of Business, 1923.*
4. Sombart, *The Order of Business Life*, 1925.
5. Gomberg, *Basis of Balance Science*, 1908.
6. Sombart, *Modern Capitalism*, Vol. II, 1921.
7. Carvalho de Medonca, *Tratado de direito commercial brasileiro*, Vol. II, 1937.
8. Müller-Frzbach, German *Commercial Law*, 1921.
9. Passow, *The Accounting of Private and Public Enterprises*, Vol. I, 3d ed., 1921.

10. Hein, *Tax and Commercial Law*, 1928.
11. Sewering, *Standard Accounting*, 1925.
12. Fisher, in *Ehrenberg's Handbook of Commercial Law*, Vol. III.
13. Simon, *The Statements of the Stock Corporation*, 4th ed., 1910.
14. Rehm, *Statements of Stock Corporations*, 2 Aufl., 1914.
15. Wieland, *Commercial Law*, Vol. I.
16. W. Schmidt, *In Stock Law* (Commentary prepared by Gadow, Heinichen, Schmidt, and Weipertz), 1939.
17. Behrend, *Commercial Law*.
18. Julius von Gierke, *Commercial Law*, 5 Aufl., 1938.

What I found with surprise was that although Dr. Tanaka has written so decisively on "the principles of regular bookkeeping" in German laws, it is noteworthy that he has never read, or at least has never quoted, even a single book out of the many entitled *The Principles of Regular Bookkeeping* that have grappled with the above principles.[6] I have no intention at all of blaming Dr. Tanaka for his failure to read books by the authors who have distinguished themselves in German academic circles since 1970, authors such as Ulrich Leffson, Heinrich Wilhelm Kruse, and Karl Peter. The reason is that such reading was physically an absolute impossibility.

What I must point out, however, is that Dr. Tanaka has not quoted a single book of reference with the phrase "regular accounting principles" in its title, of which several were published in German academic circles and taken note of ten years earlier than 1944, the date of the publication of the first edition of Dr. Tanaka's book. The books included in this category are as follows:

1. K. Hast, *Regular Accounting Principles for Fixed Assets*, 1934.
2. A. Krause, *Regular Accounting Principles for Pension Obligations*, 1935.
3. E. Streit, *Regular Accounting Principles for Reserves*, 1936.
4. K. Welland, *GoB für Wechsel, Schecks und Akzepte*, 1936.
5. N. Dietzen, *Regular Accounting Principles for Hidden Assets*, 1937.
6. H. K. Vellguth, *Regular Accounting Principles for Pending Transactions*, 1937.

A second point of surprise was that, as far as literature regarding tax jurisprudence is concerned, Dr. Tanaka read only a single book, or at least quoted only one book, *Tax and Commercial Law*, written by Mr. Hein in 1928. Nevertheless, an objective clue appeared before Dr. Tanaka's very eyes. Dr. Tanaka wrote: "Mr. Hein has indicated that regular bookkeeping is not only 'a concept of fact,' but also 'a concept of law' at the same time."[7] It is noteworthy that Mr. Hein's book was published nine years after the enactment of the German Fundamental Taxation Law *(AO)*.

What is more, Dr. Tanaka even quoted the fifth edition of a book entitled *Dynamic Balance Sheet*, in which Mr. Schmalenbach stated that the law demanded that "artificial rules" that had been called regular bookkeeping would be applied generally, and that "professional" was elevated to become "a lawful norm."[8] These arguments made by Mr. Hein and Mr. Schmalenbach, as was pointed out later by Mr. H. Kellenbenz of Cologne University, were made against the background of the circumstances of the times, during which an epoch-making phenomenon occurred—the legalization of a nationwide unified standard of bookkeeping techniques resulting in a far-reaching advance of bookkeeping in regard to the problem of industrialization of Germany. I wonder why Dr. Tanaka failed to visualize the point mentioned above.

The Fundamental Taxation Law *(AO)*, drafted by Enno Becker, had been enacted a long time before (1919). Dr. Tanaka, however, did not notice that the concept of the principles of regular bookkeeping was embodied in the German Commercial Code, and that these principles were really those that had originated in the tax law. It seems to me, therefore, that Dr. Tanaka, who was sincere in this respect, might have speeded up his theoretical organization by making almost no use of various works of scholarship regarding "proper" tax jurisprudence. Dr. Tanaka, who just missed seeing the truth of the matter under his nose, failed to notice the position of his standing and had to make an about-face. The actual circumstances of the inmost motives that caused Dr. Tanaka to make such an about-face cannot be ascertained any more, because he passed away a long time ago.

If the reader is kind enough to allow me to surmise, it seems that Dr. Tanaka probably had to reverse himself because of the restricted situation he was in, a situation caused by his own subjectivity. In other words, he had been restricted subjectively by the descriptions regarding the judicial precedents relating to the principles of regular bookkeeping that had been made before 1918, all of which were contained in Schmalenbach's book. He was restricted by the logic of the descriptions regarding the judicial precedents that had been made up to the year before the Fundamental Taxation Law *(AO)* was enacted, under which the national unification of the standard on the techniques of bookkeeping was legalized.

I assume, therefore, that it might have been the truth of the matter that as a result of Dr. Tanaka's condition, described above, he failed to conduct an inquiry into many of the BFH's judicial precedents regarding the limitation of the contents of the principles of regular bookkeeping made during the period of twenty-five years from 1919, when the *AO* was enacted, to 1944 when Dr. Tanaka's book was first published. Dr. Tanaka did not refer at all to twenty-five years' worth of judicial precedents regarding German taxation, made during the period from 1919 to 1944. It is my firm conviction, therefore, that if Dr. Tanaka might have had a chance to look over the various works of scholarship I listed earlier, along with the judicial precedents regarding German taxation made for the past twenty-five years, his theory undoubtedly would not have been limited by subjective self-restriction and it would have been an entirely different one.

Notes

1. Kotaro Tanaka, *Logic of the Laws Concerning Balance Sheet* (reprint, June 1946), p. 36.
2. Ibid., pp. 37–38.
3. Ibid., pp. 38.
4. Article 33 was the provision regarding the obligation of preparing "a list of property" and "balance sheet," while Article 34 was the provision regarding "method of entry" for "a list of property."
5. Tanaka, *Logic of the Laws*, p. 61.
6. "The principles of regular bookkeeping" are abbreviated *"GoB"* in German literature.
7. Tanaka, *Logic of the Laws*, p. 145.
8. Schmalenbach, *Dynamic Balance Sheet*, p. 362.

6

Critical Review of the Opinions of Respectable Japanese Scholars: Part I

In the Zen sect in Japan, there is a legend of an idea of reason that has been handed down from generation to generation: "When a disciple's opinion exceeds that of his master, he is worthy of being recognized for the first time as a full-fledged man." This legend means that when a disciple's opinion excels that of his master, he is worthy of being sanctioned for the first time as an independent man. I believe that we who are out of office and are free professionals grow by receiving our debt in learning from the direct and indirect guidances of many scholars. Only when we can exceed the opinions of our respected teachers, can we come of age for the first time. Then we can repay our indebtedness in learning to their kind services.

The above opinion, however, may be a self-involved conception, because I have been brought up breathing the severe and clean atmosphere of the Zen sect. At any rate, I would like to move on to a review of the subject matter below. On account of limited space, I will not mention most of the honorary titles of the scholars mentioned hereafter.

New Theory of a Balance Sheet
by Michisuke Ueno, Vol. 1, 11th ed., 1942, published by Yuhi Kaku

In this book Ueno labels the principles of regular bookkeeping that were prescribed by Article 38 of the German Commercial

Code "orderly bookkeeping principles," and he writes that "orderly bookkeeping herein means double-entry bookkeeping."[1] An understanding that the said principles of regular bookkeeping are also the principles of the law and an understanding of said principles' relation with verifiable bookkeeping records are completely lacking.

Laws Concerning Accounting for Taxation
by Saichi Chu (Professor, Nihon University, and Lawyer), 6th ed.

Chu states that the term " 'the principles of regular bookkeeping' only indicates the technical direction of bookkeeping due to the nature of the provisions, and that, therefore, it is difficult to interpret that the term goes beyond that."[2] As he bases his work on the same understanding that Ueno does, he can also receive the same criticism as Ueno.

New Accounting
by Dr. Koichi Sato, 21st ed., 1967

Sato states: "The interpretation of these principles has been assigned to civilian scholars and a man of business. Consequently, these principles under the German laws should be interpreted in the wider sense that these principles are the method of accounting management which has generally been practiced in business as a custom."[3] Moreover, Sato confesses that the threefold structure that is embodied in the principles of regular bookkeeping is beyond his comprehension. Sato's statement is a fallacy that is out of the question.

Theory of Financial Accounting Principles
by Katsuji Yamashita, a reprint, 1957

Yamashita states that from the above interpretation, it has to be concluded that "the so-called principles of regular bookkeeping in the German *Commercial Code* have, in themselves, no definite contents, and that, in a manner of speaking, these principles should be admitted as the all-inclusive principles that exert action on bookkeeping and the preparation of a balance sheet."[4] Yamashita further states that "what is actually meant by the term 'the principles of regular bookkeeping' is that they are actually the principles that guarantee that bookkeeping has to have verification power—'verification power' for business transactions made in the past."

Yamashita proposes a change, moreover, in the wording of the principle with the statement that "it is not necessarily appropriate to use the expression 'the principles of regular bookkeeping,' and I think it more appropriate to express it as 'the principles for "orderly" bookkeeping.'" In so saying, Yamashita proposes a change in the title. Yamashita ends his explanation in twelve pages in Chapter V, "Principles of Regular Bookkeeping," with this statement: "It is a mistake to accept the perfunctory interpretation that only double-entry bookkeeping has been consistent with orderly bookkeeping principles."

It is a startling misunderstanding that gainsays the truth for Yamashita to conclude that the principles of regular bookkeeping in the German Commercial Code have no definite content in themselves. I think there is no need, therefore, for me to give more proof of Yamashita's misunderstanding of this matter. I would like to take my hat off, however, to Yamashita's declaration that "since the German Commercial Code of 1897, there has been no mistake that the principles of regular bookkeeping have been adopted."

To be exact, in the first half of the original text of Article 38 of the German Commercial Code, which was enacted on May 10, 1897, the expression "regular bookkeeping" was definitely indicated, and Article 38 of the German Commercial Code of 1900 was a mere successor to Article 38 of the German Commercial Code of 1897.[5]

Modern Accounting
by Dr. Kiyoski Kurosawa (Professor Emeritus, Yokohama National University), 6th rev. ed., 1978

Under the subject "Critical Review of the Principles of Regular Bookkeeping," Kurosawa quotes the opinion of Dr. Kotaro Tanaka concerning the principles of regular bookkeeping and states that "there is a bit of legal scholastic prejudice about his opinion." He also writes, "Dr. Tanaka has acknowledged the logical system only in the law, and he has taken for granted that accounting is no more than a technical system." Kurosawa further states that Tanaka's "self-complacent view is excessively legal and scholastic, and that accounting also has its own logical system which is on a level with the law's, just as the law is organized by both logic and techniques."

I have found with keen pleasure that, under the pretext of criticizing Dr. Tanaka, Kurosawa seems to have vented the long-harbored anger of accounting scholars against scholars on jurisprudence. As one of a crowd of curious spectators, I welcome Kurosawa's criticism with cheers. However, Kurosawa's conclusion that "in this way, 'the principles of regular bookkeeping' under German law is a clean slate which cannot be defined legally, and that it has become clear that it merely means the comprehensive commitment of the law to actual business practices in accounting" is nonetheless an error.

The principles of regular bookkeeping are a concept found in the German Commercial Code, and these principles are not only in accounting but also in German tax jurisprudence. That these principles are a concept of German tax jurisprudence is evidenced by the existence of Article 5 of the German Income Tax Law and Article 29 of the Enforcement Regulations, which were created as explanatory regulations for Article 5. It is also shown by the fact that since the enactment in 1919 of the Fundamental Taxation Law *(AO)*, which was drafted by Enno Becker, who was not only a justice of the BFH but also a representative scholar of tax laws, its Article 208 has prescribed "Regular Bookkeeping, Proof of Books," and its Article 162 has definite provisions regarding the contents of the principles of regular bookkeeping. It is also incontrovertible that there have been numerous judicial precedents regarding the contents of the principles of regular bookkeeping.

Scholars of civil and commercial laws tend to look down on taxation as merely a "procedural" law. This academic attitude, however, is only arrogance, just like a bubble floating on the surface of water. Why do the scholars of commercial laws in Japan conclude that it is the regulations that cannot be defined from a legal viewpoint, disregarding or neglecting the provisions of tax laws that have been enforced continuously for some tens of years since they were enacted? May the reason for their doing so be that they would not dare to recognize the tax law as a law? Or did they fail to notice the very existence of such laws in the sphere of taxation law? Whatever the reason, the result is that they do not view the legal standards in one country as a whole.

Among those who practice Zen in this country, the word "Tan-ban-kan," which appears in the book *Denkoroku*, is well-known. This word specifically indicates a person who can see only one side of a thing because of his carrying a piece of board. I think, therefore, that scholars of accounting all together should not depend on the erroneous theory of "Tan Ban Kan" as truth.

An Introduction to the New Accounting
by Tetsuzo Ohta and Masutaro Arai (Professor, Seikei University), 9th ed., 1978

Ohta and Arai maintain that in the regular bookkeeping principles of the German Commercial Code, the phrase "the principles that have a fixed order" is used, however, "the German Commercial Code does not make its contents clear."[6]

There is no "Daijodan-no-kamae" at all, which is literally translated "holding a sword over one's head," concerning these German laws. They do not touch at all on whether or not there are any definite and detailed legal standards. This attitude may be a tactic by which errors can be avoided by "nonperformance."

Theory of Financial Accounting
by Dr. Toshio Iino (Professor, Chuo University), 36th ed., 1979

Iino states: "The principles of regular bookkeeping are those regarding the whole accounting" and they have the same meaning as "the principles regarding regular bookkeeping and the preparation of 'financial statements' in German laws."[7] Moreover, Iino says they have the same meaning as "impartial accounting practices." It is not clear, however, whether Iino understands that the principles of regular bookkeeping have a "threefold structure." In particular, Iino states that the principles in the German laws are "the terms that are found in the regulations of the German Stock Law," however, he fails to indicate the numbers of the articles of that regulation.

My research indicates that among the regulations in the German Stock Law, those that contain the term "regular accounting principles" are Articles 149, 154, 155, and so forth. There is no term "the principles for the preparation of financial statements" in these articles, however; there is only the term "yearly balance sheet and the profit and loss statements at year's end" in Article 148. Therefore, I think that Iino's statement that "the terms . . . are found in the regulations of the German Stock Law" is not appropriate.

Moreover, the origin of the principles of regular bookkeeping, as a general perception, should consistently be noted as Paragraph 1 of Article 38 of the German Commercial Code. However, Iino failed to point this out. On the contrary, Iino tries to explain the concept by offering the idea that the Stock Law is one of the sources that has been quoted in various laws and branched out therefrom. I would like to ask Iino whether he would maintain that the principle of regular bookkeeping has nothing to do with merchants who do not fall under the scope of the Stock Law?

Please allow me to digress here from the main subject for a while. I would like to draw the reader's attention to the book *Bookkeeping and Tax Accounting* (subtitled *Text and Workbook for Business and Fiscal Officials*), which was written by Harald Schmidt, a governmental director and councillor of the government of the Federal Republic of Germany. This is a reference book that seems appreciative of those who are engaged in actual business practice as I am. Schmidt makes the following statement: "It can be said that the principles of regular bookkeeping have been constituted by the custom in commerce." Furthermore, these principles have been in existence as the law that has been codified. For instance: "The good accounting principles could have resulted from commercial practice. They can even be codified by a law. Examples of creating legal norms concerning accounting principles are Sections 2 through 7 of 162 of the Tax Code. The courts are also bound by this (Article 20, Section 3, GG)."[8]

When the legal system of the Federal Republic of Germany is examined from a comprehensive viewpoint, it is found that the Commercial Code itself, in Article 38, has made it clear that the principles of regular bookkeeping are the standards on which a merchant should perform his obligation to make an entry. The major content of these principles, however, has been the system under which the realization of these contents has been entrusted to other laws or legal standards. Therefore, when anyone who is an authority in Japan ceases his pursuit after checking only the German Commercial Code and exclaims, "No definite provisions have been found at all! It is a blank paper!," what happens next is that the honor of the senior great scholars must be saved. It has been a virtue of scholars and the custom in Japan to do this. It thus seems to me that a curious phenomenon begins to occur in which "one dog barks a false alarm and a thousand others take up the cry."

I firmly believe, however, that there is no advance of civilization at all unless there is a breakdown in the commonsense knowledge that has been handed down, and that there is no progress in learning when there is no critical analysis of the theories propounded by our senior scholars. Among those who practice Zen, there is a traditional concept of "Kininozomitewa-shi-nimo-yuzurazu"—in the presence of an opportunity to do otherwise, a disciple cannot defer to his master's opinion. There has been a tradition in Zen practice, therefore, that a disciple takes advantage of such an opportunity and gives a punch to his master, who is then extremely pleased with his disciple's action.

Those who confine themselves to the "ivory tower" are in a position in which they are expected to direct and influence, through their disciples, the consciousness of many millions of people of a nation. Therefore, I sincerely wish that these ivory-tower dwellers would lead a moderate, ascetic life in the practice of Zen until they could finally be spiritually awakened. They could then write their books and be engaged in education with a mental attitude in which their innermost hearts have not a speck of egotism. They could follow the example of the ex-Emperor of Hanazono (1297–1348) who once exclaimed that "there should be no solid earth that has had not a speck of dust on it." Incidentally, I think it worth our close attention that Harald Schmidt quoted "in parentheses" Paragraph 3 of Article 20 of the Fundamental Law of the Bonn Constitution. The reason is that, irrespective of his position as one of the directors of those persons who are engaged in administration, he expressly quoted this Paragraph 3 of Article 20 of the Bonn Constitution that has prescribed the great principles of the doctrine of the administrative laws. His attitude is a special one, however, and has no precedent among similar authors. I am deeply impressed once again with this person's seriousness and modesty as a public servant in the eyes of the law. My digression has gone on long enough, and we should return to our main subject.

Basic Accounting
by Dr. Yasuichi Sakamoto (Professor, Osaka Gakuin University), 20th ed., 1979

Sakamoto states that "as regards a certain kind of property that was dealt with by the principles of regular bookkeeping, it sometimes happens that in spite of the real existence of such property on the date on which its balance sheet was actually made, its 'book-value' turns out to be zero."[9] In this way, Sakamoto used the principles of regular bookkeeping only with regards to when the existence of the "off-book asset" was admitted. That is to say, he has given the impression that he has ended his explanation by skimming over only one side of the principles of regular bookkeeping.

New Edition of Accounting
by Dr. Shinkichi Minemura (Professor, Keio Gijuku University), 1976 ed.

Regarding the principles of regular bookkeeping, Minemura repeats the phrases, exactly as they are stated in the first general principles of Corporate Accounting Principles, that provide that "financial accounting should make correct books of account regarding all transactions made in accordance with the principles of regular bookkeeping."[10] Minemura, moreover, has not added even a syllable of his own opinion regarding the wording mentioned above. Therefore, it seems to me that the definition of the principles of regular bookkeeping will become a problem again.

Modern Financial Accounting
by Dr. Kyojiro Someya (Professor, Waseda University), rev. 55th ed., 1979

Someya states that the principles of regular bookkeeping originated in the principles of regular bookkeeping that were prescribed by the German Stock Law. The principles under the German law, however, have meant the comprehensive application of the law to business accounting practice.[11]

Someya further states that the principles of regular bookkeeping in Corporate Accounting Principles, on the contrary, have had the definite meaning that signifies that the above-mentioned principles prescribe the procedure through which a transaction record and a financial statement should be prepared, and the said principles constitute the very basis on which the "principle of accuracy" should be based. I would like to counter Someya's views with the following points:

First, the proposition that the principles of regular bookkeeping originated in the principles of regular bookkeeping that were prescribed by the German Stock Law indicates an insufficient recognition of a historical fact on Someya's part. As has already been explained, the above proposition originated in Article 38 of the German Commercial Code.

Secondly, in regard to Someya's proposition that "the said principles have meant the comprehensive application of the law to business accounting practice," some persons may think that the discussion of this proposition will differ from one person to another. It is a fact, however, that in the Federal Republic of Germany, the Commercial Code and other laws and legal standards are prescribed far more definitely, minutely, and strictly than those in Japan.

In the third place, the proposition that Japan's Corporate Accounting Principles have allowed the principles of regular bookkeeping in Japan to take definite meaning contrary to the German laws only manifests the fact that Japan's Corporate Accounting

Principles uses the term "the principles of regular bookkeeping" in a way that suffers from a distortion from a theoretical viewpoint of history. And this has not been discovered yet.

Finally, Someya's conclusion—that what is meant by the prescription of the procedure for the preparation of a transaction record and a financial statement, and the laying of the foundation of the "principle of accuracy" are the very reasons Japan's Corporate Accounting Principles have "definite meaning" in comparison with German laws—cannot be accepted, because it gainsays the actual fact.

Accounting
by Nobuichiro Nakamura (Professor, Konan University),
1st ed., 1979

Nakamura states that in the general principles of the Corporate Accounting Principles in Japan, the "principles of regular bookkeeping" are prescribed, and that the principles of regular bookkeeping are considered to be concerned with the "principle of clarity" and the "principles of objectivity."[12] Furthermore, Nakamura explains that the principles of regular bookkeeping demand that financial accounting should make correct books of account regarding all transactions made, that is, recording in the books of account should be carried out in an orderly manner in accordance with verifiable evidence regarding all the economic phenomena to be recorded.

In the first place, Nakamura fails to point out that the concept of the principles of regular accounting is a literal translation of Article 38 of the current German Commercial Code from the viewpoint of the theory of evolutionary history. Also, Nakamura entertains the idea of considering the principles of regular bookkeeping as only one of the general principles of this country's Corporate Accounting Principles.

Secondly, Nakamura understands this concept in a surprisingly narrow sense as "comprehensiveness," "possibility of verification," and "orderliness of accounting record." Finally, Nakamura adopts only an ambiguous expression about the strength of "orderliness" or standardization. As far as I can determine, it can safely be said that Nakamura fails to grasp the outline of this concept.

Theory of Bookkeeping
by Dr. Kazuo Takamatsu (Professor, Soka University), new rev. ed., 4th ptg., 1978

Takamatsu writes: "As the accounting system in an enterprise, plural methods of accounting have not been carried out in parallel, but one calculation order has been formed with bookkeeping as its center in combination with all other methods of accounting, and this accounting order has become the customary practice that has been generally accepted in industrial circles. For this reason, bookkeeping is called 'regular bookkeeping' when its contents are represented by a comprehensive accounting system with double-entry bookkeeping as its center."[13]

My criticism of Takamatsu's opinion is as follows. In the first place, Takamatsu says "regular bookkeeping," but he does not say "the principles of regular bookkeeping." There can be no doubt, however, that he indicates the latter. If this is so, it is a serious error when Takamatsu concludes that "bookkeeping" is equal to "regular bookkeeping." The reason is that as a factual problem, "bookkeeping" is in no way equal to "regular bookkeeping." It is generally recognized that the "principles of regular bookkeeping," which originated in the German Commercial Code, is a collective term for the principles regarding bookkeeping that have the character of historical development.

For example, the legal standards regarding "entry" that signify "principles for double-entry bookkeeping," including "derivative laws," did not exist at all before 1954; these standards came into existence later through the decisions of Germany's Federal Finance Court (BFH).[14]

Systematic Theory of Financial Statements
by Dr. Tadahiro Yamamasu (Professor, Keio Gijuku University)
and Mr. Tsuyoo Shimamura (Professor, Meiji Gakuin
University), Theory Sec., rev. ed., 1978

Yamamasu and Shimamura state that since the end of the nineteenth century, the German Commercial Code has demanded that "a merchant have an account book in which his business activity and property condition is entered clearly in accordance with the principles of regular bookkeeping."[15] They also state that "in the same way, in the German Stock Law, it is required that the documents regarding the annual settlement of accounts be prepared in accordance with the principles of regular bookkeeping."

Furthermore, Yamamasu and Shimamura draw the conclusion that as far as the German Commercial Code is concerned, from the outset, the definite contents of the principles of regular bookkeeping are hardly shown in the law. They assert that the German Commercial Code abstains from indicating, of its own accord, the details of the definite contents of the principles of regular accounting by taking the step of committing the interpretation of these principles to the financial way of thinking, to the customary practices in accounting that are accepted to be fair and adequate among tradespeople.

Yamamasu and Shimamura also conclude that the principles of regular bookkeeping that are found in the German Commercial Code have *a character that is akin to the provision on a clean slate* for the purpose of giving *comprehensive approval* to various types of standards that have been generally accepted to be fair and adequate in financial accounting. The principles, in themselves, do not have a character that is enough to be positioned as the fundamental principle of taking the form of a record that supports accuracy.[16]

Yamamasu and Shimamura's description is contradictory in my view for the reason mentioned earlier. Their description is "the quoted portion" of the provisions of Paragraph 1 of Article 38 of the German Commercial Code and those of Paragraph 1 of Article 149 of the German Stock Law. The provision of the first part of Paragraph 1 of Article 149 of the German Stock Law has prescribed that "the annual statement must comply with the principles of regular bookkeeping (good accounting principles)." This particular provision is not, therefore, different from the purport of these authors' explanation. The problem, however, lies in the portion following the provisions quoted above.

In the first place, why is it possible for Yamamasu and Shimamura to reason that, as the law, the German Commercial Code of its own accord keeps from directing the details of the principles and adopts a measure by which the law entrusts the principles to financial thinking, or the customary practices in accounting? In the Federal Republic of Germany, there are many books whose titles include "the principles of regular bookkeeping." The German *Dictionary of Tax Law and Tax Studies*,[17] the German *Dictionary of Business Economics*,[18] the German *Dictionary of Accounting*,[19] the German *Dictionary of Economics*,[20] and the German *Dictionary of Financial Economy*[21]—all these dictionaries devote many pages to explanations of the "principles of regular bookkeeping." I presume that my reader is already aware that as the laws in Germany, detailed regulations have been mainly prescribed by codes other than the Commercial Code and by legal standards.

The second point is Yamamasu and Shimamura's conclusion that as these principles have a character that is akin to "the provision on a clean slate" for the purpose of giving comprehensive approval, they do not have the character to be positioned as a fundamental principle in the form of a record that supports accuracy.

In May 1979, I received a copy of *Income Tax Law* (12th ed., 1978), written by Eberhard Littmann, who was the Director General of the BFH. The book had been revised and enlarged to a three-thousand-page volume, twice the size of earlier editions. Dr. Littmann devoted forty-six pages (Vol. 1, pp. 295–341) to the clarification of "the principles of regular bookkeeping." This enlarged edition was set in such a small type size that a magnifying glass is required to read it.

The authors of *Systematic Theory of Financial Statements* would be surprised if they looked at the full particulars of the text regarding the "principles of regular bookkeeping" in the German laws and the legal standards. They would find that the contents of said text and standards are composed of positive law standards whose quantity far and away exceeds the full text of the Corporate Accounting Principles in Japan. I believe that the groundless conclusions arrived at by these Japanese scholars should be absolutely avoided for the advancement of learning.

My third point is that, in the material quoted above, Yamamasu and Shimamura have deleted the Japanese term "Kigyo-kaikei" (financial accounting) from the phrase "the standards for financial accounting that have generally been accepted to be fair and adequate" that has been indicated in Article 1 of the Regulations on Financial Statements and in Article 4 of the Ministerial Ordinance Regarding Audit Certificates. They have added, however, the Japanese term "Kaku-shu-no" (various). Judging from the context of these authors' statements, they have hinted indirectly at and used the concept of financial accounting standards that have generally been accepted as fair and adequate. The problem is, therefore, that they have positioned the concept either as the concept of the "principle of regular bookkeeping," which was prescribed by Article 57 of the Enforcement Regulations for the Income Tax Law, or as the concept that has nearly the same denotation as that of the concept in the Corporate Accounting Principles in Japan.

If these authors were in a position to make a positive demonstration that the phrase "financial accounting standard that has generally been accepted to be fair and adequate" is not a Japanese translation of the provision of "generally recognized principles of accounting," which is prescribed by Article 446 of the United States Internal Revenue Code (IRC), that would alter the case. If they were to admit instead that the phrase in question is the Japanese translation of the exact phrase in Article 446 of the IRC, the matter would become more serious instead. The reason is that the provisions of this code prescribe only four kinds of accounting methods, namely: 1) "Incurred Basis," 2) "Cash Basis," 3) "Production Method," and 4) "Mixed Basis," and the provisions establish no other standards than the above four methods.[22]

This means that, as far as United States laws are concerned, there is no accounting standard that has put the restraint upon the United States as the law. This is due to the fact that various standards, other than the above-quoted four accounting methods in the United States regarding the "entry" and "settlement of accounts," have all been entrusted to what these authors describe as "the customary practices in accounting in merchants' circles."

It is not German laws, therefore, but United States laws that have been entrusted to the customary practices in accounting in merchants' circles. The concept of "generally recognized principles of accounting" under the American laws is, moreover, as these authors state, the concept that "had the character that is

Opinions of Respectable Japanese Scholars: Part I   71

akin to the provision on a clean slate for the purpose of giving a comprehensive approval." When this concept is reviewed as "the denotation" of the concept itself, the United States's concept is broader than that of Japan's Corporate Accounting Principles or the concept of the principles of regular bookkeeping that are prescribed by Article 57 of the Enforcement Regulations for the Income Tax Law.

As for the German Stock Law *(AktG)* quoted by these authors in their book, I have a copy of the Stock Law of September 6, 1965, with commentary by Baron von Godin and Dr. Hans Wilhelmi (4th ed., 1971), which is nearly twenty-two hundred pages long. Touching on the principles of regular bookkeeping, the authors state:

> Good accounting principles are in essence unwritten law, in which the commercial experience of centuries has been collected, a law which is not yet completed today, but rather is constantly developing. In more recent times, it has also been influenced by court decisions and business administration science. Books which outwardly conform to the law are assumed to be kept in a regular way.[23]

At this stage, the reader should have an understanding of why the concept of the principles of regular bookkeeping has a threefold structure.

Notes

1. See p. 378.
2. See p. 27.
3. See p. 125.
4. See p. 55.
5. See Kuno Barth, *The Development of German Balance Sheet Law*, Vol. 1, p. 247, for the original text of the former Commercial Code of 1897.
6. See p. 23.
7. See p. 41.
8. See p. 69.
9. See p. 214.
10. See p. 175.
11. See p. 32.
12. See p. 99.
13. See p. 10.

14. See Federal Tax Sheet, 1954, III, S. 298.
15. See p. 107.
16. Italics mine.
17. See *Dictionary of Tax Law and Tax Studies*, 2d ed., Vol. I, pp. 714 ff.
18. See *Dictionary of Business Economics*, 1974, pp. 1011 ff.
19. See *Dictionary of Accounting*, 2d ed., pp. 702 ff.
20. See *Dictionary of Economics*, Vol. 2, pp. 69 ff.
21. See *Dictionary of Financial Economy*, 1976, p. 1477.
22. See IRC, Sec. 446–C.
23. See p. 486.

7

Critical Review of the Opinions of Respectable Japanese Scholars: Part II

Revised Accounting
by Mr. Shiro Tajima (Professor, Komazawa University),
published by Kunimoto Shobo, 4th ed., June 15, 1977

Under the heading "The Principles of Regular Bookkeeping," Tajima takes the stand that these principles are the ones that have been expressed thus: "Corporate Accounting should make correct books of account regarding all the transactions made in accordance with the principles of regular bookkeeping." He quotes, just as it is, the very wording of the provisions from Paragraph 2, General Principle 1 of Corporate Accounting Principles.[1]

I think, however, that Tajima's explanation does not constitute an explanation of this matter logically, because there is a term in his explanation that has to be explained. At the same time, there is no evidence to support Tajima's theory that "the principles of regular bookkeeping," which have been indicated in the Corporate Accounting Principles of this country, are a concept based on an illusion. Tajima concludes, however, that "there is no such kind of bookkeeping known by the name of 'regular bookkeeping.'"

Article 29 of the Guidelines, which is the authoritative regulation regarding "the principles of regular bookkeeping" prescribed by Article 5 of the Hessian Income Tax Law, has a provision with the title "Regular Bookkeeping," whereby the variety of bookkeeping is specifically limited. I wonder how Tajima views this point in particular. Moreover, he concludes that "it does not necessarily mean double-entry bookkeeping." From the theoretical viewpoint of evolutionary history, this provision did not mandate double-entry bookkeeping; however, the judicial precedent of the German Taxation Court has now established that it means the principles of double-entry bookkeeping including the "mixed method."[2] I cannot help but say, therefore, that Tajima has also failed to notice this fact.

Finally, the author has tried to position the term "the principles of regular bookkeeping" as the Japanese equivalent of the German term "Grundsätze ordnungsmäβiger Buchführung" ("regular accounting principles"). He asserts that this is not only the principle regarding entries in books of account but also the principle that constitutes the very basis for the preparation of financial statements. If this is so, I feel the author should follow the rightful method of using the corresponding term in German. I have not noticed any indication of this, however.

Tajima seems to have failed to notice, moreover, the fact that the principles of regular bookkeeping have a threefold structure and that these principles are subject to the strict limitation of the outline of principles by the positive law. It can safely be said, therefore, that the last sentence in Tajima's book is only barely correct: "In this sense, it can safely be said that regular bookkeeping is a 'compound principle' instead of a simple principle."

A Textbook of Accounting
by Dr. Yoshio Numata (Professor, Komazawa University), 8th rev. ed., 1978, 10th ptg., published by Dobun Kan

Under the heading "Principles of Regular Bookkeeping," Numata states that "the principles of regular bookkeeping" is a term that has been newly coined by the Corporate Accounting Principles, and that "the said principles have been created, to a certain extent, by the advocate for the Corporate Accounting Principles."[3] No explanation about this particular matter has ever been given, however. As a general theory, these principles have nearly the same meaning as "the principles of 'orderly bookkeeping' that are prescribed by the German Commercial Code, and ... they are said to mean that 'the entry shall be made systematically and clearly' as prescribed by Article 33 of this country's revised Commercial Code."

With the above views in mind, I would like to make the following comments. First, in regard to Numata's conclusion that "'the principles of regular bookkeeping' is a term that has been coined by the Corporate Accounting Principles," it may safely be said that the above expression will be a startlingly precise one when we venture to decide without hesitation that the term "the principles of regular bookkeeping" is not a Japanese version of the German term "Grundsätze ordnungsmäßiger Buchführung" ("regular accounting principles"), which is prescribed in Article 38 of the German Commercial Code.

Secondly, the same is also true in the case of the conceptional regulation about which Numata said that it had been created, "to a certain extent, by the advocate for the Corporate Accounting Principles." There is no way of inquiring into Numata's level of understanding of this concept regarding the German laws, because he only remains within the bounds of introducing commonly accepted theories, and he himself has not developed any substantial theories regarding the principles of regular bookkeeping in the German Commercial Code.

It is an illusion, as I have explained before, that the concept of "the principles of regular bookkeeping" in this country's Corporate Accounting Principles is the Japanese version of the German term "Grundsätze ordnungsmäßiger Buchführung" ("regular accounting principles") in the German Commercial Code. When this premise is eliminated, therefore, the statement that the term is newly coined by the Corporate Accounting Principles and that it was created, to a certain extent, by the advocate for the Corporate Accounting Principles is sharply and admirably asserted.

Numata has pointed out, moreover, that "the Corporate Accounting Principles have taken care not to mention the relationship between books of account and financial statements."[4] In this connection, I feel that Numata's characteristic logical acuteness emerges. I have to admit, therefore, that the proposition that the term "the principles of regular bookkeeping" is not the Japanese version of the German term prescribed by Article 38 of the German Commercial Code, on which this author has tacitly placed his premise, will be a little difficult for us to understand from the viewpoint of this country's history of accounting.

Theory of Financial Accounting
by Dr. Kiyomitsu Arai (Professor, Waseda University), published by Chuo Keizai Sha, 45th enlarged ed., February 1979

Arai states the following: "The principles of regular bookkeeping are those that demand that: 1) for the sake of formality, the recording of books of account shall be conducted in accordance with fixed necessary conditions, and 2) as a substantial principle, the organic connection between books of account and financial statements, and between mutual financial statements shall be maintained." In this connection, the phrase "fixed necessary conditions" in the first stipulation indicates: a) "all-inclusive character," b) "verifiability" c) "orderliness," etc. That is to say, the principles of regular accounting demand that all accounting transactions should: a) be made in one accounting period, b) be based on the fact of actual transactions, or on other verifiable evidence, and c) be recorded continuously and systematically.

The phrase "organic connection between books of account and financial statements, and that between mutual financial statements" in the second stipulation indicates that financial statements should be inductively prepared from books of account that meet the conditions deemed necessary. In regard to mutual financial statements and, especially, income statements and balance sheets, the latter should be "a connecting ring" with the former in accordance with the "doctrine of derivative method." As an explanation depending on reason, it may safely be said that Arai's is generally well organized.

The problem is that when both the accounting standard that is generally recognized as fair and appropriate, prescribed by Article 4 of the Ministerial Ordinance Regarding Audit Certificates, and the accounting standard that is generally recognized as fair and appropriate, prescribed by Paragraph 4 of Article 22 of the Corporation Tax Law in this country, are supposed to mean the Corporate Accounting Principles, it may be justified to regard the Corporate Accounting Principles as having the character of the source of law. The Corporate Accounting Principles only state, however, that "corporate accounting should prepare accurate books of account concerning all the transactions in accordance with the principles of regular bookkeeping."

However carefully the phrases that have been described in the Principles are analyzed in detail, it may not be possible to deduce how Arai's explanation, cited above, can be fully covered. In other words, Arai tries to logically outline here a summary of the structure of the principles of regular bookkeeping in Germany. What is important here, however, is that he fails to touch on the problem of "timeliness" in making an entry. Paragraph 1 of Article 146 of the German Fundamental Taxation Law *(AO)*, Paragraph 2 of Article 43 of the German Commercial Code, and Article 29 of the Enforcement Regulations for the Income Tax Law—all these provisions stipulate this particular point accurately and strictly.

Arai does not understand that this particular point is utterly different from "timeliness" in the United States's Accounting Principles. In view of the threefold structure of the principles of regular bookkeeping, however, even though Arai can generally describe the principles that have evolved historically in merchants' customary bookkeeping, how about his inquiry into the principles of regular bookkeeping especially in regard to the positive law standard?

Why does Arai not feel the reason for advocating "the lack of the law" in this country? Furthermore, since the author grasps the fact that both Article 130 of the Corporation Tax Law and Article 155 of the Income Tax Law have acknowledged the "verifiable bookkeeping records" of books of account, why is he unable to declare that this constitutes the very "connotation" of the principles of regular bookkeeping? In this sense, we must conclude that this author still only partially understands the principles of regular bookkeeping.

New Theory of Financial Statements
by Dr. Tatsuo Inoue (Professor, Chuo University, C.P.A.),
published by Chuo Keizai Sha, 72d rev. ed., 1978

According to Inoue, the principles of regular bookkeeping originated in the "regular accounting principles" prescribed by the

German Commercial Code (Articles 38 and 129). The "principles of regular bookkeeping" have substantial contents, including accounting principles. Acknowledging the existence of the principles in customary business practices in corporate accounting, the Commercial Code has made a comprehensive commitment, under the name "regular accounting principles," to the customary practices in general.

This German practice can be thought to approximate the phrase "fair practices in accounting" in the provisions of Paragraph 2 of Article 32, which was prescribed when Japan's Commercial Code was revised in April 1974 and provides that "concerning the interpretation of the regulations regarding the preparation of books of account, 'fair practices in accounting' shall be taken into consideration." The principles of regular bookkeeping that are prescribed by Japan's Corporate Accounting Principles, however, are different from those in the Commercial Code in Japan. The Corporate Accounting Principles state that the principles of regular bookkeeping demand that "in accordance with verifiable evidence, all the transactions shall be recorded completely and accurately in systematic books of account," and that the record of books of account shall be put in order on a generalized basis through the periodic measurement and classification whereby the financial statements "should be prepared."

In regard to Inoue's explanation, I would like to make the following comments. First, there may be a misprint. Article 129 of the German Commercial Code has nothing to do with the principles of regular bookkeeping. The title of Article 129 is "Defense Objectives of the Corporate Member (Partner)" and not "Principles of Regular Bookkeeping." Secondly, although it is a trifling matter, there is no word "der" in the wording of the principles of regular bookkeeping contained in the provisions of the German Commercial Code, from which the term "regular accounting principles" has come. This reminds me of "Edo-sen-ryu" (a short, satirical poem) that implies that "Uguisuno-hitokoemo-nen-o-irenikeri" (literally translated, "A voice from a Japanese nightingale makes us think it is necessary to pay careful attention to everything we hear").

Thirdly, the theory of comprehensive commitment has been "an oral tradition of misunderstanding" regarding the principles of regular bookkeeping, which clearly shows that Inoue has been simply using hearsay or the groundless theories of other persons for his own convenience as far as "the principles of regular bookkeeping" are concerned. Fourthly, as Inoue has said, what is stated in two of the general principles is the principle of record. Therefore, why can it be said by Inoue that it means that thereby the financial statements "should be prepared?" One can accept the proposition that "there has been a characteristic theory of bookkeeping and accounting which is peculiar to Bookkeeping and Accounting." It should not be understood by us, however, that in the above theory any intermediary principles cannot be shown.

Reviewing Inoue's theory in this way, it seems that as he states that "the principles of regular bookkeeping prescribed by the Corporate Accounting Principles are different from this," he seemingly recognizes that the principles of regular bookkeeping in the German Commercial Code are different from those prescribed in the Corporate Accounting Principles. It may be concluded that Inoue will not be able to indicate the real differences between the principles in Japan and in the German laws. The reason is that all the procedural principles regarding this author's statement, quoted earlier, up to where he says "are different from this" and "it means that it should be prepared" have all been included in the principles of regular bookkeeping as a current legal concept in the German laws.

Accounting
by Dr. Yoshio Aida (Professor, Keio Gijuku University), 1976 ed., published by Kunimoto Shobo

Aida states that "the Provision in General Principles 2," which prescribes that "Corporate Accounting should prepare correct books of account with respect to all the transactions made in accordance with the principles of regular bookkeeping," is what we call the principles of regular bookkeeping.[5] From a logical viewpoint, however, this statement is not an explanation because "to be explained" has also been included in Aida's explanation.

It seems to me that Aida takes the stand that the principles of regular bookkeeping mentioned by the German laws and those prescribed by the Corporate Accounting Principles are entirely different. Furthermore, Aida examines the "principles of regular bookkeeping" in two ways: in both broad and narrow senses. Under the heading "The Principles of Regular Bookkeeping" he states that, in the broad sense, the principles of regular bookkeeping tend to be synonymous with "fair business practices in accounting." It sometimes happens that the principles are understood to have the same meaning as the term "fair and appropriate accounting standards." Furthermore, Aida states that the principles are generally understood literally as the principles regarding "the entry."

He further states that those who understand the principles as an accounting standard tend to be of the opinion that this is demanded in the provisions of the Corporate Accounting Principles. I think Aida tries to explain the principles in the broad sense by introducing various opinions on this particular matter. At the end of his explanation, Aida says that it can be considered problematic whether "the accounting standard that has been generally recognized as fair and appropriate" should be considered to have the same meaning as that of the principles of regular bookkeeping. Where the phrase "generally recognized principles of accounting," stipulated by Article 446 of the United States's Internal Revenue Code (IRC), is supposed to be the original text of the accounting standard generally recognized as fair and appropriate (this is the expression of Paragraph 4 of Article 22 of the Corporation Tax Laws), the "connotation" of the accounting standard is different from that of the principles of regular bookkeeping in the German laws. The reason is that the latter does not acknowledge accounting through the "mixed method" that has been acknowledged by the former.

The principles of regular bookkeeping, which are different from those in Germany, will—unlike Article 446 of the IRC—not acknowledge the "mixed method." (This means that sales and purchase should be made by "actual basis accounting" and that others should be conducted by "cash basis accounting.") In his explanation of the principles of regular bookkeeping in the narrow sense, Aida states that in order to be "regular" the following characteristics are required: "all-inclusive character," "verifiability," and "orderliness." Furthermore, he states that, even in the case of "single entry bookkeeping," if the entry is kept in good order, it can fall under the principles of regular bookkeeping. He also states that, at the same time, the principles of regular bookkeeping mean the doctrine of "mixed method." I think that Aida's understanding is full of subjective reasoning. There is no indication that he understands "the threefold structure."

Commentary on Accounting Principles
by Dr. Shigeyoshi Kimura (Professor, Soka University), 8th ed., June 1963, published by Chuo Keizai Sha

Kimura makes the following statement:

The regulation that is equivalent to this provision [General Principle 2 of the Corporate Accounting Principles] has been in existence in Japan's Commercial Code, and its Article 32 prescribes that "a merchant shall provide books of account in which daily transactions and all other matters affecting property shall be entered therein systematically and clearly. ..." [Paragraph 1 was quoted, omitting its "provisos"]. Paragraph 1 of Article 38 of the German Commercial Code is equivalent to the above provision of the Commercial Code of Japan. As to the item "to be entered systematically and clearly," the German counterpart provides that it is to be made evident according to the principles of regular bookkeeping. In view of the correspondence of the terms and expressions used, it may safely be said that General Principle 2 of our Commercial Code and Article 38 of the German Commercial Code are of the same purport. In other words, General Principle 2, Article 32 of our Commercial Code, and Article 38 of the German Commercial Code prescribe nearly the same matter.[6]

Under the heading "Study of Related Literature," Kimura states, moreover, that the so-called principles of regular bookkeeping are among the principles whose contents are the most unclear in the Corporate Accounting Principles. The major problematic points in the principles of regular bookkeeping are:

1. What is really meant by "the principles of regular bookkeeping"? That is to say, are they the principles that dictate the form of recording in accounting, or are they those that dictate even the "contents" of the record?

2. What is indicated by the term "the form of recording"? In conjunction with "the form of bookkeeping," does this term indicate a specific form of bookkeeping (i.e., double entry bookkeeping), or does it indicate a fixed necessary condition, irrespective of the form of bookkeeping? Moreover, what is the necessary condition?

Dr. Kimura then reviews the theories advocated by the following professors: Dr. Katsuji Yamashita (Kobe University), Dr. Yoshio Numata (Komazawa University), Dr. Toshio Iino (Chu University), Dr. Kiyoshi Kurosawa (Yokohama National University), Dr. Yasuichi Sakamoto (Osaka-Gakuin University), Dr. Minoru Emura (Tokyo University), the late Dr. Koichi Sato (Waseda University), Dr. Tatsuo Inoue (Chuo University), and the late Shoichi Ito (Komazawa University).

The reader should pay careful attention to the point that in the first part of Kimura's theory, quoted in this chapter, Kimura's intention was to explain General Principle 2 of the Corporate Accounting Principles. An explanation of the concept of the principles of regular bookkeeping itself was not intended at all. At the end of the first part of the quote, it is very important to note, however, that Kimura concludes: "General Principle 2, Article 32 of our Commercial Code, and Article 38 of the German Commercial Code prescribe nearly the same matter."

In this concluding statement, the author reveals his own level of understanding of the principles of regular bookkeeping. Kimura describes the concept of the principles of regular bookkeeping as a single, self-inclusive concept that has a complete meaning in itself by indicating that the principles of regular bookkeeping of Article 38 of the German Commercial Code are a singular form of "a principle" and that it has prescribed the same thing as Article 32 of our Commercial Code. In other words, this author has failed in his understanding of this concept as a collective term of a group of principles regarding bookkeeping, which continuously develops from a historical perspective.[7]

In this respect, therefore, Kimura makes his first error. Next, as if he has taken the position of a spectator, Kimura proposes a problem with the statement that the so-called principles of regular bookkeeping are among the principles whose contents are the most unclear in the Corporate Accounting Principles. Furthermore, he treats the concept of "the principles of regular bookkeeping," which appears in General Principle 2, as if it is a concept that constitutes a part of the "Grand Code of Laws" that will be in effect forever.

It is an unshakable historical fact that numerous scholars in Japan, to say nothing of Kimura, have translated the term "Grundästze ordnungsmäßiger Buchführung," which was prescribed by Article 38 of the German Commercial Code, as "various principles of regular bookkeeping," or "a principle of regular bookkeeping." Considering that our Corporate Accounting Principles were drawn up as an "Interim Report" on July 9, 1949, by the Countermeasure Investigation Committee for the Corporate Accounting System of the Economic Stabilization Board, it is extremely irrational to conclude that the concept "the principles of regular bookkeeping," which appears in the General Principle of our Corporate Accounting Principles, is the unique creation of Japanese scholars and unexpectedly in accord with the terms of Article 38 of the German Commercial Code.

As stated earlier, in view of the fact that Dr. Kotaro Tanaka, Japan's leading scholar on the Commercial Code, positioned the German Commercial Code as "the mother" of the Commercial Code in Japan, it should be said that the extent of the unreasonableness of such a conclusion can be known. As a consequence, at this juncture I wish to draw the following conclusion. The Japanese scholars who were engaged in the preparation of the "Interim Report" did not know that at that time, the principles of regular bookkeeping of Article 38 of the German Commercial Code were already a historical reality in Germany—the definitive legal standard regarding bookkeeping—and that this standard included, in addition to the Commercial Code, many principles among various positive laws and judicial precedents.

The reason I am confident that this deduction is correct is that it can be proved by a historical fact. Among accounting scholars in Japan, almost none have pointed out the real existence and the many-sided character of the definite positive law standards that exist regarding the principles of regular bookkeeping in Germany.

This is really the basis for my argument and the assertions I have made so far that the concept of the principles of regular bookkeeping, found in Japan's Corporate Accounting Principles, has been used on the basis of a sort of an illusion.

At any rate, on July 14, 1954, the Deliberative Council for Corporate Accounting of the Finance Ministry made public a document entitled "Partial Revision of the Corporate Accounting Principles and the Standing Rule of Financial Statements," in which the Council stated that "it has begun to be admitted that it will be necessary to correct the inadequacy of the terms used, the disunited wording, and other points." In so doing, the Council confirmed publicly that the Corporate Accounting Principles should not be treated as "a canon" of everlasting fame, and the Council also concluded by saying that "these explanatory notes were adopted as a tentative conclusion as the result of this Council's investigative deliberation."

The Council made a declaration that one of the fundamental characteristics of the explanatory notes regarding the Corporate Accounting Principles was their provisional character. The Council ended its conclusion with the statement that "these notes are to be further supplemented and modified by cautious research and study in the future ... and it is scheduled to present these notes for widespread criticism by the public in general." In view of these facts and circumstances, it does not follow that "the Deliberative Council for Corporate Accounting of the Finance Ministry also had the understanding that our Corporate Accounting Principles, in a broad sense, are eternally unchangeable principles upon which modifications or corrections should not be carried out."

If such is the case, it must be said that under the subject "Study of Related Literature," it is an error for Professor Shigeyoshi Kimura to take the position of trying to discover problems only in the explanation of given sentences and terms. For instance, the author poses the questions: What is really meant by "the principles of regular bookkeeping"? What is indicated by the term "the form of recording"? What is the necessary condition? In Germany, for example, in the Fundamental Taxation Law *(AO)*, which is one of the laws and regulations prescribing the content of the principles of regular bookkeeping, namely, in Paragraph 1 of Article 146 of the *AO*, the following stipulation appears: "The postings and other required entries are to be done completely, accurately, orderly, and on time."

It is quite natural that accounting records should have the characteristics of "perfectibility," "truthfulness," and "orderly clarity." However, have our scholars ever discussed that the demand for "timeliness" is also one of the important principles of regular bookkeeping?

An Outline of Accounting
by Dr. Shigeo Aoki (Professor, Waseda University, President, The Japan Society of Accounting), published March 20, 1978, by Chuo Keizaisha

Aoki states that, like the "principles of regular bookkeeping" prescribed in General Principle 2 for Corporate Accounting, it is the principle of regular bookkeeping that dictates that "regarding all the transactions made, Corporate Accounting should prepare correct books of account in accordance with the principles of regular bookkeeping."[8] The author also asserts that the principle of "truthfulness" (the principle of "regular accuracy") mentioned earlier, when it is connected with these principles of regular bookkeeping, can be technically substantiated. He states, moreover, that the principles of regular bookkeeping dictate that the historical record of transactions should be conducted in good order and systematically in accordance with a fixed rule. The principles of regular bookkeeping, however, do not always indicate "double-entry bookkeeping." It may be considered, Aoki writes, that double-entry bookkeeping is the most typical regular bookkeeping.

In regard to Aoki's statements I must comment as follows. In the first place, it has been repeatedly pointed out that the above statements made by Aoki do not constitute a logical explanation, because the term to be explained is included in the explanation Aoki makes concerning the concept of the principles of regular bookkeeping. Secondly, as Aoki made no statements at all on the circumstances of the evolutionary historical theory regarding the concept of the principle of regular bookkeeping, I have no way of gauging his understanding of whether this concept was created by this country's scholars, or whether it is an imported concept that originated in the German tax law and was popularized generally by adoption into the German Commercial Code, Stock Law, and so forth.

Thirdly, it seems to me that Aoki tacitly explained that the concept of the principles of regular bookkeeping in this country's Corporate Accounting Principles is entirely different from the principles of regular bookkeeping in the Federal Republic of Germany. This is clear from his opinion that the principles of regular bookkeeping should technically substantiate the principle of "accuracy." In the Federal Republic of Germany, the principle of "accuracy" has been no more than a principle that constitutes an important substance of the principles of regular bookkeeping.[9] Finally, there is no way for me to know whether or not Aoki has really understood the threefold structure embodied in the principles of regular bookkeeping, which I have maintained so far, because Aoki has not made a single statement about a "threefold structure."

Notes

1. See p. 26.
2. Federal Tax Sheet 1954, S. 298.
3. See p. 34.
4. See p. 35.
5. See p. 69.
6. See p. 23.
7. *Dictionary of Tax Law and Tax Studies,* Vol. 1, 1972, p. 543.
8. See p. 75.
9. Ulrich Leffson, *Principles of Regular Accounting,* 4 Auflage, 1976, S. 104.

8

Fair Accounting Practice in the Commercial Code of Japan

Critical Review of Scholars Representing the University of Tokyo, Tohoku University, and Kyoto University

The 1974 revision of the Commercial Code of Japan adopted for the first time in history the term "fair accounting practice" (Article 32 [2] of the Commercial Code in Japan). Viewed from the context of the law, it was a concept that made its appearance abruptly, a term that cannot be found in books previously published by accounting scholars in Japan. I assume that its appearance came about because the members of the Commercial Code section of the Legislative Council of the Ministry of Justice had taken the articles at the beginning of Chapter 5, "Books of Account," into consideration and had decided that it would be justifiable and in keeping with the style of the German Commercial Code, the "mother law" of the Commercial Code in Japan, to include the text of the provision "obligation of bookkeeping" of Article 38, placed at the opening of Chapter 4, "Commercial Books," of the German Commercial Code, which is a general and inclusive regulation that prescribes "according to good accounting principles."

Why was the expression "in accordance with the principles of regular bookkeeping," which is similar to Article 38 of the German Commercial Code, not adopted just as it is? As a man of business who is not part of the government, there is no way for me to know the real reason for this particular matter. My opinion is, however, that as most of the committee members were lawyers, they could not grasp the farsighted wishes of the accounting scholars and they failed to catch the trend of those similar phrases that are scattered throughout the given literature.

Some examples of these phrases follow: "The standard of corporate accounting that is generally accepted as fair and appropriate" (Article 4 of the Ministerial Ordinance Regarding Audit Certificates); "the standard of accounting that is generally accepted as fair and appropriate" (Article 22 of the Corporate Income Tax Law); "in accordance with the principle of double-entry bookkeeping" (Article 53 of Enforcement Regulations for the Corporation Tax Law); "in accordance with the principles of regular bookkeeping" (Article 57 of Enforcement Regulations for the Income Tax Law). Moreover, as the so-called Corporate Accounting Principles are generally understood as the principles of accounting in a joint-stock corporation, these committee members may have decided that the term "Corporate Accounting Principles" could not be used as a unified and inclusive regulation for merchants in general. As a result, I suppose, the term "fair accounting practice" may have been expediently coined.

What do Japanese scholars of the Commercial Code think of the term "fair accounting practice?" Professor Tsuneo Ootori of the University of Tokyo, for example, states that a practice can be described as a fair accounting practice if it is in accord with the objective of preparing books of account, that is, if it is in accord with the purpose of clarifying the conditions of a merchant's property and loss and profit in business. He further states that the Corporate Accounting Principles are the outcome of summarizing what has been generally accepted as fair and appropriate in routine practice in accounting and that it can be considered as such in the inclusive regulation of Paragraph 2 of Article 32 of the Commercial Code.[1]

According to Professor Eizo Hattori of Tohoku University, moreover, a "fair practice in accounting," prescribed by Paragraph 2 of Article 32, means a practice that is considered appropriate and reasonable in view of the objective of books of account to clarify the financial status, or operating results, of an enterprise. In this connection, the Corporate Accounting Principles, mainly in regard to joint-stock companies, have been understood as "the summarization of what is generally accepted as fair and appropriate from among those practices that have been developed as routine practice in the actual business of corporate accounting." As far as a joint-stock company is concerned, therefore, compliance with the Corporate Accounting Principles will mean adhering to a fair accounting practice. Hattori also states that, in regard to enterprises other than joint-stock companies, "it is conceivable that there are many instances in which these enterprises may have no difficulty in applying, for the most part, the Corporate Accounting Principles."[2]

Kenichiro Osumi, an honorary professor at Kyoto University, states: "The regulations of Paragraph 2 of Article 32 of the Commercial Code have been established for the purpose of adjusting the Commercial Code and the Securities and Exchange Act. Therefore, for this purpose, there is a precondition that the Corporate Accounting Principles, which form the basis for the regulation of financial statements in accordance with the Securities and Exchange Act, are recognized tentatively as fair accounting practice." He states further that "among those [practices] that have been developed as routine in corporate accounting, the Corporate Accounting Principles are a summary of what has been generally accepted as fair and appropriate. From this it can be understood that the so-called fair accounting practice in Paragraph 2 of Article 32 of the Commercial Code includes the Corporate Accounting Principles in regard to accounting and books of account in human society."[3]

I do not have any doubts at all that the Corporate Accounting Principles, as the audit standard for certified public accountants, has become widespread and permanently fixed. I think it would be good, for the most part, for the three scholars just mentioned to position the Corporate Accounting Principles as constituting the contents of "fair accounting practice," as shown in Paragraph 2 of Article 32 of the Japanese Commercial Code. I wish to raise an objection, however, to the point these three scholars argue as the mediation principle, the view that "from among those [practices] that have been developed as routine in the actual business of corporate accounting, the Corporate Accounting Principles are a summary of what is generally accepted as fair and appropriate." This proposition is no more than the uncritical transfer of the proposition found in No. 2 of the writing made public in *Concerning the Establishment of the Corporate Accounting Principles*, which was announced simultaneously with the Corporate Accounting Principles as an interim report of the Corporate Accounting System Countermeasure Investigation Commission of the Economic Stabilization Board in July 1949.

It is a kind of fantasy to say that the Corporate Accounting Principles are a summary of what has been generally accepted as fair and appropriate in actual accounting practice. The first piece of evidence is clear when we take a look at the following:

As the corporate accounting system in this country, as compared with those in Europe and America, has had enough room for further improvement, and has been extremely disorganized, . . . it is an urgent problem in this country to improve and unify Japan's corporate accounting system. Therefore, it is intended to establish and maintain, first of all, the Corporate Accounting Principles so as to provide a scientific basis for the democratic and healthy development of the nation's economy in this country.

That is, the Corporate Accounting Principles have been formulated through a political intention through which, for the purpose of improving and unifying the accounting system in existence, an accounting standard was to be established to provide the very basis for the sound development of the Japanese economy.

The second proof can be found in the various statements "Regarding the Partial Revision of the Corporate Accounting Principles," made by the Corporate Accounting Council. The statement made in November 1963 indicated that "the partial revision of the Corporate Accounting Principles, this time . . . was primarily intended to make a revision so as to cope with the revision of the calculation regulation in the revised Commercial Code," and thus acknowledged that the partial revision this time had nothing at all to do with a summary of actual business practice in accounting. Furthermore, the provision "fair practice in accounting should be taken into consideration" was newly provided for in Paragraph 2 of Article 32 of the Commercial Code, and a statement regarding the audit of big enterprises by certified public accountants, which was made in August 1974, said that "in preparation for the development of such circumstances . . . as shown under separate sheet, it is decided to carry out the partial revision of the Corporate Accounting Principles."

For the third piece of evidence, we can look at the writing of Dr. Kurosawa, who personally participated in drawing up the Corporate Accounting Principles. In No. 12 of his series "Historical Material: The Accounting System in Japan," he states: "What is referred to here as 'this Commission's Recommendation' indicates the Corporate Accounting Principles, which were made public a month and a half earlier than the *Report on Japanese Taxation* by the 'Shoup Mission.' . . . In the beginning, our conception of intending to establish the Corporate Accounting Principles was surrounded by the voices of foes on all sides, the success or failure of which was nothing other than an adventure."[4] I feel it is a common Japanese malpractice to patch up the facts with apparently made-up stories in official documents released by governmental agencies. I believe that, knowingly or unknowingly, to enter such matter in a textbook is not an appropriate scholastic action.

The Formulation of the United States Corporate Accounting Principles

In comparison with the above example in Japan, the corporate accounting principles that have been published by the American Institute of Certified Public Accountants (AICPA) seem to be honest and straightforward. The corporate accounting principles in America are called *Generally Accepted Accounting Principles*. They were made public in October 1970. At the beginning of these principles, referring to the nature of the American accounting principles, the following appears:

Generally accepted accounting principles incorporate the consensus at a particular time as to which economic resources and obligations should be recorded as assets and liabilities by financial accounting, which changes in assets and liabilities should be recorded, when these changes should be recorded, how the assets and liabilities and changes in them should be measured, what information should be disclosed and how it should be disclosed, and which financial statements should be prepared.[5]

I feel this statement may be the very truth in the accounting principles.

It should particularly be noted that these corporate accounting principles, as announced by AICPA, have been approved by *Accounting Series Release No. 4*, issued by the Securities and Exchange Commission (SEC). Notification No. 4 states: "The AICPA Special Committee on Opinions of the Accounting Principles Board defines generally accepted accounting principles as those 'having substantial authoritative support.' " The Securities and Exchange Commission in America has been granted strong authority for establishing regulations, by Article 19 of the Securities Act (1933), by Article 11 of the Securities and Exchange Act (1934), and especially—in regard to accounting records and financial statements—by Article 17 of the Securities and Exchange Act:

Anyone who violates the above laws and provisions, under Article 24 of the Securities Act, will be subject to imprisonment for a term of less than five years, or a fine of not more than $5,000, or both, and under Article 32 of the Securities and Exchange Act, imprisonment for a term of less than two years, or a fine of $10,000, or both, and in the case of specialized traders in securities exchange, a fine of not more than $500,000.

The reader may already known that the United States Securities and Exchange Commission mandates severe penalties. According to *On Corporations*, written by Henry Winthrop Ballantine, a professor at the University of California, the reason for granting such authority for establishing regulations and for the enactment of the Securities Act and the Securities and Exchange Act, which have severe penal provisions, was that during the Great Depression (1929–1933), the investing public suffered a severe loss amounting to a total of $25 billion due to unlawful accounting practices and illicit manipulation in securities transactions.[6] The reader can thus see that the *Generally Accepted Accounting Principles* that were established by the AICPA incorporated the consensus and that the "generally accepted accounting principles" are supported by authoritative power and have a normative binding power, justified by the *Accounting Series Release No. 4* issued by the Securities and Exchange Commission.

I do not intend to say that, even in the case of an "incorporated general consensus," it is the outcome of the simple decision of a majority vote, which has often been observed in the Association of Tax Practitioners in present-day Japan. Dr. Carl S. Shoup, touching on the Corporate Accounting Principles of Japan, stated in the Shoup Mission's *Report on Japanese Taxation* that "their strength lies in the calibre of the personnel and the quality of their work."[7] He is of the opinion that the nature of the effectiveness of Japan's Corporate Accounting Principles is affected by the caliber of the individual specialist who participated in the establishment of the Corporate Accounting Principles and the quality of his achievements in the academic circles of accounting.

Needless to say, the Corporate Accounting Principles in this country are not laws and ordinances. Consequently, they do not have the character of the source of the law. I think, however, that only Article 4 of the Ministerial Ordinance Regarding Audit Certificates began to pursue conformity to "the standard of corporate accounting that is generally accepted as fair and appropriate." A governmental agency, the Corporate Accounting System Countermeasure Council of the then Economic Stabilization Board, which was later transferred to the Corporate Accounting Council of the Ministry of Finance, prescribed that the Corporate Accounting Principles begin with "a summary of what has been generally accepted as fair and appropriate." I think the Corporate Accounting Principles of Japan became a semi-statute system of standards and then a secondary source of the law.

As I have said, the Corporate Accounting Principles in this country are not laws and ordinances, and, for the sake of formality, they do not have the character of the source of the law. From this particular viewpoint it may safely be said that, compared with the American *Generally Accepted Accounting Principles*, which have the support of public power by the *Accounting Series Release* of the Securities and Exchange Commission that has an independent authority for establishing regulations, Japanese accounting principles are inferior to the American ones as far as respectability goes.

The *Report on Japanese Taxation* by the Shoup Mission recommended that the Review Council should be changed to "an independent commission established under the general jurisprudence of the Ministry of Finance," and, furthermore, the report stated: "We also urge that the Securities Exchange Commission exercise strongly its substantial powers to bring about an improvement in the accounting methods of business firms."[8] At the present time, the Review Council has been reduced to an organ of the Ministry of Finance, the sole mission of which is investigations and the performance of examinations (The Certified Public Accountants Law, Articles 35–42). The Securities Exchange Commission changed its name to the Securities and Exchange Council; it too has become an organ of the Ministry of Finance, and its only mission is deliberation and investigation of securities (Securities and Exchange Act, Articles 165–70).

It is to be regretted by the state and the people that, contrary to the fair direction that had been expected from the Shoup Mission, such degradation and degeneration caused an error in placing the role of dealing with big nationwide problems—such as the concentration of power in the hands of the bureaucrats, development of the Certified Public Accountants' system, and improvement in the accounting methods of business firms—in the hands of the Japanese bureaucrats. From the point of view of accounting in regard to such cases as the *Fuji Sash Co.* case, the *KDD* case (Kokusai Denshin-Denwa Co., Ltd.), or the *Denden Kosha* case (the Nippon Telegraph & Telephone Public Corporation), if the Securities and Exchange Commission in Japan had been given strong authority along with the direction that was initially recommended by the Shoup Mission, it is not difficult to imagine that these cases would not have occurred at all, or if they did occur, the circumstances would have been considerably different.

The scope of the authority for establishing regulations regarding accounting by the Securities and Exchange Commission in the United States of America is extended, not only to the political parties, but also even to United States governmental agencies. The scope of the authority of the principles of regular bookkeeping in the Federal Republic of Germany, like those in America, is also extended, even to the methods of accounting records to be made by the federal agencies. As I have already touched on this point, I will omit a repetition of the explanation here.

British Accounting Principles

It may safely be said that in regard to their orderliness, the Corporate Accounting Principles of Japan are akin to the *Recommendations on Accounting Principles*, which were established by the Institute of Chartered Accountants in England and Wales. The copy I have is the 1975 edition, the full text of which is comprised of 151 pages. Like the Corporate Accounting Principles of Japan, the provisions regarding the preparation of books of account are hardly contained in the British recommendations, and almost all the provisions are restricted to the conditions required for financial statements, the methods of indication, the form and the extent of information to be released to the public in general, and so on. What is particularly to be noted in regard to the British *Recommendations* is as follows: Articles 151 and 157 of *AktG* (Stock Law) in the Federal Republic of Germany have made the standard forms of balance sheet and profit and loss statements statutory. Japan also prescribes standard forms of balance sheets and profit and loss statements in Nos. 1 and 2 of the "Standard Forms" of the Regulation on Financial Statements.

In contrast, however, the British *Recommendations on Accounting Principles* have concluded that "such standard forms are not the very thing to be desired." The *Recommendations* reasons as follows: "Businesses are so varied in their nature that there must be flexibility in the manner of presenting accounts. A standard form to suit every industrial and commercial undertaking is neither practicable nor desirable. This is recognized in the Companies Act of 1948."[9] Moreover, in regard to a "true and fair view," as prescribed by Article 149 of the Companies Act of 1949, it is said that no standard form has ever been provided. As a matter of fact, Paragraph 2 of Article 149 has prescribed only that the balance sheet and the statement of loss and profit should both be in accord with the essential factors of "Schedule 8" of the Companies Act of 1948. The "Schedule 8" in question was changed to "Schedule 2" by the Companies Act of 1967; however, no standard form was prescribed. The reader should pay particular attention to the fact that in "Schedule 2" of the Companies Act of 1967, the seven sections in parentheses have been replaced in the Companies Act of 1976 by "Schedule 2."

The Substance of Fair Accounting Practice

The concept of a fair practice in accounting as prescribed by Paragraph 2 of Article 32 of the Commercial Code of Japan is, unlike the examples below, simply a general and comprehensive regulation for the merchant in a broad sense:

- The concept of a fair accounting practice, as dictated by Article 38 of the German Commercial Code, has the power of "proper order" in all fields that are in need of accounting records in the Federal Republic of Germany.
- The Securities Act of 1933 in the United States claims, as a legal standard, "completeness" and "truth" of books of account, irrespective of the size of an enterprise, the difference between a corporation and an individual person, or the difference between a political party and a state agency.

Moreover, the corporate accounting principle that has been included in the concept of "fair accounting practice" is the principle in accounting that actually exercises, substantially, its normative power, in regard to a joint-stock company, especially only in regard to a large-scale joint-stock company. The calculation regulations in the Commercial Code (precisely speaking, the regulations regarding a joint-stock company's balance sheet, loss and profit statement, and schedule) are the legal standards in accounting that have been applied to a joint-stock company and a limited company (Articles 43 and 146 of the Limited Responsibility Company Law).

When it comes to the above, therefore, a problem may arise in regard to the accounting standard that should apply in the case of a non-joint-stock company or a limited company. Needless to say, from the text of the law, it is a simple matter to say that "it is a fair accounting practice." I wonder, however, what the Councilor, Civil Affairs Bureau, of the Ministry of Justice in Japan would answer, if he were asked the question. What would be the answer of those persons in the sectional meeting of the Commercial Code, the Judicial System Council, of the Ministry of Justice? I suspect they would be perplexed.

The reason is that the concept of a "fair practice in accounting," as prescribed by Paragraph 2 of Article 32 of the Commercial Code of Japan, has a character in common with the concept of "the principles of regular bookkeeping" as prescribed by Article 38 of the Commercial Code, which was enacted prior to 1919 in the Federal Republic of Germany. In 1919 when Enno Becker, who drafted the Imperial Tax Code, made a statute of "the 'substance' of the principles of regular bookkeeping, or orderly bookkeeping," the definite contents of the standard had not been presented until that year. The principles of regular bookkeeping were established for the first time in Article 162 of the Imperial Tax Code in 1919 as an itemized substance. The state approved comprehensively an idea merchants had cultivated for a long time, a sound and fair practice regarding the entry; that is, it was generally understood that "the principles of regular bookkeeping" in Article 38 of the German Commercial Code were only articles of law in which the state expressed its approval, in a carte blanche manner, of merchants' 'sound and fair practice in accounting,' which lacked specific rules or principles and required documentation.

As a consequence, Japanese scholars of the Commercial Code actually had to seek shelter in an empty, hazy, and abstract conceptual regulation by explaining that "a fair practice in accounting" means that, in view of the objectives of books of account, which clarify financial status or the results of the business operation of an enterprise, it is the practice in accounting that is judged to be fair and appropriate.[10] This means that in the hearts of the committee members who comprised the Section Meeting of the Commercial Code, the residue of Professor Kotaro Tanaka's "theory of a carte blanche regulation" was still in existence.

In other words, the committeemen of the Section Meeting of the Commercial Code did not know that, in the tax laws in the Federal Republic of Germany, there existed detailed statutory regulations indicating the substance of the principles of regular bookkeeping. In 1976, moreover, these statutory regulations were introduced into Chapter 4, "Books of Account," of the German Commercial Code, Paragraph 2 of Article 43 of which actually prescribes: "Entries in books and other required notations are to be done in a complete, accurate, timely, and orderly manner." They did not know this fact. If they actually knew it, they should have quoted it.

I do not think that the excellent Japanese scholars of the Commercial Code are ignorant of this fact. Therefore, in addition to the previously mentioned books, I checked the following list of books:

Seiji Tanaka (honorary professor, Hitotsubashi University), *All-revised Detailed Discussion of General Rules of the Commercial Code* (1978, Keiso-Shobo ed.).

Takeo Suzuki (honorary professor, University of Tokyo), *New Edition of the Commercial Code* (1978, Keiso-Shobo ed.).

Yoshinori Hasui, comp., *General Rules of the Commercial Code—Commercial Transaction Law* (1980, Horitsu Bunkasha ed.).

Seiji Tanaka, comp., *New Edition Commercial Code*, 4th rev. ed. (1978, Chikura-Shobo ed.).

Masao Takahima (professor, Keio-Gijuku University), *General Rules of the Commercial Code, The Commercial Transaction Law* (1976, Keio-Tsushin ed.).

Seiji Tanaka and Ryosuke Kita, *Commentary, General Rules of the Commercial Code*, rev. ed. (1975, Keiso-Shobo ed.).

Kenji Sanekata and Toshiro Shima, comps. *General Rules of the Commercial Code* (1980, Seirin-Shoin Shinsha ed.).

Shuzo Toda (professor, Chuo University), *General Rules of the Commercial Code* (1980, Bunkyu-Shorin ed.).

Teruhisa Ishii, *General Rules of the Commercial Code*, rev. ed. (1979, Kobundo ed.).

Yoshinori Hasui, Toshio Sakamaki, and Harumi Shimura, comps., *Lecture on General Rules of the Commercial Code* (1980, Seirin-Shoin Shinsha ed.).

Setsu Tatsuta (professor, Kyoto University), comp., *Summary Explanation of the Commercial Code* (1980, Yuhikaku ed.).

Katsuro Kamiyanagi, Masahiro Kitazawa, Tsuneo Ootori, and Akio Takeuchi, comps. *General Rules of the Commercial Code, Commercial Transaction Law* (1980, Yuhikaku ed.).

Tsuneo Ootori, Ichiro Kawamoto, Masahiro Kitazawa, Yoh Sato, and Shuzo Toda, *Practice, the Commercial Code (General Rules,*

Commercial Transactions), rev. ed. (1976, Seirin-Shoin Shinsha ed.).

Choshichi Hoshikawa, Kogoro Yamaguchi, Wataru Horiguchi, and Toshio Sakamaki, comps., *General Rules of the Commercial Code, Commercial Transaction Law*, rev. ed. (1979, Hogaku-Shoin ed.).

After reviewing all the above books, I was truly disappointed. I had to doubt my own eyes many times. It was shocking to me that none of the scholars listed above touched on the concept of "the principles of regular bookkeeping" under Article 38 of the German Commercial Code, which is equivalent to the Japanese concept of a "fair practice in accounting"—not an empty, obscure, and abstract concept, but a concept of statutory law, detailed exposition of which has been in existence in German taxation laws for more than sixty years. Nor had they mentioned the fact that the concept of "the principles of regular bookkeeping" had actually been adopted in Article 43 of the German Commercial Code.

How do these Japanese scholars view the situation in recent years in which deplorable incidents in accounting have happened repeatedly? As Japanese politicians have become tradesmen, they may have lost their capability for serious thinking about the formation of the destiny of the state and the people. Nay, prior to their appearance on the main stage of politics, they may have left behind, somewhere, this essential attribute.

I hope that the reader will think about this matter. It is the managers, not professional accountants, who first take a look at the original records of transactions. Professional accountants, however, whether they are tax practitioners or licensed tax accountants, are in the position of receiving accounting materials at a later time. Whether or not perfect "completeness" and "truth" of accounting materials can be secured is dependent entirely on the inner hearts of the managers. Why does the commercial code or the taxation law assume an attitude of prescribing in a dignified manner the perfect "completeness" and "truth" of the entry as the text of legal provisions? What are they afraid of? What trouble are they afraid of? What is standing in their way? Those who live in Japan should wish sincerely that all should be able to lead a clean and sound life with confidence.

If the reader agrees, I urge him to join our movement for establishing a law under which not only all merchants but all those responsible for accounting records will be under the obligation to secure, just as people in Europe and America are, perfect "completeness" and "truth" in all records. Article 53 of the Enforcement Regulations for the Corporation Tax Law prescribes "regarding all the transactions which exert influence on property, liabilities, and capital." This article is an afterthought, however, and is not in the original law. Article 32 of the Commercial Code, which predated the revision that was made in 1974, mentioned "all matters that should exercise influence on assets." I do not know why, but the five letters "Its-Sai-No-Ji-Ko" ("all matters") have been deleted from the revised Commercial Code. Did they think it unnecessary to continue the essential element in accounting that indicates "completeness" in records of transactions, because this element had taken root securely in a "fair practice in accounting"? Such a conclusion is nonsensical! It is high time for us to curb the disgraceful incidents in accounting that occur repeatedly.

Article 34 of the French Commercial Code prescribes: "Est puni d'un emprisonnement de un a cinq ans et d'une amende de 240,000 a 4,800,000 francs, ou de l'une de ces deux peines seulement, tout commissaire qui a sciemment donné ou confirme des informations mensongeres sur la situation de la société, ou qui n'a pas révélé au procureur de la République les faits délictueux dont il a eu connaissance." Article 400 of the Stock Law, under the heading "Incorrect Representation," proscribes a falsehood in financial statements, while Article 403, under the head "Offence against the Obligation of Report," proscribes a falsehood in an audit report; these matters warrant imprisonment for a term of less than three years or a fine. R. V. Jhering, the nineteenth-century German jurist said, "The goal of law is peace; the means thereto is struggle." It is now high time to put this into practice.

From a theoretical viewpoint, when the Calculation Regulations of our Commercial Code are revised, I would like to see the substantive enactment of principles making financial statements conform to the highest standards regarding corporate accounting. In regard to practical business, I would request the establishment of penal provisions that are on the same level as those of Britain, America, Germany, and France. These provisions should provide not only that "entries should be made in an orderly and clear manner," but also that "in books of account, it is necessary that matters should be entered in the manner of complete comprehensiveness, truthfulness, timeliness, orderliness, and clearness." I believe that only by doing this can we reduce the number of disgraceful accounting-related incidents that occur repeatedly.

Notes

1. Tsuneo Ootori, *The General Rules of the Commercial Code*, p. 237.
2. Eizo Hattori, *General Rules of the Commercial Code*, p. 351.
3. Kenichiro Osumi, *General Rules of the Commercial Code*, p. 219.
4. *Accounting* (Dec. 1979), p. 99.
5. *AICPA Professional Standards*, Vol. 3, Accounting as of July 1, 1976, p. 7261.
6. Henry Ballantine, *On Corporations*, p. 874.
7. App., Vol. IV, D52.
8. Dr. Carl S. Shoup, *Report on Japanese Taxation*, Vol. II, p. 224.
9. *Recommendations on Accounting Principles*, 18. "Presentation of Balance Sheet and Profit and Loss Account," p. 49.
10. Hattori, *General Rules of the Commercial Code*, p. 351.

Part Three

9

Calculation Regulations in the Federal Republic of Germany: Part I

Itemized Discussion of the Principles of Regular Accounting

As I said earlier, Dr. Kotaro Tanaka, a prominent scholar representing Japanese academic circles on the subject of commercial laws, made a fatal error in grasping the concept of the "principles of regular bookkeeping" prescribed by Article 38 of the German *Commercial Code*. This has led to irrevocable damage in the subsequent development of accounting theories and the accounting system in Japan. The Imperial Tax Code *(RAO)* was drawn up by Enno Becker and enacted on December 13, 1919. With the enactment of this particular law, the Federal Republic of Germany had, for the first time, itemized and detailed regulations as a positive law regarding the principles of regular bookkeeping.

It was around the middle of November 1921, when an item-by-item explanation of the Imperial Tax Code was published by Enno Becker. I regret that I do not have a copy of this first edition. I have obtained, however, the original text of the second edition of this book, which was published in August 1922. In the Preface to the second edition, Enno Becker stated that "the second edition is similar to the first edition, which quickly sold out." Although he mentioned a number of disputes that had taken place and the utilization of judicial precedents, he did not mention that the law had been revised. Thus it may safely be said that the text of the law as it appears in this second edition is identical with the law as it was first enacted.

Critical Review of Paragraphs 1 and 2 of Article 162

Article 162 at the beginning of the Imperial Tax Code had the following textual organization. Paragraph 1 of this article prescribes as follows: "Whosoever is responsible for keeping the books, or making notations according to the tax laws, should observe the following regulations." In the revision of Paragraph 1 made in August 1965, the phrase "according to the regulations of 160 and 161 or otherwise" was inserted after the word "whosoever." In the current law, which took effect in January 1977, however, the entire text of this Paragraph 1 has been deleted. This was done only to avoid duplication with another provision that prescribes the person responsible for making an entry.

Paragraph 2 dictates as follows: "The entries in the books are supposed to be conducted continuously, completely, and accurately. The taxpayer should use a living language and the characters of same." This paragraph had not changed until 1977, when the current law was enacted. Under the current law, the first part of Paragraph 2 was moved to Paragraph 1 and, moreover, what had been Paragraph 7, regarding the entry of cash, was moved next to the latter part of Paragraph 2 so that it became part of Paragraph 1 of Article 146, which now reads as follows: "Posting and other required notations are to be done completely, accurately, and in a timely and orderly manner. Cash receipts and disbursements should be entered daily." In this instance, as I touched on it earlier, the first problem is the meaning of the term "timely." According to the German dictionary *Duden*, "zeitgerecht" ("timely") means "rechtzeitig" ("on time") (Vol. 10) and "pünktlich" ("punctually") (Vol. 8). That is, "timely" means that an entry is to be made "within a rightful time" and "punctiliously." As it is prescribed that cash should be recorded on a daily basis, daily records of receipts and disbursements and confirmation of balance are indispensable.

The point at issue leads us only to the "timeliness" of the entry of "credit transactions"—transfer transactions, in the terms of bookkeeping. In regard to this, I have already stated that Article

Calculation Regulations: Part I   107

29 (*EStR* 29) of the Enforcement Regulations provided an explanation of Article 5 of the German tax law under the subject "Regular Bookkeeping." Its Paragraph 2 begins with the following regulation: "All business transactions are to be posted in registers in a timely and orderly manner. The timely posting of business transactions—with the exception of cash transactions—does not require daily posting. However there must exist a temporal relationship between the transactions and their posting in account books." This is the wording of the Enforcement Regulations, enacted by the Federal Minister of Finance, who had adopted the decision of the Federal Finance Court that was handed down in 1965.

The regulation prescribes that a cash transaction be entered on the day it occurs and that a transfer transaction, whenever it occurs, does not have to be entered on the same day. The principle of "timeliness," however, should still apply to transfer transactions and their entry. The time limit for the "timeliness" of the entry of a transfer transaction is defined as the end of the month after the month which includes the day on which the transactions occurred. The *EStR* prescribes this particular relation by using the following expression in the middle part of Paragraph 2: "One cannot object, as long as the credit transactions of one month are posted to the register before the end of the following month."

The demand for "timeliness" not only refers to the time limit for the entry of transactions, it also clarifies the limit of approval for the "regularity" of books of account, to say nothing of the time for presenting financial statements. This matter can be known by taking a look at another part of this court decision. The court decision states as follows: "The regularity of a commercial accounting assumes that the balance sheet and profit and loss statements are drawn up within a reasonable time after the end of the fiscal year. Bookkeeping which is reconstructed later is not 'regular,' even if it is technically correct."[1] I would guess that the reader may now see how strict the standard regarding "timeliness" is in the calculation regulations of German laws.

The Concept of "Timeliness" in American Accounting

The reader should pay special attention to this particular point, because it is remarkably different in American accounting. In his book *Detailed Explanation of the Corporate Accounting Principles*, Professor Kaichiro Banba of Hitotsubashi University has detailed the concept of "timeliness" to which he has added: "picking up, from American literature, the thing that is considered as the constituent element of general principle in this country's accounting principles."[2] I assume that the "timeliness" to which Professor Banba refers in this instance is ".20 0–5. Timeliness" in "AC Section 1024, Objectives of Financial Accounting and Financial Statements," which was established in October 1970, as "Statement of the Accounting Principles Board" by the AICPA.[3] I think, however, it simply states that in regard to information about a corporation's financial accounting prepared for the respective economic judgments of stockholders and creditors, being informed of such information *a little earlier than usual* is one of the seven major quality objectives.

The American principle of "timeliness" has not been based on the conception that a time limit be established in regard to entry and so forth. In order to establish the sound development of Japan's economy, whether the German model of establishing "timeliness" or the American model of "timeliness" is more desirable has already become self-evident. To sum up, it can be said that this matter will result in a problem of insight and capacity of the legislators, the persons who have to draw up the law. I hope the reader clearly understands this point in particular. The reason distinct legal standards exist in regard to the timeliness of entries and so forth in the Federal Republic of Germany is that there is a legal relation in which its legislation constitutes the inside and outside relationship with jurisprudence that approves the verifiable bookkeeping records of books of account. Recognition of this point has been clearly indicated in judicial precedents. I would like, therefore, to touch on it later.

Critical Review of the Opinions of Herbert Brönner

As stated above, Paragraph 7 of Article 162 of the original law was moved to the latter part of Article 146. What was the text of the law when it was enacted? The text, which follows, was different from the existing law in several ways: "Cash receipts and disbursements should be posted at least daily in commercial transactions." The point I want to make is that a positive law standard to the effect that "the entry of cash transactions should be made at least once a day" has been in existence in Germany's legislation since 1919. In the sixty years since the enactment of this positive law standard, although the paragraph was moved to the latter part of Article 146 of the new law, the substance of this particular standard has not changed.

Mr. Herbert Brönner, a certified public accountant and licensed tax practitioner in Berlin, states that it has been a tenet of regular bookkeeping for merchants that the entry of cash transactions should be made in a cashbook.[4] The authority for his statement, I suspect, must be the judicial decision that was handed down by the Federal Finance Court on March 6, 1952 (the twenty-seventh year of Showa in Japan). According to *Tax Court Decisions in Catalog Form*, by Dr. Otto Schmidt of Cologne, a copy of which I happen to own, the essential point of this judicial decision was as follows: "Regular commercial bookkeeping requires the posting of cash transactions in a cash book." Brönner further states as follows: "The BFH-U of 1 October 1969 (IR 73/66 *BStBl* 1970 II S. 45) once more thoroughly addresses the regularity of cash accounting. It requires regular cash accounting."[5] He states this, but he does not introduce the contents of the decision of this court.

Mr. Brönner quotes as many as 1,543 cases, with the dates of the court decisions, the dates on which the court opinions were published, and the case numbers, the judicial decisions that have been handed down over the past fifty years from January 1921 to January 1971.[6] It is regrettable that his discussion of the limitations of court decisions is inadequate. For example, the court decision handed down on October 1, 1969, states as follows: "When recording each individual cash receipt and disbursement, the requirements of a business's cash account do not, as a rule, include the responsibility of a running record of the cash on hand and its representation in the books or documents. This is different, however, when the daily over-the-counter receipts are determined (when permissible) by a cash report, a treasurer's report." As a result of this court decision, it has been clarified that the amount of cash on hand varies whenever payment and receipt of money are made;

however, there is no obligation to make an entry of the amount of cash on hand.

Mr. Brönner's book, as one might expect, is the work of a businessman, and he devotes 83 pages to a discussion of *Handelsbilanz* and 281 pages to *Steuerbilanz*. He also devotes 349 pages to an analysis of the "individual posting of the balance and of profit and loss statements," especially the theory involved in each, and he freely quotes judicial precedents. Among the books in this category, his is brilliant. My only criticism is that he has been inaccurate in his quotations from the relevant judicial precedents.

A book entitled *Tax Code: Tax Court Code Secondary Laws* (12th ed., 1977), coauthored by Rolf Kühn, a lawyer, certified public accountant, and tax practitioner, and by Heinz Kutter and Ruth Hormann—judges of the Financial Affairs Court—also suffers from the incompleteness of its quotations from the judicial precedents. It is superior to Brönner's book, however, in the accuracy of its quotations. In addition to the limited nature of the quotes from the judicial precedents, clarity is lacking in this book just as it is in Brönner's.

If I were to pick up the gist of the major court decisions from the above-mentioned *Tax Court Decisions in Catalog Form*, relying only on the dates and the numbers of the court decisions, the following summary of the court decisions could be made: "Cash accounting in which cash receipts and disbursements are recorded on the next business day is still considered proper, if compelling business reasons prevent the posting on the same day, and when it can be determined with certainty from the bookkeeping records, how the cash on hand has developed." In the pursuit of the calculation regulations of an enterprise and the legal condition of entries in the Federal Republic of Germany, one often encounters situations in which the decision in a trial endeavors to judge and demonstrate, elaborately, the existence or nonexistence of "regularity." Germany has legislation which dictates that when a corporation's calculations and entries are found to have "regularity," the fact itself has "probative force" under the law. This concept must appear an unexpected, perhaps even unorthodox method to those who are primarily familiar with American accounting and American tax law.

Secondly, I would like to introduce the essential points of the court decision which both Brönner's book, *Die Bilanz,* and Kühn, Kutter, and Hormann's *Tax Code* have quoted. On May 12, 1966, the Federal Finance Court handed down the following decision: "The principles of regular bookkeeping do not, as a rule, require that retail merchants who generally sell wares over-the-counter to customers who are not personally known to them record the cash receipts individually." A principle governing entries that is considered nearly the same as the substance of this court decision has also been made statutory in Japan. It is the provisory clause among items of sale, No. 11 of the items mentioned in books of account by a corporate body that is planning to obtain approval for filing a blue return, Separate Table No. 20 of the Enforcement Regulations for the Corporation Tax Law. The provisory clause prescribes as follows:

In sales in cash by a corporate body conducting retail sales and other activities similar to retail sales, as to those items that cannot conform to the text of this regulation, in place of it, the daily amount of sales in cash and the person or persons to whom the sales were made [may be entered], or as to those whose customers cannot be entered, and, among such items as the name of an article, the content of other presentations made, the quantity, unit price, or amount of money, those items which cannot be entered may be omitted.

In a remarks column, No. 1 in these Enforcement Regulations, it is prescribed that "in the sales in cash by a corporate body which conducts retail sales and acts similar to retail sales, as to those which cannot be based on the regulation of the proviso shown in the above, only the total amount of daily sales in cash may be entered, when the approval to do so was obtained from the Chief of the Taxation Office concerned." This Japanese regulation is applicable to the statutory conditions of entries in Germany.

What is important here is the fact that it was in May 1966 when this court decision was handed down in the Federal Republic of Germany. Sixteen years earlier, conditions governing entries, especially the point at issue, were made statutory in Japan. Thus, in this Japan was ahead of the Federal Republic of Germany.

Personal Views on the Judicial Precedents Concerned

In regard to cashbooks, the following judicial precedent cannot be overlooked. It is the juridical decision of the German Finance

Court that was handed down on July 13, 1971. The gist of this decision is as follows: "It is not necessary to save the records of the origins of receipts, if their contents are recorded in a cashbook kept in the form of consecutively listed daily cash reports immediately after the transfer of the daily receipts." The relation between the storage of records and the condition of a cashbook is restricted by this judicial decision. The reason this decision was handed down is that, in the Federal Republic of Germany, the principles of regular bookkeeping as general categorical propositions are majestically provided for in the positive laws.

In addition to this judicial precedent, there is another that does not appear in Brönner's book and that is concerned with the handling of cash. It is a judicial precedent that was handed down by the Federal Finance Court on October 20, 1971. The gist of this decision, which was written by the judge who had actually handled the case, runs as follows: "If special cash(books) are kept in addition to the main cash register, regular bookkeeping requires the existence of secondary ledgers for individual special cash accounts. In a special cash account must be included contributions made to the entrepreneur."[7]

In cases where several safes are used, a "memorandum" of cash for each safe is required. It will be necessary to take into consideration that the memorandum itself is to be treated as an object for "regularity" in bookkeeping, together with the following, which has been prescribed by Item 1, Paragraph 2 of Article 29 of Income Tax Guidelines: "No specific bookkeeping system is prescribed. However, the bookkeeping system chosen must guarantee the recording of all business transactions and assets." It can be said, therefore, that what is meant by recording all transactions and property has been extended even to a demand for "regularity" in entries in current cash deposit journals that should correspond to supplementary cash registers.

Declaration of "Conclusiveness" by a Delegated Order

Special attention should be paid to "Einführungserlaß zur *AO* vom Oktober 1976," which is known as a delegated order and is said to have the secondary force of law under German tax juris-

Calculation Regulations: Part I 113

prudence. At the beginning of Paragraph 1 of Article 146 under the heading "Regularity Requirements for Bookkeeping and for Records," the following appears: "Only regular bookkeeping has probative force." That is, Article 146 proclaims that in the Federal Republic of Germany, only the calculations, records, and books of account that are precisely based on the principles of regular bookkeeping are "verifiable bookkeeping records." As Dr. Klaus Tipke of Cologne University has said: "The required testimonial proof must be honored. Evaluation of testimonial proof before the presentation thereof is not permitted."[8]

In regard to this point in particular, for those who are particularly interested in this matter, I would recommend looking at a 180-page book, *Proof in Tax Law*, by Wolfram Birkenfeld who was a judge of the Tax Court in Berlin. Birkenfeld discusses this matter in considerable depth. I trust the reader will understand that the concept of books of account as "verifiable bookkeeping records" cannot be conceptualized in American and British accounting and under American and British tax jurisprudence, and that provisions that acknowledge "verifiable bookkeeping records" are currently in existence in Japan's tax laws.

Critical Review of Paragraphs 3 and 4 of Article 162

To return to a critical review of the text of Article 162, Paragraph 3 of the article states: "Business books should contain no accounts that are registered under false or invented names." The text of this provision remained unchanged for fifty-eight years after its enactment in 1919 until January 1977. In the current *AO*, however, the following provisions have been inserted as Paragraph 2 of Article 146:

Books and the otherwise required records are to be kept and stored within the jurisdiction of this law. This does not apply to places of business (business establishments) outside of the jurisdiction of this law that are required to keep books and records by local law, as long as they fulfill this requirement. In this case and in the case of subsidiary companies outside of the jurisdiction of this law, the results of the local bookkeeping must be taken over by the bookkeeping of the business establishment here insofar as it is of importance for taxation. In this case the tax law regulations within the jurisdiction of this law are to be followed and to be marked in the books.⁹

This particular provision has no connection at all with Paragraph 3 of Article 162 of the former *AO*. Furthermore, Paragraph 4 of Article 162 stated: "Insofar as it is customary in the business, the books are to be bound and given consecutive numbers on each leaf or page." This provision was also unchanged until January 1, 1977. In the new law that took effect on that date, this provision does not appear. Article 10 of the French Commercial Code prescribes that serial numbers and initials be entered in a journal book and a general ledger, gratis, by a judge of the commercial court, a judge of the ordinary local court, the mayor, or the deputy mayor.[10]

Such a demand, however, has not existed in the French Tax Laws. It may not be a serious problem to make an entry of an essential factor or a condition for books of account in the Tax Law or in the Commercial Code. What is important is whether or not the essential factor or condition has been given as a positive law. What is problematic is the fact that the state has legalized it as the living standard of the people. I attach special importance to the fact that, in accord with changing times, the state has resolutely made this step. This provision in the French Commercial Code, however, has raised an obstacle to the popularization of the recently developed computerized accounting. The fact that, prior to the use of books of account, merchants were under the obligation to obtain a serial number and the initials of official agencies means that all those books of account that have been turned out by computers should be considered only as subsidiary books.

As a result, a situation has been created in which the actual "livre-journal" and "livre-d'inventaire," both of which are required for the entry of transactions on a sequential basis in accordance with Article 8 of the French Commercial Code, should be disposed of as scrap, whenever their records are completed every month. This includes all the books mentioned above that have been used up to the previous month. Otherwise, due to the books of account and various tables that computers have turned out, on a large scale, the storage locations for merchants' books of account will become just like the stacks in a library.

Mr. Michel Bossard, a public accountant and resident of the CCMC Data Processing Center, the largest such center in France, talked about this matter with me. Mr. Bossard visited TKC together with Mr. Heinz Sebiger, the president of DATEV, which is the largest data processing center in the Federal Republic of Germany. They visited Japan for the purpose of organizing a combined association of large data processing centers in Japan, Germany, and France. We spoke on the electric train heading for Kinugawa Hot Spring on March 31, 1980.

France and Italy

Unlike in France, the fundamental requirements in regard to the preparation of books of account and the maintenance of the records of a business are dictated by Civil Law in Italy. All enterprises, excluding minor merchants, should provide daily journals and inventory books. And every year all businesses must draw up balances and profit and loss statements.[11] Up to this point, nothing seems particularly strange. Also prescribed, however, is that when merchants' books of account are initiated, serial numbers must be entered on each page, and each leaf should be stamped by a registration office and, in cases when a special law so prescribes, by a notary public.[12] Finally, every year the merchants' books of account are to be inspected by the registry office or a public notary office.[13]

The fact that a court, a city office, a registry office, and a public notary office are involved with books of account and accounting records conveys a particular kind of conception regarding bookkeeping, even to us Japanese. The fact that the Italian Civil Law demands "Klarheit" and "Correctness" in indicating the financial situation of an enterprise and in the character of financial statements gives me the impression that the financial statements to be submitted, or to be made public by an enterprise, must in general have the character of substantial obscurity or at least a shade of a darker tone in themselves.[14] Giving due consideration to the fact that books of account have never been acknowledged as "verifiable bookkeeping records" in Italy, my sense about this particular point may be considered reasonable.[15]

Critical Review of Paragraph 5 of Article 162

The original text of Paragraph 5 of Article 162 says:

No blank space should be left in places that are to be described according to the rule. The original contents of an entry should not be rendered illegible by crossing out or in any other way; the entry should not be erased, nor should any other modifications be undertaken whose nature would make it uncertain whether they had been made as the original entry or not until later.

At this point there is a matter that weighs, just a bit, on my mind. This original text of Paragraph 5 of Article 162 is the exact text of the provision that appears on page 204 of the second edition of the book published in 1922 by Enno Becker. However, in Volume 2 of Dr. Otto Schmidt's *Tax Court Decisions in Catalog Form* (24 vols., Cologne), from which I quoted earlier, the words "An Stellen, die in der Regel" appear. The word "in" has been added.

This finding made me suspicious. I therefore collated Schmidt's text with the full text of Paragraph 5 of Article 162 of the *AO* as it appears in *Tax Laws: A Collection of the Texts with Notes and Index* (24th ed., 1972). The latter text is identical with the provisions transcribed by Enno Becker. Because Germans are supposed to be accurate in their scholarship, I thought an inaccuracy could not be possible. Finally, I checked the original text of Article 162 as it appears in *Wirtschaftsprufer-Handbuch*, published in 1973 by the Institute of Chartered Accountants in Germany, which should be an authority on this matter. As might be expected, Paragraph 5 begins with the opening passage "An Stellen, die der Regel nach," in which the word "in" does not appear.

In conclusion, I knew that German scholars, like those in Japan, had frequently made mistakes in their theories, however, they also made mistakes even in their grammar. In this particular instance, it is a clear error from the point of view of German grammar to insert "in" in this particular expression, because doing so duplicates the sense of the word "nach." In this connection, this particular article has been eliminated in the new law.

To return to the subject at hand, Paragraph 5 of Article 162 was not touched in the revision in 1965. However, it has been deleted in the new law.

Critical Review of Paragraphs 6 and 7 of Article 162

Paragraph 6 of the text of Article 162 provides: "Wherever this is customary in business, books should be kept in ink. If the taxpayer makes entries from temporary records, the latter should be kept. Vouchers should be numbered and kept as well." This provision had also not been revised since its enactment in 1919. It was deleted, however, from the new law that went into effect in January 1977.

Paragraph 7 of the text of Article 162 was enacted in the original *AO* in 1919 and also appeared in the revision made in 1965: "Cash receipts and disbursements should be recorded at least daily in the conduct of business." In the 1977 law, however, this provision was transferred to Paragraph 1 of Article 146, as I stated earlier, and it was modified slightly: "should be written down daily." The substance of this provision, however, has not changed at all. The reason this can be said is that the term "festgehalten" can be interpreted as the mere entry of receipts and disbursements and the balance, but it also means *collation* with the balance of actual cash in hand.

Dr. Eberhard Littmann, who was identified earlier as the presiding judge at the Federal Finance Court in Munich, has stated, however, in his *Income Tax Law:* "At any time, it must be possible to compare the recorded cash on hand with the actual amount based on the records in the cashbook (see also *BFH v. 9. 10. 1952, BStBl 1954 III S. 71; 10. 12. 1953, BStBl 1954 III S. 82.*)"[16] That is, the provisions regarding the "daily entry obligation of receipts and disbursements" of the former law were incorporated into the standards through general interpretation, including even the *obligation of* daily *collation* of the balance of actual cash in hand, as a matter of course by this decision of the BFH and other official documents while the original law was in effect. Such being the case, it can be concluded that its substance has not changed at all.

Critical Review of Paragraph 8 of Article 162

When it was enacted in 1919, Paragraph 8 of Article 162 provided: "The books, records, and business papers (insofar as they are of importance for taxes) should be kept for ten years. This time period begins at the end of the calendar year in which the last entry is made in the books or records or in which the business papers are created." This provision, however, at the time of its revision on August 2, 1962, and at the time of its enforcement on August 8, 1965, was revised as follows:

Books, inventories, balance sheets, records according to Section 1, business letters received, copies of business letters sent, journal vouchers, business papers that have tax significance, and other documents are to be kept in order. That is
1. Books, inventories, and balance sheets for ten years,
2. Records, business letters received, copies of business letters sent, journal vouchers, and other documents for seven years, as long as a shorter time period is not specified in other tax laws.

The period of time begins at the end of the calendar year in which the last entry was made in the book in which the inventory was recorded, the balance was determined, the business letter was received or sent, the voucher came into existence, or the records or other documents were created.

In the new law that went into effect on January 1, 1977, these provisions were removed from Article 146, in which entry conditions were made statutory, and were incorporated into Article 147 with the addition of a new subject, "Regulations for the Preservation of Documents." Furthermore, the provisions underwent a remarkable change. In the first place, Paragraph 1 of Article 147 of the current law states:

The following documents are to be preserved in order:
1. Books and records, inventories, balance sheets, as well as the explanations required for understanding them and other documents of the organization,
2. Business letters received,
3. Copies of business letters sent,
4. Journal vouchers,
5. Other documents of tax significance.

And Paragraph 2 of Article 147 runs as follows:

Except for the balance sheet, the documents listed in Section 1 can also be stored on a computer storage disk or another data medium, when this is in accordance with the principles of regular bookkeeping and when it is certain that the copies or data

1. Are identical in appearance with the received business letters and vouchers and in content with the other documents, when they have been made legible.
2. Are available during the period of time they are to be preserved and can be made legible at any time within a reasonable time.

If the documents listed in 146, Section 5, have been produced on a data medium, the data can be stored printed out instead of in the data medium; the printed documents can also be preserved according to Sentence 1.

The length of time of preservation and the scope of the materials to be preserved have, moreover, been prescribed by Paragraph 3 of Article 162, the original text of which will be referred to later. The materials listed in No. 1, Paragraph 1, of Article 147 are to be preserved for ten years, and the scope of the materials to be preserved has been enlarged to some extent. As to those materials not listed in No. 1, they are to be preserved for six years, just as before.

Adapting to the Age of Computerized Accounting

The reader may be perplexed by suddenly coming across a reference to "Paragraph 5 of Article 146" at this stage, considering that I have not given the contents of Paragraph 5 of Article 146. This is nothing but a slight confusion that is the result of the rearrangement of the text of the provisions of the former law at the time when the new law went into effect. It is undeniable that one of the major aspects of the conversion from the old law to the new one was the coordination of a sudden change in the economic community, especially due to computer-aided accounting. Article 162 of the Imperial Tax Code ended with the following Paragraph 9 in 1919: "The tax office can check whether books and records are being kept continuously, completely, and correctly in form and contents." At that time, to establish such standards of order was considered sufficient. It was a time when no one could even dream about the future overwhelming popularity of computer-aided accounting. Paragraph 5 of Article 146 of the new law is put in the statutory form that follows:

The books and other required records can also consist of the orderly filing of the vouchers or can be kept on data media, insofar as these forms of bookkeeping, as well as the process used, conform to the principles of regular bookkeeping; as concerns records that are only to be kept for tax purposes, the reliability of the method used is determined according to the purpose the records should serve in taxation. In keeping the books and other required records on data media one must be especially careful that the data are available during the time period records are to be kept and that they can be made legible within a reasonable period of time (Sections 1 through 4 apply accordingly).

As the reader can see, the text of this provision is a modern revised version of the principles of regular bookkeeping, especially considering account today's economic community, which centers on computer-aided accounting. The principles of regular bookkeeping, as the itemized theory of a positive law, have gradually changed along with the changing times.

Subsequent Revision of Article 162

Thus far I have introduced the full text of Article 162 of the Imperial Tax Code, which was drawn up by Enno Becker and enacted in 1919. Since then the Tax Code has been modified several times. The most thorough revision, however, was the one made in August 1965. Although a transitional version, standing between the early law and the current one, this law was enforced for twelve years and is the nucleus of the current law. As this is so—and considering the old proverb "Carrying knowledge into new fields"—it is necessary to examine the full text of the 1965 version of Article 162.

In the revision made in 1965, the following provision was inserted into Article 162 as Paragraph 9:

The copies of business letters sent (copies, carbons, or other permanent copy of the wording on a computer storage disk) must agree with the originals. The other papers mentioned in Section 8, No. 2, are to be kept in the originals. They can also be kept in the form of reduced-size copies that are identical with the originals. This applies also to journal vouchers insofar as the filing of these records replaces the keeping of journals and ledgers. If, because of this, documents can only be kept in a form that is not readable without aid, then the party must produce at his own cost the required number of reproductions readable without aid to the tax officials or to the court. In the case of investigation or tests in the rooms of the business, the required reading machines for reduced-size copies are to be provided.

This provision shows that by August 1965 the Federal Republic of Germany had a positive law regulation that dealt with the preservation of accounting materials by microfilm and with computer-aided accounting. With minor revisions in its wording and organization, this Paragraph 9 was incorporated into Article 147 in the current law that has been in effect since 1977.

Notes

1. *BHF VI 154/63 U; Urt. 5. 3. 65; BStBL III 1965. 285.*
2. See p. 11.
3. *AICPA Professional Standards,* Vol. 3, July 1, 1976, p. 7226.
4. *Die Bilanz nach Handels- und Steuerrecht,* 8 Auflage, 1971, S. 502.
5. See p. 502.
6. See pp. 754–78.
7. *BFH IR 63/70; Urt. v. 20. 10. 71.*
8. *Tax Law* (8th ed), p. 526.
9. Deutsches wissenschaftliches Steuerinstitut der Steuerberater und Steuerbevollmächtigten e.V., *AO-Handbuch* (1981), p. 50.
10. Code de Commerce, art. 19.
11. Codice civile, art. 2214, 2217.
12. Ibid., art. 2215, 2421.
13. Ibid., art. 2216, 2421.
14. Ibid., art. 2423.
15. Testo unico, art. 117. 118.
16. Eberhard Littmann, *Das Einkommensteuerrecht,* 12 Auflage (Neuester Stand Groβformat, 1978), Band I, S. 321–123a.

10

Calculation Regulations in the Federal Republic of Germany: Part II

Critical Review of Paragraphs 3, 4, and 6 of the New Tax Code *(AO)*

Paragraph 3 of Article 146 of the current Tax Code *(AO)*, which constitutes the nucleus of the calculation regulations of the tax laws of the Federal Republic of Germany, stipulates: "The entries and other required records are to be made in a living language. If any language other than German is used, tax officials may require translations. If abbreviations, numerals, letters, or symbols are used, then the meaning must be unambiguously indicated for each."

I have already touched on the point that this term "a living language," which means "ordinary language," had already appeared in Article 32 of the German Commercial Code that was enacted in 1961. Computer-aided accounting, or business processing by a computer, utilizes symbols and marks. In Japan, a revision of the law may encompass these phenomena, however, I am sorry that the positive laws regarding accounting or tax laws in my country have no provisions that correspond to this particular German provision.

Paragraph 4 of Article 146 has the following expression: "An entry or record may not be changed in such a manner that the original contents can no longer be determined. Such changes must not be undertaken whose nature makes it unsure whether they are part of the original entry or not made until later." The alteration of original records in accounting has frequently caused difficulties in tax examination in Japan. The legislative framework that encompasses this problematic sphere will be instructive to Japan.

As we have already looked at Paragraph 5 of Article 146, we can now examine the last paragraph of Article 146. Paragraph 6 stipulates: "The regulations of order also apply whenever the proprietor keeps books and records that have taxation significance, without being required to do so." Unlike the present situation in Japan, the Commercial Code and the Tax Laws in the Federal Republic of Germany spell out strict and realistic legal provisions regarding the determination of the limits of responsible persons for the statutory obligation of bookkeeping, the details of which we will consider later. As those enterprisers who are hovering above or below the line of this limit, regardless of whether they are corporations or legal persons, feel uneasy about committing a "violation of the duty to keep books" under the German Penal Code, under which a prison sentence of less than two years or a fine can be imposed, I think these regulations are necessary.[1] Dr. Erich Samson, a professor at Kiel University, wrote the sections on the Penal Code and the Code of Criminal Procedure in *Steuerstrafrecht mit Steuerordnungswidrigkeiten*. I will touch on the Tax Penal Code later in regard to the principles of regular bookkeeping.

Critical Review of Paragraphs 3, 4, 5, etc., of the New *AO*

I stated earlier that Paragraph 8 of Article 162 of the 1919 law was revised and incorporated into Article 146 of the 1965 law, and that it was again revised and incorporated into Article 147 of the 1977 law under the new heading "Regulations for the Preservation of Documents." I have, however, introduced only Paragraphs 1 and 2 of Article 147. Some modifications in regard to the period for the preservation of materials have been made in Article 147 in order to cope with computer-aided accounting; in the current law, the sphere of expression in the legal provisions has been enlarged as far as Paragraph 5. Paragraph 3 prescribes:

The documents listed in Section 1, No. 1, are to be preserved for ten years, the other documents listed in Section 1 are to be kept for six years, as

124 Calculation Regulations: Part II

long as a shorter period is not permitted by other tax laws. The period of time to keep records does not expire, however, insofar and as long as the documents have significance for taxation for which the period of assessment has not expired. 169 Section 2, Sentence 2 is not valid.

The original text of the second sentence of Paragraph 2 of Article 169, which appears at the end of Paragraph 3, states: "The statute of limitations is ten years, insofar as a tax has been evaded, and five years if it has been reduced by involuntary negligence." In this instance, the term "statute of limitations" is a concept that is generally unfamiliar to the Japanese. The title that has generalized the new law from Article 169 to 171 is "2d Expiration of the Statute." The title refers to the time period that must elapse before the credits and debits to be considered for taxation have become legally final.

Paragraph 4 of Article 147 of the new law states: "The period of time begins at the end of the calendar year in which the last entry was made in the book, the inventory was taken, the balance determined, the business letters received or sent, the voucher came into existence, or the records or other documents were created." A calendar year terminates at exactly twelve midnight of December 31 of that year. From the viewpoint of Japanese phraseology, however, we have to say, "from January 1, next year." I feel that there can be a simpler form of expression, instead of making such a detailed limitation, which is too depressing for the Japanese. It should be taken into consideration that underlying the phraseology there is a difference of national character between these two nations.

Finally, Paragraph 5 dictates:

Anyone who keeps documents only in the form of copies on microfilm or on other data media, is required to provide, at his own expense, the necessary apparatus and aid required to render the documents legible. At the request of the fiscal authorities, he is to print the documents immediately, in full or in part and at his own expense, or he is to provide reproduction legible without aid.

The "Regulations for the Preservation of Documents" of Article 147 of the new law comes to an end with this Paragraph 5.

I must remind the reader: "The proof of the pudding is in the eating." In Article 162 of the 1919 *AO*, Paragraph 9 completes the text of the provisions related to the authority of tax offices to examine books of account and records. The purpose of the legal control of these provisions is different from that of the Paragraph 9 that appears in the revised 1965 version. Paragraphs 9 and 10 of the 1919 *AO* became Paragraphs 10 and 11 in the 1965 revision. Paragraph 10 of the newly revised law in 1965 states:

The tax and revenue office may inspect as to whether books and records are being kept continuously, completely, and accurately regarding form and content. This inspection is also permitted to the extent that it does not concern the condition (circumstances) of the persons or businesses whose books are audited, but rather is concerned with clarification of the condition of the employees who are or have been in the employ of these persons or businesses.

Paragraph 11 states:

In a large business, a regular company audit should be undertaken by appropriately trained officials or experts of the finance administration. The audit should in every case include the period of time back to the last audit conducted. When a business conducts an audit for the first time, the finance administration shall determine the period of time that the audit must include.

Both Paragraphs 10 and 11 are included in Article 193 of the current law, as they have been absorbed in Paragraph 1 of that Article.

Under the title "Admissibility of an External Audit," Article 193 prescribes:
(1) An external audit is permitted in the case of taxpayers who own a commercial, agricultural, or forestry business or who are self-employed.
(2) In cases of taxpayers other than those indicated in Section 1, an external audit is permitted a) to the extent that it concerns the obligations of this taxpayer to pay taxes on behalf of another or to withhold or pay out taxes, or b) if extreme circumstances require clarification for tax purposes and an audit at the office is not practical due to the nature and extent of the circumstances to be examined.

I think that Paragraphs 10 and 11 in the revised law in 1965 and Article 193 of the current law do not correspond in view of their respective connotation and extension; they simply have the relationship of probable correlation.

126 Calculation Regulations: Part II

In the *AO-Handbuch* (Munich: C. H. Beck,1977; page 62), subtitled *Writings of the German Scientific Tax Institute of Tax Advisors and Tax Representatives, E.V.*, there appears a section "Imperial Tax Code and Its Secondary Laws in Comparison with the Tax Code, AO 1977." At page 66, Paragraphs 10 and 11 of Article 162 of the Imperial Tax Code appear side by side with Article 193 of the new law, a rough arrangement. It is clear that there is no logical correspondence between them, and that Article 193 of the new law has undergone such a transformation that it may be said to be a newly created article of law.

Criticism of Professor Leonard Peez

Professor Leonhard Peez, the author of *Principles of Regular Data Processing in Accounting* (Wiesbaden: Th. Gabler Press, 1975), writes: "We find the clearest references to the principles of regular bookkeeping and a codification, incomplete however, of formal principles in the following regulations." He then cites the following seven sources of law:

1. 38 through 47a *HGB*.
2. 149 through 161 *AktG*.
3. 41 and 42 *GmbHG*.
4. 33 through 33h *GenG*.
5. 5 *PublG*.
6. 160 through 163 *AO*.
7. 5 *EstG* (with Abschn. 29 *EStR*)

As this book was published in 1975, the author naturally quotes the provisions of the Imperial Tax Code prior to the revised law of 1977. This obviously could not be helped. However, I think it regrettable that compared with the various sources of laws that have been cited in the *Wirtschaftsprufer-Handbuch*, which was compiled by the Institute of Chartered Accountants in Germany, this book is incomplete. Furthermore, on page 58, the book quotes, as "prefunctory principles," articles of the German Commercial Code from 38 through 47a *HGB* as the first source of law. On page 54, however, it indicates Articles 39 and 49, from among the principles of regular bookkeeping that have been prescribed by Article

38 of the German Commercial Code, as *materielle* principles, which is an error because it contradicts itself.

Professor Peez's book is, nevertheless, an extremely helpful reference book, because it carries, as an appendix, the full text of the material on calculation regulations in the Commercial Code. This "Outline of a Revision" was made public as *Paper 7/261 of the German Bundestag, 7th Session.* Attention should be paid to the fact, as a conspicuous feature, that the concept of "the principles of regular bookkeeping" in German accounting has been constituted as a versatile concept of positive laws, not only in the Tax Code and the Commercial Code but also in various sources of laws. The reason is that using the concept "the principles of regular bookkeeping" as a single term, it has the character of having appeared on the main stage as a positive law by carrying the demand for the formulation of specific social standards that are peculiar to each source of a law.

The Origin of the Statutory Obligation of Bookkeeping

At my elbow, there is a book that explains the German Commercial Code, a book which is, I believe, the most comprehensive in the Federal Republic of Germany. It is comprised of six volumes with over forty-five hundred pages and was published by Walter de Gruyter & Co. in Berlin—*Commercial Code,* Commentary begun by Hermann Staub, continued by members of the Imperial Courts (3d ed., revised by Superior Court Judge Dieter Bruggemann, Celle; President of the Senate of the Federal Court of Appeals Robert Fischer, Karlsruhe; retired Superior Court Judge Paul Ratz, Munich; Wolfgang Schilling, Esq., Mannheim; and Professor Hans Wurdinger, Hamburg). Pages 439 through 463 of Volume 1 are primarily devoted to an explanation of the German Commercial Code. At page 442, the following is particularly noted:

33ff is not a remedial statute in the sense of 823 Sec. 2 *BGBl.*[2] Here the merchant's obligation for bookkeeping, under business law or professional law, comes into possible conflict with his obligation under civil law and certainly with such duty in tax laws. In each case the objective is different; this definitely determines the content of the individual responsibility. . . . The obligation to keep books (according to civil law) is based on contract—business contracts, agreements of profit sharing—less often on law; subsidiarily in the cases of 713,[3] *(716 Abs. 11),*[4] *740 Abs. 2,*[5] *1413*[6] *BGBl)*

The Civil Code, as a general law for a citizen's life, assumes the responsibility for the demand for "orderly bookkeeping," which has been necessitated by individual and separate living relations in order to cope with versatile aspects of living. As the Civil Code is the law among citizens, it may have a character based on contract. On the contrary, Tax Law has to assume the responsibility for establishing, as a standard, the existence of systematic, unified, and detailed bookkeeping whose primary object is adequate decisions on taxable capacity in the relationship between "the ruler" and "the governed." It seems to me that *Commercial Code,* the book mentioned above, is truly farsighted in its opinion that Article 38 of the German Commercial Code places a merchant's obligation of bookkeeping in a position of constant competitiveness between both the Civil Code and the Tax Laws.

The Statutory Obligation of Bookkeeping for Those Who Are Not Merchants

In regard to the bill to amend the calculation regulations in the German Commercial Code that was made public by the German National Assembly, this bill did not affect Paragraph 1 of Article 38. I have already touched on the point that as the "obligation to keep books," which is based on the "principles of regular bookkeeping" prescribed by Paragraph 1 of this German Commercial Code, has been understood to have the character of a public law, in case of any violation of it, there is a legal provision under which the violator will incur a penalty of imprisonment of less than two years or a fine, in accordance with Article 283b of the German Penal Code.

Due to the limits of space, I will not introduce this provision here but will postpone it to some other time. I am concerned, moreover, that Paragraph 1 of Article 38 may be misunderstood to the effect that someone who is other than a merchant—for example, an agricultural worker or a forester—has no "obligation to keep books," because Paragraph 1 of Article 38 of the German

Commercial Code only prescribes for "each merchant." Article 19 of the Introductory Law for the Tax Code, which was enacted on December 14, 1976, contains a provision in regard to the "bookkeeping obligation of farmers and foresters," according to which anyone who has an annual income of more than DM 120,000 has the obligation of making regular entries and of making lawful "regular balance sheets."

Our Japanese government has long held an ambiguous attitude in regard to the "obligation of bookkeeping" and the tax payments of farmers, foresters, and so forth. It is my opinion, however, that the Japanese government should make a decision that the demands of the times do not allow this attitude on this particular matter. If the Japanese government still takes the position that there is a social value in this ambiguity, then what more can be said about this attitude?

Paragraph 2 of Article 38 of the German Commercial Code is the provision that mandates the orderly preservation of correspondence regarding transactions. In the draft of the revision, what was to be preserved was clarified and enlarged through the addition of a total of three phrases, for example, "Abschrift" (which means a "copy") and "andere Datenträger" (which means "other data medium"). In Article 41, the revised draft resulted only in the deletion of the term "an inventory of a property." In Article 42, there are no conspicuous points of revision. What was revised on a large scale were Articles 43 and 44.

Paragraphs 1 and 2 of Article 43 of the German Commercial Code

Article 43 is a legal provision under the heading "The Keeping of Business Books." Its nucleus, in what was hitherto Paragraph 1, prescribed that in making an entry in commercial books and other necessary records, a merchant should use "ordinary language," and this nucleus has not changed. Only the expression "und der Schriftzeichen einer solchen" (which means "and these letters") has been deleted. A second sentence has been newly added to this Paragraph 1: "If abbreviations, numerals, letters, or symbols are used, a meaning must be unambiguously determined for each." It is clear that this new addition is intended to cope with the age of electronic computers.

The following sentence, which was revised in 1976, has been inserted in Paragraph 2 of Article 43: "Entries in books and other required records must be conducted completely, accurately, and in a timely and orderly manner." I have already touched on "timeliness" in this particular instance. If this provision, as a categorical proposition, is not introduced into our Commercial Code, this country's commercial law scholars, the Justice Ministry authorities, and the members of the Diet will not, for a long time, be able to avoid the censure that they are incompetent and unfaithful. One should not flatter mass psychology in a fawning manner in establishing legal standards, whatever they may be. Just like a doctor who assumes full responsibility for the medical treatment of a patient by overcoming the patient's temporary anguish, those who are connected with legislation should take full responsibility for the formation of the "soundness" in our society.

I believe that this attitude has been the principle object of the "philosophy of law" since the days of Plato. Because of limited space, I must postpone introducing the revised bill regarding the calculation regulation, Paragraph 3 of Article 43 of the German Commercial Code below. I will, however, share with my readers the fatal defects in the current Japanese Commercial Code, which I must touch on here.

What Is Meant by the Concept of the "Small Merchant"

Article 3 of the Revised Enforcement Law in Japan's Commercial Code prescribes the legal provision that defines the small merchant. The provision states that the "small merchant" in Article 8 of the new law means a merchant whose capital is less than 2,000 yen and whose business is not a company.[7] Frankly speaking, this article is a part of Japan's Commercial Code that is hidden away and not much spoken about. I have become intensely aware of this because I am a business practitioner in accounting. Because of this legal provision—Article 8 of Japan's Commercial Code — the concept of a small merchant who is exempted from the obligation of regular bookkeeping has been substantially disseminated. The obligation to keep books of account, which is prescribed by Article 32 of Japan's Commercial Code, has become an unreasonable thing, simply because this particular article is not accompanied by penalty provisions, such as Articles 12 and 19 of the British Companies Act of 1976, Article 24 of the U.S. Securities Act of 1933, Article 32 of the U.S. Securities and Exchange Act of 1934, Article 379 of the German Tax Code, and Article 283b of the German Penal Code.

Irrespective of levels of scale, the scope of the accounting practices of Japanese enterprises has been weakened. This means that the Civil Code has become the instrument that has produced numerous tax evaders and persons who do not file their taxes. This trend has contributed in a big way to the collapse of national finance.

The Frequency of the Revision of the Commercial Code and Its Special Characteristics

Just before I wrote this chapter, I received a copy of a book that was published by C. H. Beck in the Federal Republic of Germany on January 1, 1980, the title of which was *Beck's Text Edition* (rev. ed., 1980). Upon opening it, I discovered that the *Business Law Book, Outline of a Revision* (rev. ed.), which was made public by the National Assembly of the Federal Republic of Germany and had been quoted in Leonhard Peez's *Principles of Regular Data Processing in Accounting* (1975, S. 166 ff.), especially the portion regarding the calculation regulations, had already been made a statutory law and had been integrated into the existing German Commercial Code after revisions of the provisions in the draft bill were made twice.

I must, therefore, make a correction here with my deep apologies. The current German Commercial Code, which was enacted on May 10, 1897, has been revised frequently, as many as fifty times during this century. I am deeply touched by the courageousness of the German legislature that is implied by the frequency of their revisions. I am uneasy, however, that their work of revision has never extended to the names of the laws. For example, it was on July 29, 1976, when the provision in the first sentence of Article

41 of the current German Commercial Code became legalized, the original draft of which was made public and revised by the German National Assembly. The name of the revised law was First Law to Combat Business Crime. Under this law, the revisions of the said provisions of the Commercial Code were made and announced by *BGBl*, I, 2034. In the same way, the revisions of Paragraph 2 of Article 38, the revisions of Articles 43, 44, and 47a, the addition of Paragraph 2a to Paragraph 2 of Article 39, and the deletion of Article 44a and Article 44b of the German Commercial Code—all these were made in the revision of the Enforcement Law of the *AO* that was enacted on December 14, 1976, the results of which were made public by *BGBl*, I, 3341.[8]

In my survey of the revisions of the German Commercial Code that were made on fifty occasions, I have found only thirteen times when the revision of the Commercial Code was indicated in the name of the law. The most conspicuous example is the big revision made in 1973 involving changes in more than a hundred articles. This revision was implemented by a law entitled "Proclamation Concerning the Implementation." This writer cannot help being astonished at this. We will have to keep our eyes on *BGBl* at all times. The saying "So many countries, so many customs" is certainly true.

Notes

1. Klaus Franzen, Brigitte Gast-De Hann, and Erich Samson, *Steuerstrafrecht mit Steuerordnungswidrigkeiten*, 2 Auflage (Munich: C. H. Beck'sche Verlagsbuchhandlung, 1978), S. 587.

2. This is the regulation concerning damage compensation to a business as the result of an unlawful act, and it is equivalent to Articles 709 and 710 of the Civil Code of Japan.

3. This is the regulation regarding the rights and obligations of the persons who are administering the affairs of a company.

4. This is the regulation concerning the rights of inquiry and inspection of a syndicate member. It should be especially noted that the expression "the books of business and the company's papers" has been included in the text of this provision.

5. This is the provision acknowledging a partner's participation in the result of uncompleted business affairs. This is equivalent to Paragraph 3 of Article 681 of the Civil Code of Japan.

6. This is the text of the provision regarding the relationship between a wife's liability and her bringing property ("property brought into the marriage"). Moreover, page 443 has the following description: "The obligation to keep books for taxes, as opposed to that given case by case according to civil law, is not formed independently."

7. The amount of money was changed to 500,000 yen by the revision in 1981.

8. Beck'sche Textausgaben HGB, 63 neu bearbeitete Auflage, Stand: 1. Jan. 1980, S. 1135.

11

Calculation Regulations in the Federal Republic of Germany: Part III

The German Commercial Code Revised in 1980

Considering the order of my arguments, I should now introduce the full text of the revision of the German Commercial Code that has been made a positive law. In the course of drafting the provisions of the revised law, which appeared in *Paper 7/261 of the German Bundestag, 7th Session* and was made public by the German National Assembly, several modifications and additions were made. I wrote earlier, for example, that "in Article 41, the revised draft resulted only in the deletion of the term 'an inventory of property,'" the reason for which was simply that the revised draft stated such. When I checked the text of the provisions of the positive law of the Commercial Code as of January 1, 1980, however, I found that the words "unter Angabe des Datums" ("with an indication of the date") had been added to the first sentence of Article 41, the entire text of which read: "The balance sheet is to be signed and dated by the merchant." Thus, with this addition to the first sentence, the obligation of affixing one's name to the inventory was removed but the obligation of indicating a day, month, and year was added.

Furthermore, Paragraph 2a was added to Article 39, which was itself left untouched in the revision. Paragraphs 1 and 2 of Article 39 were not changed prior to World War I. Some of my readers may already be familiar with these paragraphs, but for the benefit

Calculation Regulations: Part III

of the younger generation, I will introduce them here. Paragraph 1 prescribes:

At the time of the opening of business, a merchant has to make an accurate entry of such items as fixed property, credits and liabilities, amount of cash, and other items of property, and, at the same time, put a value on each item of property and make a "balance sheet" [this is the translation for "Abschluβ," which indicates the relation between property and liabilities—au.].

Paragraph 2 states:

In the next place, at the end of each business year, a list of property and a balance sheet are required to be drawn up. The term of a business year should not exceed twelve months. The preparation for the inventory of property and a balance sheet should be conducted during the period that corresponds to the progress of appropriate business operations.

The following Paragraph 2a was added to the text:

When listing the inventory, the extent of the property according to type, amount, and value may also be determined based on random sampling with the aid of accepted mathematical statistical methods. The process must follow the principles of regular bookkeeping. The stated value of an inventory compiled in this manner must equal that stated value of . . . a physical inventory.

Reading through this added text must convince my readers of the following. The Federal Republic of Germany has tried to make the calculation regulations as precise as possible. This German endeavor seems an extension of what Eugen Schmalenbach once said, "That which is professional is a lawful norm."[1]

I think, however, that the competent authorities in Japan are apt to excuse this by saying that this legislation in Germany is the inevitable result of the racial traits of the Germans or the Germanic race, and that such legislation would not necessarily be compatible with the disposition of the Japanese. It is my wish that the Japanese authorities take charge of the legislation and the revision of laws by concentrating their thoughts on one point by which Japan's course will be directed in a truly beneficial way— beneficial not only to the state but also to the Japanese people— that they overcome their initial instincts, because the law essentially has the power of forming social order in itself. At any rate, my readers should realize that in the Federal Republic of Germany, the Germans have been attempting to gradually make the calculation regulations as precise as possible by adapting these regulations to the phenomenal change of the times.

In the second place, in the provisions of Paragraph 2a, it has been prescribed that "the process must follow the principles of regular bookkeeping." In regard to the definite contents of the methods of disposition or "the way it should be," however, this provision does not indicate any specific provisions of any positive law. That is, the concept of the "principles of regular bookkeeping" has not been made a positive law in all its "connotations" and "extensions" in regard to this particular theory. Thus the theory of the "threefold structure" of this concept, which I have maintained from the beginning, has objective appropriateness in itself.

According to a book of research on the German Commercial Code, which was published on February 20, 1956, by the Foreign Laws Research Association of Kobe University (published by Yohi-Kaku, Vol. 1 of a reprinted ed. [1st ed.], p. 105), Paragraph 3 of Article 39 prescribes as follows:

> Due to the nature of his business, in the case where a merchant, in each business year, has any commercial goods in stock that cannot be entered properly in an inventory of a property, he may make such an entry in the course of two business years. His obligation of preparing a balance sheet every business year should not be disturbed by this two-year business entry.

This provision, however, was totally deleted by the revision made on August 2, 1965. At this time, Paragraphs 3 and 4 were newly established. As of January 1, 1980, the texts of these provisions have been left unrevised. The original text of Paragraph 3 states:

> In compiling the inventory at the end of a fiscal year, a physical inventory of the items of the property is not necessary at this point in time, as long as the amount of the items of property can be determined in type, amount, and value by another process that follows the principles of regular bookkeeping even if it does not include a physical inventory at this point in time.

Finally, the original text of the provisions of Paragraph 4 prescribes:
> In the inventory at the end of a fiscal year, items of property do not need to be recorded if:

Calculation Regulations: Part III 137

1. The merchant has recorded their possession by type, amount, and value in a special inventory based on physical inventory or other process permitted by Section 3, and which has been conducted for one day within the past three months before, or the first two months after, the end of the fiscal year, and,
2. ... that, based on the special inventory by applying a process of extrapolation or... which follows good accounting practice, it is certain that the amount of property items on hand at the end of the fiscal year at this point can be valued in a regular way.

I have been a bit puzzled by the fact that in the book *Business Law Book, Commentary* (Vol. 1, p. 463 [Berlin: Walter de Gruyter & Co., 1967]), an error appears in the text of the provisions in Paragraph 4 of Article 39: "Vermögensgegengegenstände" should appear as "Vermögensgegenstände." Moreover, the book also made the error of indicating Item No. 1 as "der beiden ersten Monate" ("the first two months"). Both expressions may be of the same meaning. As the matter is concerned with the expression of the text of law, however, it seems undesirable to notice such frequent mistakes.

Such mistakes, however, are a trifling matter. I prefer to emphasize that I am deeply impressed that such ultramodern technical methods in present-day accounting as "perpetual inventory method," or "cost reversal method," have been made positive laws in the German Commercial Code. Is seems to me that those persons who are concerned with legislation in the Federal Republic of Germany are replete with the attitude of Josui Kuroda (1546–1604), a feudal daimyo who became a Christian in 1583 and wrote the famous book of ethics *Five Principles of Water*. In this book he wrote in regard to the property of water: "Water seeks its own future course at all times."

Paragraphs 1 through 3 of Article 40 were unchanged before World War I. Paragraph 1 prescribes that "a balance sheet should be indicated in the German currency." Paragraph 2 states that "in drawing up an inventory of property and a balance sheet, all items of property and liabilities should be added up with the prices that are attributed at the point of time when the said preparation is to be made." Paragraph 3 states that "uncertain credit should be added up by the estimated amount to be collected, and irrecoverable claims should be deducted." The provisions of the current

138 Calculation Regulations: Part III

Paragraph 4, which was modified by the revision made on August 2, 1965, are as follows:

Insofar as this conforms to the principles of regular bookkeeping, one may, in preparing the inventory and balance sheet:
1. Collect as a group items of property of approximately equal value or similar type, for which an average value (based on the type of property or other circumstances) is known,
2. assess items of the capital assets, as well as raw materials and supplies of the stock, with a constant amount and a constant value, if their amount is subject to only minor fluctuations in size, value, and composition. However, every three years as a rule a physical inventory must be conducted.

Article 40 comes to an end with Paragraph 4.

I have already touched on the revision of Article 41. As far as Article 42 is concerned, I believe that at a certain point after World War II, expressions like "eines Landes" ("of a Land") may have been changed to "eines Bundesstaats" ("of a federal state"). In regard to this, I think it very strange that the "Charts of Modifications of the Tax Law Book" in *Beck's Text Edition* (63 Auflage, S. 1132 ff.) omit this and so does *Business Law Book, Commentary* in the chapter "History of Business Law."

The text of this article, I believe, existed before World War I and remained unchanged, except for the partial modifications of particular expressions mentioned above. This particular provision prescribes that "in the case of an enterprise belonging to the state, federal states, or a domestic self-governing body, the administration that should draw up the final report on the financial accounts by a method that is different from the provisions of Articles 39 to 41 should not be restricted." In short, this article prescribes that only the report on the final accounts should not be restricted by the German Commercial Code, and, therefore, other articles such as those prescribing entry conditions, and so forth, are to restrict these public business entities.

Consequently, and as will be explained in detail later, the penalty in regard to an infringement of the "entry obligation," which is prescribed by Article 283b of the Penal Code of the Federal Republic of Germany, should naturally be applied. The Federal Republic of Germany, moreover, is a state that has observed strictly, unlike Japan, the "principle of the legality of administration." There are detailed regulations regarding the form of the report on the final settlement of accounts in "Regulation for Owners/Operators, November 21, 1938" (Paragraph 2 of Article 18 of the Laws and Regulations mentioned above). As this is not my main subject, however, I will not detail them here.[2]

As I have already mentioned, what was chiefly changed were Articles 43 and 44. As to Article 43, however, I have introduced my readers only to Paragraphs 1 and 2. I will continue my review here. In Paragraphs 3 and 4 of Article 43, and in the draft of the revision of these paragraphs that was made public by the German National Assembly, there has been no change at all. The text of Paragraph 3 states: "The entries and other required records are to be made in a living language. If any language other than German is used, the tax officials may require translations. If abbreviations, numerals, letters, or symbols are used, then the meaning must be unambiguously indicated for each." This particular provision had never existed before. Judging from the logical sequence of this provision, however, it will be clear that such a special provision is not necessary in Japan's Commercial Code.

The following provision in statutory form is found in Paragraph 4:

The business books and other required records can also consist of the orderly filing of vouchers or can be kept on other data media insofar as these forms of bookkeeping, as well as the process used, conform to the principles of regular bookkeeping. In keeping the books and other required records on data media one must be especially certain that the data are available during the period the records are to be kept and that they can be made readable at any time within a reasonable period of time. Section 1, sentence 2, and Sections 2 and 3 apply accordingly.

The necessity for making records of account on data media available must be considered indispensable and will soon be a matter of course for those enterprises that have installed excellent small electronic computers.

On February 24, 1964, the "Management Standard of Computer-Aided Accounting," which was based on Article 6001 of the U.S. Internal Revenue Code, was enacted into law—Revenue Procedure—in the United States. Those Japanese people who avail themselves of the spiritual structure of the "affluence" ("amae") of this nation, a trend that has been popularized or even strengthened at present, or those who try to find the source of the vitality of our nation in the present ambiguity of our legal standards—how do they view the demand for the "Accounting Management Standards" that is common with advanced nations? These standards have been worked out, one by one, by the International Accounting Standards Committee, which was organized by a group of nine developed nations, of which Japan is a member. Do the Japanese intend to choose the way of the orphan among the advanced countries by shutting eyes and ears to these demands? It is indeed a matter of deep concern.

Paragraph 1 of Article 44, whose full text has been entirely revised, follows:

Each merchant is obligated to retain the following documents in an orderly manner.
1. Business books, inventories, balance sheets, along with the instructions necessary to understand them, and other documents of organization.
2. business letters received,
3. copies of business letters sent,
4. vouchers for posting in the books to be kept according to 38 Section 1.

The original text of Paragraph 2 states "Business letters are only pieces of writing which concern a business transactions." Paragraph 3, which is a long article, prescribes:

The following documents are to be preserved in order: Books and records, inventories, balance sheets, as well as the required explanations for understanding them and other documents of the organization. . . .

If documents based on 146 Section 5 have been produced on data media, instead of the data media the data can also be stored printed out; the printed documents can also be preserved according to Sentence 1.

As stated above, the Revenue Procedure, which established the "Management Standard of Computer-Aided Accounting" in the United States, makes it an obligation to furnish an "audit trail" (Article 2) and to draw up "visible and legible records" (Article 4). There are no specific provisions regarding the period of preservation of accounting records and business correspondence in the United States. The fact that specific provisions do not exist corresponds to legal provisions that declare that there is no prescribed period concerning "false declaration" or "nondeclaration" in the United States.[3]

Paragraph 4 of Article 44 prescribes: "The documents listed in Section 1, No. 1, are to kept for ten years." And Paragraph 5 of Article 44 states: "The period of time for keeping records begins at the end of the calendar year in which the last entry in the book is made, the inventory is listed, the balance sheet determined, the business letter received or sent, or the journal voucher produced." These paragraphs are the end of Article 44. Former Articles 44a and 44b were deleted, as was made known when the revision went into effect on December 14, 1976. Leonhard Peez's *Principles of Regular Data Processing in Accounting* (1975) contains (beginning on p. 166) the draft of the revision of the German Commercial Code that was announced by the German National Assembly. It is clearly stated on page 168 of this book that in the draft of this revision, "Articles 44a and 44b are revoked."

The ten-volume *Industrial Accounting in Programmed Form* was published by the Business Administration Press, Dr. Th. Gabler, in Wiesbaden. The text of this book was supervised by, among other professors, K. F. Bussmann in Munich, Jörg Bottler in Gießen, Peter Horvath in Darmstadt, and Dr. Herbert Kargl in Mainz. Volume 9, *Trade Balance Sheet, Tax Balance*, was published the year after Peez's book was published. Despite the clear statement in Peez's book, Volume 9 made the error of carrying the full text of Articles 44a and 44b (see p. 297). It seems to me that the tendency to neglect close examination may not be limited only to university professors in Japan.

Regarding the Two Ordinances

Due to space limits, I cannot include the contents of two ordinances or ministerial notices that are related to the main subject of this study. I have touched on the point that a ministerial notice ("Erlass") under German law is a secondary source of law. The first of these is BMWF-Erlass of December 21, 1971,[4] which is concerned with the disposition of microfilms. The other is BMF Ordinance of January 26, 1973, regarding the concept of data storage, which is prescribed under the heading "Regular Bookkeeping," in Paragraph 6 of Article 29 of the *EStR* that was enacted in 1969. The full texts of these two ordinances can be found on pages 163 and 166 of Professor Peez's *Principles of Regular Data Processing in Accounting.*

Books of Account and Their Probative Power

I have so far hardly touched on Law No. 32 of March 27, 1890, in which there was already an obligatory provision in regard to the preparation of books of account. This Commercial Code was then revised by Law No. 9 on March 4, 1893, in which Chapter 4, "Books of Account," had provisions that were more detailed than those of the existing law—a total of eleven articles (from Article 31 to Article 41). One provision worthy of special mention here appeared in Article 31 and prescribed: "each merchant . . . *should have the responsibility for making preparations for complete books of account,*" thus indicating that the legal provision requiring the "completeness" of books of account was already in existence in Japan. I assume that this provision in Article 31 may have been influenced by the fact that Article 28 of the General German Commercial Law of 1861 imposed conditions on books of account under which German merchants were responsible for the preparation of them.

The revised Japanese Commercial Code of 1893, furthermore, prescribed in Article 39, the "probative power" of books of account. The concept of "probative power" as stated earlier, was a legal concept that had already been adopted in Articles 34 and 36 of the above-mentioned German Commercial Code; it dated even further back to 1794, namely, to the sixth year of Kansei under the rule of the Emperor Kokaku, which happened to be the seventh year under the regime of Ienari Tokugawa, the eleventh Shogun of the Tokugawa clan in Japan. It was in 1794 that the Prussian General Common Law (Law of the Land) was enacted. The above legal concept of "probative power" had already been adopted in Articles 566, 569, and 605 from among the text of provisions that legalized bookkeeping regulations for merchants.

The Misunderstanding of Our Accounting Scholars

There is what appears to be an unavoidable error in the theory of a Japanese scholar whose article appeared in the July issue of *Accounting* (Vol. CXVIII), the bulletin of the Japan Society of Accounting. Examining Paragraph 1 of Article 149 of *AktG*, which prescribes that "a statement of accounts in a business year should be *in conformity with* the principles of regular bookkeeping," he concluded that this particular provision "looked like a repetition of" the principles of regular bookkeeping as prescribed by Article 38 of the German Commercial Code, and that, conditionally, it was quite a "clumsy way of making rules." He stated, moreover, that this provision gave him "the impression of having been swayed" by the historical concept of the principles of regular bookkeeping that had been the tradition of the German Commercial Code since 1898. Furthermore, he stated that books of account themselves were only the internal evidence of the statement of final accounts in a fiscal year. He also wrote that the principles of regular bookkeeping had been prescribed in Article 147 of the British Companies Act of 1948, the regulations of which were inseparable from the "principle of a true and fair view."

In the first place, Article 147 of the British Companies Act of 1948 is the provision that was abolished by Paragraph 12 of Article 12 of the Companies Act of 1976 and lost its validity.[5] Secondly, the concept of the principles of regular bookkeeping is not the one that originated in the German Commercial Code of 1897. It is, in fact, the concept that originated two years earlier in Article 19 of the Hessian General Income Tax Law.[6] In the third place, I am extremely dubious about this scholar's attitude that this particular provision "looked like a repetition of" the principles of regular bookkeeping. Sparing no efforts in my research, I have found that the term this scholar mentioned, "zu entsprechen-entspricht" ("to conform to"), appeared not only in Article 149 of the *AktG* but also in Article 26 of the Federal Banking Law and in Articles 141, 146, and 147 of the Tax Code of 1977. In Article 41 of *GmbHG*, the expression "zu sorgen" ("to care for") these principles is used. In Article 33b of the Union Law *(GenG)*, the expression "zur Anwendung" ("for application") is used, while in Article

5 of the "Law of Opening to the Public," the word used is "gelten" ("to be valid"), and in others there are alternative expressions. To make a long story short, I must emphasize the legislative fact that the "principles of regular bookkeeping," as a generic term that has a threefold structure, has functioned as a pivotal concept in all spheres of society in which there is a need for entries in books of account.

Finally, this scholar stated that the books of account themselves were only the internal evidence of the statement of final accounts in a business year. I have already mentioned the views of Dr. Klaus Bierle, senior lecturer at the University of the Saarland, Saarbrücken, who wrote about the principles of regular bookkeeping in the *Dictionary of German Tax Jurisprudence*, and the opinion of Professor Ulrich Leffson of Münster University, who wrote the section on the principles of regular bookkeeping in the *Dictionary of Business Economics*. Their statements clearly show that the "principle of vouchers" is included in the concept of the principles of regular bookkeeping and that such a concept formed the basis of their own judgments that no postings be made without vouchers. I would also like to state here that the "principle of a true and fair view" in the British Companies Act of 1948 is a mistranslation and misunderstanding on the part of several Japanese scholars. I will discuss this point in particular, however, later in this study.

The Concept of the Small Businessman, the Disposition by Notification, and the Standard of Form

I said earlier that the provision about the concept of small merchants in Article 3 of the Enforcement Law of the revised Commercial Code in Japan is the "secret part" of this country's Commercial Code. The reason is that apart from in the Meiji, or the Taisho era in Japan, nowadays, a small merchant whose capital is less than 2,000 yen (in 1981 this amount was raised to 500,000 yen — au.) does not exist at all in Japan. The existence of this particular provision itself, therefore, has removed the limits on who is responsible for making an entry, and it has made the entry obligation under the Commercial Code a mysterious thing indeed.

Article 8 of the revised Commercial Code, which was enacted

by Law No. 49 on March 7, 1899, described "a small merchant" as follows: "The regulations regarding commercial registration, trade name, and 'commercial books' shall not be applied to anyone who sells an object door to door, or on the road, or to *other small merchants*." Regarding the scope of "and other small merchants," it was prescribed that what the term encompassed "should be provided for by an Imperial ordinance," by Article 7 of the Enforcement Law of the Commercial Code, which became effective on the same date the revised Commercial Code was enforced. I leave the judgment of which is the more logical and practical of these two laws in my reader's hands.

In German law, persons who are responsible for the entry obligation are defined by both the Commercial Code and the *AO*. To make a long story short, when a person who has been exempted from the entry obligation is reviewed from the standpoint of the Commercial Code, he is "a small merchant" who has been defined by Paragraph 1 of Article 4 of the German Commercial Code. However, under the revision made in March 1953, this provision has been changed as follows: "The regulations concerning firms, business books, and proxies do not apply to the person whose business entity neither in manner nor extent requires a business operation set up in a commercial (businesslike) way."

That is, terms such as "craftsmen" or "small business" that appeared in the former text of the law were deleted. In Paragraph 1 of Article 141, moreover, the *AO* in 1977 prescribes under the heading "Bookkeeping Obligation of Certain Taxpayers": "Entrepreneurs as well as farmers and foresters . . . are also obligated to keep books for these businesses and to make balance sheets based on annual inventories even if there is no bookkeeping obligation under 140."

What is important here is that the existence or nonexistence of the entry obligation makes a diverging point for *confirmation* by government taxation offices, that is, the diverging point for the existence of the administrative action called "notification," which was prescribed by Paragraph 2 of Article 141. The standard was as follows: (1) Excluding nontaxable sales and sales that are covered by the provisions of Nos. 8 and 9 of Article 4 of the Amount Sold Taxation Law (Article 4 prescribes provisions of tax exemption regarding procurement, delivery of money and property, and specified consumption, and these provisions are extended to No. 27—au.)—the entry obligation comes into existence in a business year when other sales exceed DM 360,000. When other sales are less than DM 360,000, there is no entry obligation at all. Or, (2) when business assets exceed DM 100,000, there is an entry obligation, while there is no obligation when business assets are below DM 100,000. Or, (3) when the value of property used for agricultural or forestry purposes exceeds DM 100,000, there is an entry obligation, while there is no obligation when property is valued at less than DM 100,000. Or, (4) when a profit from business (not "net profit"—au.) exceeds DM 24,000 in a business year, there is an entry obligation, while there is no obligation for a profit of less than DM 24,000. Or, (5) when the profit gained from agricultural and forestry industries in a business year exceeds DM 15,000, there is an entry obligation, while there is no obligation for one of less than DM 15,000. It was prescribed, therefore, that whether the entry obligation exists should be decided by whether or not each circumstance falls under one of the above five different standards. This "standard of form" was revised later on, the details of which follow:

Items 1 and 2: Remain unchanged.

Item 3: The economic value of the flat land to be used for agricultural and forestry purposes (to be decided in accordance with Article 46 of the Evaluation Law) which exceeds DM 40,000 in a business year.

Item 4: The profit gained from business ("ordinary expenditure," as it is called in Japan) which exceeds DM 36,000 in a business year.

Item 5: The profit gained from agricultural and forestry business operation which exceeds DM 36,000 in a calendar year.[7]

An important point here is that the standard amount of the recurring profit for Items 4 and 5 cannot be grasped after the end of a fiscal year or a calendar year. This is because the existence of the above-mentioned administrative action—the "notification"—to be taken by the Government Taxation Offices constitutes a decisive factor in this particular matter. At this point in time, "administrative action by notification" does not exist in the tax laws concerning income in Japan.

In the case of Japan, it may safely be said that the state itself has produced "no-return applicants on income" on a large scale. Through the recognition of the above five standards for entry obligation, the reader should be able to understand the strong intention of the state to impose the principle of fairness of taxation on the people in the Federal Republic of Germany. In this connection, I would hope that my reader understands that those who have tried to obstruct the principle of justice in taxation on the strength of a mysterious theory of the national character that implies that, irrespective of our high educational standards, we are a nation that has been maintained by the principle of "coaxing in complying with a request," are only those who hope for the preservation of an unfair tax system that is valuable for themselves.

Tax Evasion

As to the guarantees of the calculation regulations that have been outlined so far, I must first touch on acts punishable under tax law. In this connection, the *AO* in 1977 prepared a total of forty-four provisions, ranging from Article 369 to Article 412. Article 369 is primarily concerned with the definition of "acts punishable under tax law." It is a conspicuous point, however, that Paragraph 2 of Article 369 prescribes that "for punishable acts concerning taxes the general criminal laws apply," thus linking together clearly "felonies concerning taxes" and the German Penal Code. And Article 370 defines "tax evasion." Paragraph 1 of this article lists the following three points, to be punished by imprisonment of up to five years or by a fine:

1. Unlawful or incomplete declaration.
2. Concealment of an important fact.
3. Non-use of a taxable certified stamp, or a revenue stamp.

Paragraph 2 prescribes that an attempt to do any of these is punishable.

Paragraph 3 states that in especially serious cases, the offender will face imprisonment of from six months up to ten years, and it lists the following four examples:

1. Tax evasion that originates from "gross self-interest."
2. Tax evasion accomplished through the abuse of a public official's legal authority.
3. Tax evasion accomplished by taking advantage of the assistance originating from the abuse of a public official's legal authority.
4. Continuous tax evasion by counterfeiting or forging of a voucher.

It is further prescribed in Paragraph 2 of Article 378 that a fine of not more than DM 100,000 can be imposed when, "acting in violation of the order," a person evades taxes as defined by Article 370 by negligence ("commits the acts out of negligence"). Furthermore, Article 379 establishes the provisions of "tax risk" (under which Paragraph 1 prescribes a fine of less than DM 100,000) whereby one "commits a misdemeanor." This occurs when a person: 1) draws up an illegal voucher, or 2) fails to make an entry of transactions, or makes an illegal entry, or gives instructions to make an illegal entry.

Paragraph 2 and the rest are provisions regarding negligence in submitted various kinds of reports, and so forth. As they have no relation with the main subject of this article, however, I will omit them here. What is important here is that the concept of "tax endangerment" is not only based on a fact that occurred in the past—such as having already evaded a tax, or having already received an unlawful tax reduction or tax exemption—but also, at the stage at which it makes it possible to evade taxes, it is a concept that acknowledges the value of added penalty. It follows that, in this way, the will of the state to enforce the principle of fairness of taxation will be realized in the form of giving credence to the power of forming social order.

Violation of the Obligation of Bookkeeping and the Tax Penal Code

As I touched on earlier, Article 283b of the Federal Republic of Germany's Penal Code contains provisions for the "violation of the obligation of bookkeeping." Paragraph 1 states as follows:

A person will be punished by fine or by imprisonment of up to two years if he 1) does not keep books that he is obligated to keep by law, or keeps or alters them in such a manner that makes the review of his assets and liabilities more difficult; 2) disposes of, conceals, destroys, or damages business books or other documents that he is obligated by commercial law to keep, before the end of the legally prescribed period, and thereby, makes the review of his assets and liabilities more difficult; or 3) in violation of commercial law, produces balance sheets in such a way that the review of his assets and liabilities is made more difficult or does not produce a balance sheet of assets and liabilities or an inventory at the prescribed time.

This is the full text of Paragraph 1 of Article 283b of the German Penal Code. In this instance, the problem is the essential factor of "the prescribed time." Article 148 of the *AktG*, however, specifies the time as "in the first three months of the business year." Paragraph 2 of Article 41 of the *GenG* has a similar time-limit regulation. No. 4, Paragraph 1 of Article 240 of "Konkursordnung" also indicates a time limit. The reader may have, therefore, a doubt about whether or not the "prescribed time limit" has been determined for all merchants in Germany and whether or not there is a time limit for the preparation of a balance sheet.

It should be noted, however, that Paragraph 2 of Article 39 of the German Commercial Code stipulates only: "to be applied within the appropriate time of a regular conduct of business." Thus the Commercial Code maintains the basic attitude of entrusting the time limit to common sense, without specifying the period of time. At the same time, it should also be noted that there is a judicial precedent that "after a lapse of seven months, it does not fall under an appropriate period of time."[8] The full text of Paragraph 2 is as follows: "Anyone who acts with negligence in the cases of Section 1, Nos. 1 or 3, is punishable by fine or imprisonment of up to one year."

Paragraph 3 is a short sentence: "283, Abs 6 is correspondingly valid." Article 283 is the penal provision regarding bankruptcy. Paragraph 6 is the provision that stipulates when the actions of a bankrupt person have criminality in them, for example, the concealment of funds payable and other actions.

Article 283b of the German Penal Code comes to an end at this point. These provisions were inserted into it when the German Penal Code was partially revised on January 2, 1975.[9] I suppose that this may have resulted from the fact that the Federal Republic of Germany had come to feel very keenly the necessity for guaranteeing by penal provisions the "objective exactness" and "truth" of the entry and of financial documents due to the swift and diversified advances of international trade and commercial relations, and also in an effort to maintain the international reputation of its enterprises. This revision in the Federal Republic of Germany, however, was made in the same year Great Britain revised its laws and followed the United States's revision by forty-two years. At any rate, I have great admiration for the United States, Great Britain, and the Federal Republic of Germany. All have established legal standards that should be followed by all merchants with no relation at all to *the scope of the dimensions of the enterprises* in each country.

Japan's legislative authorities have been tacitly pressed for a revision of its current laws and regulations by the advanced countries in the world. I fear that they wish to flee this responsibility due to a lack of insight, confidence, and courage, and that they will continue to limit the applicability of the calculation regulations only to large-scale enterprises in Japan. I believe that Japan may entertain the possibility of maintaining the present system of laws under which no one assumes the responsibility for the existence of falsehood, mistake, and omission in the accounting and taxation affairs in Japan.

Now and then I cannot help but wonder who among the Japanese will take the responsibility for the formation of the destiny of our state and nation. This is my own, personal feeling, however, and I would now like to change the topic and closely review the calculation regulations that are current in the United States and England. Before my critical review, there is a problem on which I should touch. It is the existence of the Tax Penal Code in the Federal Republic of Germany. According to the German *Dictionary of Tax Law and Tax Studies*, this Penal Code was enacted early in the nineteenth century. It is a special section of the general *Penal Code*.[10] The literature relative to the Tax Penal Code that I use every day is as follows:

1. Undersecretary Römer, *Imperial Tax Penal Code and Imperial Tax Judgments*, 1927.
2. District Court Judge Hans Cattien, *Imperial Tax Penal Code and Imperial Tax Judgments*, 2d ed., 1929.
3. Klaus Kottke, *Tax Saving, Tax Avoidance, Tax Evasion*, 2d ed., 1962.
4. Gerhard Suhr and Axel Naumann, *Tax Penal Code Commentary*, 3d ed., 1977.
5. Carola Seckel, *Tax Evasion*, 2d ed., 1979.
6. Peter Spörlein, *The Taxpayer and the Tax Penal Code*, 1979.
7. Jürgen Danzer, *Tax Avoidance*, 1981.
8. Günter Kohlmann, *Tax Penal Code*, 3d ed., 1982.
9. Franz Konz, *Handbook of Tax Evasion*, Vols. 1 and 2, 1982.
10. Klaus Franzen, Brigitte Gast-De Hann, and Erich Samson, *Tax Penal Code*, 2d ed., 1978.

Notes

1. Eugen Schmalenbach, *Dynamic Balance Sheet*, 5th ed., p. 362.
2. *Business Law Book, Commentary*, Vol. 1, p. 484 ff.
3. IRC-Reg. 301, 6501 (c)-1. 1980 *Standard Federal Tax Reports*, 5446 A.
4. At that time in Germany, the Economic and Finance Ministries had not been separated.
5. Companies Act of 1976, Sec. 12 (12).
6. Kuno Barth, *The Development of German Audit Law*, Vol. 2, App., p. 102.
7. Tax Code, 9th ed., 15 Feb. 1982, dtv S. 64.
8. *BGHSt, BetrBer, 1955, 109.*
9. Klaus Franzen, Brigitte Gast-De Hann, and Erich Samson, *Tax Penal Code*, 2d ed. (Verlag C. H. Beck, 1978), p. 584 ff.
10. The Tax Penal Code is a special section of the general Penal Code.

12

The Formation of an Especially Close Connection between Civil Law and the Tax Laws

What Should Be Learned from Article 140 of the New Tax Code *(AO)* of the Federal Republic of Germany?

The reader may remember my earlier remarks about Gerd Spangemacher. I pointed out that Mr. Spangemacher, the presiding judge of the Federal Finance Court in the Federal Republic of Germany, wrote in *General Theory of Law* (5th ed., 1978) that he had high praise for Enno Becker for his historical achievements in drafting and completing the Imperial Tax Code *(RAO)*, and that it was Enno Becker in 1918[1] who had created an especially close connection between Civil Law (Citizens' Law) and Tax Law in Germany. I stated that the pivotal provisions of this close connection were Paragraph 1 of Article 160 of the former *RAO* and Article 140 of the new *AO*, and that as this article contained so much related material, I wanted to postpone discussing it at that time.

The original text of Article 140 of the revised, new *AO* of 1977 runs as follows: "Anyone who is required by laws other than tax laws to keep books and records that are important for tax purposes must fulfill the obligations incumbent upon him by the other laws, also for tax purposes." I have stated that this provision was formerly Paragraph 1 of Article 160 of the old *RAO*. There are some differences, however, in the texts of Paragraph 1 of Article

160 and this new Article 140. Furthermore, there are also some differences in the texts of Paragraph 1 of Article 160 and the original text of this law, that is, the text of 1919. Although this is a trivial matter, I would like to point out the differences here.

At the end of Article 140 of the present law the phrase "also for tax purposes" appears. In the former Article 160, the phrase appeared at the end of Paragraph 1 as "also in the interest of taxation." And in the 1919 text, this particular provision was Article 163. Furthermore, Article 163 not only had this phrase but it was followed by an independent short sentence: "162 is correspondingly valid." Article 162 was related to the general regulations of books of account, Paragraphs 1 through 9, on which I have already touched and which I will, therefore, omit here.

In regard to Article 140 (or Paragraph 1 of Article 160) in particular, it is interesting to take a look at *Imperial Tax Code: Pocket Commentary* (Cologne: Verlag Dr. Otto Schmidt KG, 1961), which was written by Heinrich Wilhelm Kruse of Cologne University and Klaus Tipke of Würzburg University.[2] Kruse and Tipke write as follows:

160 1 makes those obligations of bookkeeping and record keeping, which exist because of laws other than tax laws, tax obligations (derived from bookkeeping obligation) at the same time. This means that pertinent nontax regulations are being applied to tax law and that violations of the nontax regulations have the same consequences as violations of such regulations contained within the tax laws.[3]

My readers may now understand that the reason Gerd Spangemacher concluded that this provision formed an especially close connection between Civil Law and Tax Law was because he accepted the explanation of Drs. Tipke and Kruse.

In this connection, a document dated October 1, 1976, "Writing Concerning Introductory Regulations Concerning the Tax Code," is attached to Article 140. The substance of this particular provision cannot be completely clarified until this document has been examined in detail. As luck would have it, I have a copy of *Compendium of the Tax Code* (40th ed., Munich: C. H. Beck Press, 1980), which was issued on January 1, 1980. It was written and sent to me by a friend who resides in Heidelberg, Germany, Mr. Walter Ludwig Eckert, the president of the Tax Advisors Association of

North Baden. This is a huge reference book, containing 1063 pages. At page 232, "Book and Record Keeping Obligations Due to Other Laws" appears, the enactment of the Enforcement Regulation. In regard to Article 140:

> By this regulation the so-called nontax bookkeeping and record keeping regulations, which are also important to taxation, are made useable also for tax laws. Those that come under consideration include the general book and record keeping regulations of commercial, corporate, and cooperative law. Also included are the book and record keeping obligations for certain businesses and professors that result from myriad laws and ordinances (for example, the following books are to be kept and/or records are to be made).

At this particular point, although it is a repetition, I would like to again call your attention to the fact that the conception at the heart of this article is not in existence in the spheres of practical business or academia in Japan. It seems to me that more than sixty years ago Enno Becker must have had the "insight" that unless he prepared such legal provisions and completed the versatile formation of an especially close connection between Civil Law and Tax Law, there would be no room for conceptions such as the principle of justice in taxation and the ideology of justice in taxation.

Earlier I mentioned that Article 140 contained a great deal of material. The reason is that, under the current law, the books that are listed as "the following books" in the Enforcement Regulation of Article 140 apply to seventy different spheres of jurisprudence, resulting in a truly spectacular sight. At present, as I write this chapter, the government of Japan has been cited by the Organization for Economic Cooperation and Development (OECD) for the omission of laws and ordinances regarding the protection of privacy, and so forth. In response to this, the government has hastily made preparations to draft the indicated laws by setting up a research committee to be chaired by Professor Ichiro Kato, the former president of the University of Tokyo. I have also been invited to serve as a member of this special committee.

It seems to me that the reason Japan has been viewed as an "honor student" in its economic activities is mainly related to its preeminence in the sphere of producing merchandise. On the other

The Formation of an Especially Close Connection 155

hand, Japan's performance in the sphere of social science, regarding the consolidation of legislation, is utterly different. It will be necessary for those in high authority, therefore, to keep a close watch on these matters. It is an amazing fact indeed that through the medium of Article 140, the principles of regular bookkeeping in the Federal Republic of Germany have a profound effect on all legislation in the Federal Republic of Germany.

In regard to the first sphere of jurisprudence listed by the Enforcement Regulation of Article 140, the text reads as follows:

1. Supporting books by collectors and transporters of trash, as well as refuse disposers, according to 2, Secs. 2 and 3 of refuse proof regulation (of July 29, 1974, *BGBl*, I, 1574);

The Enforcement Regulation concerning the second sphere of jurisprudence states:

2. From enterprises in which used oil is guilded in a certain amount or the used oils according to 6, Sec. 1 of the used oil law (of Dec. 23, 1968, *BGBl*, I, 1419) with 2, Secs. 1–3 of the regulation for the implementation of the used oil law (of Dec. 2, 1971, *BGBl* I, 1939);

The third sphere of jurisprudence is shown as:

3. From pharmacies, preparation books and examination books according to 6, Sec. 4, and 7, Sec. 6 of the pharmacy business regulations (of Aug. 7, 1968, *BGBl*, I, 939);

The fourth sphere of jurisprudence is stated as:

4. From information bureaus and private investigators, records concerning the assignments given out, according to the state regulations given by individual states, as, for example, according to 1, Sec. 1 of the Bavarian information and private investigators regulation (of Oct. 19, 1964, *GVBl*, Bavaria, 188);

The Enforcement Regulation defines the fifth sphere of jurisprudence as:

5. From those in construction industries and recipients of building capital, who undertake a new construction, building books

156 The Formation of an Especially Close Connection

according to 2 of the law concerning the security [collateral] of building debts (of June 1, 1909, *BGBl*, 449);

About ten years before the enactment of the Imperial Tax Code in Germany, the law concerning the security of building debts was enacted. This was during the period Germany was an empire. At this particular stage, I hope the reader understands and admires the fact that under Article 140, when Enno Becker undertook to create a close connection between Civil Law and Tax Law, he infiltrated the system of entry obligation deeply into the national economy.

To continue, the original text of the Enforcement Regulation in regard to the sixth sphere of jurisprudence runs as follows:

6. In the case of public contracts for building, a separate construction account for each building contract by the contract taker, according to 16, Sec. 1 of building price regulation (VO PR No. 1/70 concerning prices in public contracts for building *BGBl*, 1972, I, 293);

The seventh sphere of jurisprudence is indicated as follows:

7. From proprietors of lodgings, an index of tourists (guests) according to the state law, for example, according to 18, Sec. 1 of the registration law of the state of North Rhine-Westphalia (of Apr. 28, 1950, *GVBl*, NW, 117);

In the Federal Republic of Germany, the government of a state, which is referred to as a "Länd," has the power to legislate laws that apply only to the state concerned. The "Länd" also has a notification law, under which residents are obligated to submit various kinds of reports. The legislative power of a "Länd" can be confirmed by the following provision found in Paragraph 1 of Article 70 of the current Constitution: "The states shall have the right to legislate insofar as the Constitution does not confer this legislative power on the federation" (trans. Guido Goldman, "The German Political System").

The Enforcement Regulation defines the eighth sphere of jurisprudence thus:

The Formation of an Especially Close Connection 157

8. From businesses that have insemination stations, records concerning the collection, release, and use of the sperm according to 18, Sec. 3 of the animal husbandry laws (of Apr. 20, 1976, *BGBl*, I, 1045);

The ninth sphere of jurisprudence has been prescribed as follows:

9. From enterprises that import, export, grow, harvest, manufacture and process, trade in, purchase, distribute, and dispose of substances that come under the narcotics laws and inventory books concerning the entry and exit, as well as processing, of the narcotics according to 5, Sec. 1 of the narcotics law (in this case of Jan. 10, 1972, *BGBl*, I, 1);

The tenth sphere of jurisprudence, according to the Enforcement Regulation, provides:

10. From pharmacies, doctors, and veterinarians, dispensaries, practices, and clinics, books or file cards concerning the whereabouts of narcotics (narcotics books) according to the narcotics prescription regulation, no. 15 (of Jan. 24, 1974, *BGBl*, I, 110);

The original text of the Enforcement Regulation prescribes in regard to the eleventh sphere of jurisprudence:

11. From security industry businesses (watchmen), records concerning the security contracts according to 11, Sec. 1 of the regulation concerning the security industry (of June 1, 1976, *BGBl*, I, 1341);

The Enforcement Regulation in regard to the twelfth sphere provides as follows:

12. From regional master chimney sweeps, "sweeping books" according to 14, sec. 1 of the regulation concerning chimney sweeping (of Dec. 19, 1969, *BGBl*, I, 2363);

Having read thus far, the reader may be beginning to appreciate the breadth of the concept that Gerd Spangemacher called "Civil Law." Spangemacher once said that Enno Becker formulated the legal relationship between the state as tax creditor and the citizen as taxpayer, whose legal relationship meant such a connection. Japan's business, academic, and political circles seem to have no conception of such legislation. I believe, however, that if we want the realization of "justice in taxation" in Japan in a true sense, we should learn this particular conception that Enno Becker created more than sixty years ago.

At any rate, the Enforcement Regulation of Article 140 of the *AO*, under which the obligation of recording in Civil Law should be regarded at the same time as an entry obligation in Tax Law, exercises its effectiveness in seventy different spheres of jurisprudence. As it contains so much material, I have been hesitant about introducing all of this Enforcement Regulation to you. As the subject of my argument, the probative power of commercial books, is coming next, I will continue my discussion here.

The original text of the Enforcement Regulation provides as follows concerning the thirteenth sphere of jurisprudence:

13. From proprietors and leaders of workshops for the blind, records concerning the amount and earnings of the wares of the blind and supplementary wares according to 3, Sec. 1 of the regulation concerning the implementation of the law for businesses for wares of the blind (in this case, the regulation of March 25, 1969, *BGBl*, I, 283);

Furthermore, the Enforcement Regulation prescribes as follows regarding the fourteenth sphere of jurisprudence:

14. From the bookmaker, carbon copies of the betting tickets or betting books, statements of account and contracts with the bookmaker's assistants and business books according to 4, sec. 1 RennwLottG (of Apr. 8, 1922, *RGBl*, I, 335, 393), 10 bis 13 ABRennw-LottG (Implemental Provisions for the Racing and Lottery Law of June 16, 1922, Central Paper of the German Empire);

In the Federal Republic of Germany, such kinds of records are given a legal character as records for taxation and are, therefore, records of transactions in which "completeness" and "truth" are demanded.

Any violator is treated as a tax offender (Article 369 of *AO*), and

The Formation of an Especially Close Connection 159

he is subject to penal regulations (Article 283b of the Penal Code). As the clear will of the state, "equal sacrifice" as a principle of taxation in the science of finance and the principle of fairness of taxation, viewed from tax jurisprudence, have laid down new roots in instances such as those stated above. We can take note here of the high quality of German government officials and, at the same time, of the superior quality of German statesmen.

To return to our main subject, the original text of the Enforcement Regulation regarding the fifteenth sphere of jurisprudence states as follows:

15. From firms that process butter, special records as per No. 7 of the regulation concerning milk-fat-reduction and production and export (of Mar. 26, 1974, *BGBl*, I, 785);

The Enforcement Regulation regarding the sixteenth sphere of jurisprudence indicates:

16. From denaturing enterprises (denaturing of soft wheat), records concerning the origin and storage of the soft wheat, as well as the amount of soft wheat denatured daily, according to 12, Sec. 1, No. 1, and 12, Sec. 2, No. 1 of the ordinance of the denaturing . . . of grain (of Nov. 19, 1971, *BGBl*, I, 1831);

The Enforcement Regulation regarding the seventeenth sphere of jurisprudence is:

17. From guardians, custodial books for the securities in deposit according to 14, Sec. 1 of the law concerning the deposit of securities (of Feb. 4, 1937, *RGBl*, I, 171);

The Enforcement Regulation regarding the eighteenth sphere of jurisprudence is:

18. From plants that preprocess egg products, records concerning the egg products going in and coming out, according to 5, Sec. 2, No. 2 of the egg production ordinance (of Feb. 19, 1975, *BGBl*, I, 537);

The nineteenth sphere of jurisprudence is defined by the Enforcement Regulation as follows:

160 The Formation of an Especially Close Connection

19. From proprietors of driving schools, records concerning the training of each pupil as well as concerning the fee charged according to 18, Secs. 1 and 2 of the driving teacher law (of Aug. 25, 1969, *BGBl*, I, 1336, amended by Art. 1, No. 9 of the law of Feb. 3, 1976, *BGBl*, I, 257);

The Enforcement Regulation regarding the twentieth sphere of jurisprudence is as follows:

20. From the responsible heads of the officially recognized training institutes for driving instructors, records concerning the training of each driving teacher candidate according to 28, Sec. 1 of the driving teacher law.

The Enforcement Regulation regarding the twenty-first sphere of jurisprudence prescribes:

21. From owners of motor vehicles who are required to keep traveling records or monitoring devices, log entries according to 57a of street traffic regulations (Nov. 15, 1974, *BGBl*, I, 3193);

The twenty-second sphere of jurisprudence is prescribed as follows:

22. From forestry seeding and planting businesses, registers concerning all stocks, receipts, change in stock, and issuance of seed and plant material as per 12, Sec. 1 of the law concerning forestry seed and plant material (in this case, of Oct. 29, 1969, *BGBl*, I, 2057);

The Enforcement Regulation regarding the twenty-third sphere of jurisprudence states:

23. From those entitled to gas/oil subsidies, usage books for gas/oil according to 9, Sec. 1 of gas/oil subsidy regulation of transport (of Mar. 20, 1961, *BGBl*, I, 260); 8, Sec. 1 gas/oil subsidy regulation for rail traffic (of Dec. 11, 1973, *BGBl*, I, 1900); and 8 of gas/oil subsidy regulation for street traffic (of Dec. 21, 1973, *BGBl*, I, 1962);

Having read this far, the reader must be impressed by how the Federal Republic of Germany has attempted to infiltrate the prin-

The Formation of an Especially Close Connection 161

ciples of regular bookkeeping into every class of the nation, and how faithfully the nation has attempted to understand fully that "equal sacrifice" is the taxation principle in the science of finance and that the principle of justice of taxation is the taxation principle in tax jurisprudence. Although we Japanese have gained worldwide preeminence in the sphere of the production of commodities, we should not be so frivolous as to behave arrogantly. What we have covered thus far comprises only about a third of the total spheres over which the Enforcement Regulation exercises its legal control.

To return to the Enforcement Regulation, concerning the twenty-fourth sphere of jurisprudence, the following is prescribed:

24. From businesses that deal in poultry, registers concerning the amount of poultry received and sold, according to 2 of the poultry disease ordinance (of Dec. 19, 1972, *BGBl*, I, 2509);

The Enforcement Regulation concerning the twenty-fifth sphere of jurisprudence is as follows:

25. From farmers, which sell or deliver fresh poultry meat, special records concerning the sale or delivery, according to 3, Sec. 2 of the poultry-meat exception ordinance (of July 19, 1976, *BGBl*, I, 1857);

The Enforcement Regulation concerning the twenty-sixth sphere of jurisprudence states:

26. From processing plants of the grain and feed industry under certain conditions, books concerning all business transactions, especially concerning the details of purchase, of storage of the processing, and of the sale as well as the brokerage of the product, according to 16, Sec. 1 of the grain law (of Nov. 24, 1951, *BGBl*, I, 901);

The twenty-seventh sphere of jurisprudence is prescribed by the Enforcement Regulation as:

27. From dealers of used goods and precious metals, used goods books concerning their business according to law of the federal state, for example, according to 1, Sec. 1, and 2, Sec. 1 of

the used goods regulations of the State of North Rhine-Westphalia (of Mar. 19, 1958, *GVBl, NRW* 79);

In Japan there are many instances of entry obligation in books of account and the obligation of records being made statutory in regard to special professions, for example, Article 14 of the Pawnshop Business Law, Article 34-2 of the Quarrying Law, and Article 24 of the Medical Practitioners Law. Unlike in the Federal Republic of Germany, however, there are no legal provisions in Japan under which entry obligation and the obligation of records have been positioned under Civil Law at the same time as under Tax Law for the purpose of establishing an especially close connection between Civil Law and Tax Law. Establishment of such laws in the Federal Republic of Germany, as stated above, belongs to matters that go back more than sixty years.

Whether or not such a conception should be adopted is now considered provisionally as a separate problem, but why has it happened that literature touching on such a conception and the real existence of legislation has never been found in this country? In this connection, I feel keenly the inconsistency with our study of comparative jurisprudence. The realization of the "principle of justice in taxation" is indeed a serious problem in Japan. The reason for this is that it is a social phenomenon that is in proportion to the patriotism, the discernment, and the courage to pursue what a state should be of those who are concerned with legislation in this country.

The Enforcement Regulation concerning the twenty-eighth sphere of jurisprudence prescribes as follows:

28. From operators of goods transporters, travel logs, books concerning the long distance transport of goods, dispatching and accompanying documents, and books concerning the brokerage of cargo or cargo space, according to 28, Secs. 1 and 2; 29, Sentence 1; and 32, Sec. 1 of the cargo transport law (of Aug. 6, 1975, *BGBl*, I, 2132) in conjunction with 1–3a of the regulation concerning monitoring of tariffs in long distance shipping and shipping across borders (of Sept. 30, 1974, *BGBl*, I, 2428);

The twenty-ninth sphere of jurisprudence is prescribed by the Enforcement Regulation as follows:

The Formation of an Especially Close Connection 163

29. From midwives, billing books concerning professional business, as per 10 of the second ordinance for the implementation of midwifery law (of Sept. 13, 1939, *BGBl*, I, 1764)

The Enforcement Regulation concerning the thirtieth sphere of jurisprudence states as follows:

30. From entrepreneurs who give out, transmit, or receive home piecework, lists of this work, payment registers, and payment books, according to 6, Sentence 1, and 8, Sec. 1 of the home work law (of Mar. 14, 1951, *BGBl*, I, 191), in conjunction with 9 ff. of the first ordinance for the implementation of the home workers law (of Jan. 27, 1976, *BGBl*, I, 222);

This regulation positions even the details of records of work in the home as records in tax laws. It should be understood that the above entry obligation is subjected at the same time to the restrictions of the Exemption Regulation in regard to small businesses as prescribed by Paragraph 1 of Article 4 of the German Commercial Code. Otherwise, it constitutes a violation of Paragraph 3 of Article 20 of the statute that prescribes that unless executive power and judgment are bound by law and justice, such acts will mean the destruction of the so-called principle of lawfulness of administration.

The Enforcement Regulation concerning the thirty-first sphere of jurisprudence states:

31. From producers, mixers, importers, or wholesale distributors of light, heating, or diesel fuel, books concerning the contents of tanks, out of which the suppliers can be determined, as per 5, Sec. 1–3 *BImSchV* (of Jan. 15, 1975, *BGBl*, I, 264);

The Enforcement Regulation concerning the thirty-second sphere of jurisprudence prescribes as follows:

32. From producers of hops, records concerning the hops sold and delivered, according to 6 of the ordinance for subsidies for hops growers (of Dec. 18, 1975, *BGBl*, I, 3135);

The thirty-third sphere of jurisprudence is prescribed as:

33. From entrepreneurs who produce weapons to be shipped or ship the weapons themselves, or who obtain actual control over weapons of war from another or transmit same to another, weapons books as proof of the whereabouts of the weapons, as per 12, Sec. 2 of the law concerning the monitoring of weapons of war (of Apr. 20, 1961, *BGBl*, I, 444);

Next is the Enforcement Regulation concerning the thirty-fourth sphere of jurisprudence:

34. From stockbrokers, daily journals, as per 33, Sec. 1 of the stock exchange law (of May 27, 1908, *RGBl*, 215);

The Enforcement Regulation concerning the thirty-fifth sphere of jurisprudence states as follows:

35. From warehousemen, warehouse receipt registers and stock ledgers, according to 37, Sec. 1, and 38, Sec. 3, No. 1 of the regulation concerning negotiable warehouse receipts (of Dec. 16, 1931, *RGBl*, I, 763);

At this stage, my description of the related spheres of jurisprudence has covered barely half of the total regulations. The reader may breathe a sigh of relief at this point. I hope that my reader will be patient and continue to work through this chapter. This particular matter cannot be found in accounting literature in Japan, nor in that of tax jurisprudence, much less in the science of the Commercial Code, or in business economics, and so forth. From the standpoint of securing a sound national economy, this is a problem that has considerable importance.

The Enforcement Regulation provides concerning the thirty-sixth sphere of jurisprudence:

36. From income tax advisors, special records concerning receipts, disbursements, and assets, as per 21 of tax advisors law (of Nov. 4, 1975, *BGBl*, I, 2735);

Article 21 of the Tax Advisors Law in the Federal Republic of Germany states the following: "The Income Tax Advisor must record all receipts and disbursements consecutively and completely. The records are to be kept without delay and in the German language." Karl-Heinz Mittelsteiner, the president of the Association of Licensed Tax Practitioners in Hamburg, coauthored *Steuerberatungsgesetz Handkommentar* with Horst Gehre. In this work, Mittelsteiner states: "In general, the Income Tax Advisor [Associations] do not fall under the bookkeeping regulations as per 161 ff of the tax code."[4] Such being the case, the recording obligation, which does not fall generally under the entry condition of *AO*, has again been positioned as the entry obligation under the tax laws via Article 140 of *AO*. In the concept of civil law, which Gerd Spangemacher discusses in his book *General Theory of Law*, the professional law, known as the Licensed Tax Practitioner's Law, has naturally been included.

To continue with our examination of the regulations, the Enforcement Regulation concerning the thirty-seventh sphere of jurisprudence states as follows:

37. From manufacturers of aircraft, records concerning the regular implementation of sample tests, according to 23 of testing regulations for aircraft (of May 16, 1968, *BGBl*, I, 416);

The Enforcement Regulation regarding the thirty-eighth sphere of jurisprudence prescribes:

38. From aeronautical technical firms, records concerning the conducting of inspections of aircraft, as per 38 of testing regulations for aircraft;

The Enforcement Regulation concerning the thirty-ninth sphere of jurisprudence follows:

39. From owners of aircraft, records concerning the at cost flights subject to authorization, routes flown by airplanes, and cost per flight hour, according to 72 of the air traffic permit ordinance (of Nov. 28, 1968, *BGBl*, I, 12630);

The fortieth sphere of jurisprudence is prescribed as follows:

40. From firms that process skim milk powder, special records concerning the quantity of skim milk powder received, issued, and on hand according to 7 of the skim milk price reduction regulation (of Feb. 19, 1976, *BGBl*, I, 346);

166   The Formation of an Especially Close Connection

The Enforcement Regulation concerning the forty-first sphere of jurisprudence indicates:

41. From brokers, loan and investment agents, builders and building consultants, information concerning the contracts and/or building projects according to 10 of the agent and builders ordinance (of June 11, 1975, *BGBl*, I, 1351);

Having read through the above regulations, my reader must recognize the German attitude that even in the professional occupations fraudulent acts are possible. The Federal Republic of Germany, however, demands righteousness in its legislation. It is highly desirable that the power of the law applies to all economic fields, without exception, because a human being is neither God nor a devil.

The Enforcement Regulation regarding the forty-second sphere of jurisprudence prescribes:

42. From metal dealers, business books (metal books) concerning their purchases as per 6, Sec. 1 of the law concerning trade in base metals (of July 23, 1926, *BGBl*, I 415) and the applicable state ordinances, for example, according to 4 of the regulation of the state of North Rhine-Westphalia concerning trade in base metal and retail trade in scrap (of Mar. 19, 1958);

The Enforcement Regulation governing the forty-third sphere of jurisprudence is as follows:

43. From firms of the milk and fat industry, books concerning all business transactions, especially concerning details of purchase, storage, processing, and distribution as well as the brokerage of certain products, according to 23, Sec. 1 of the milk and fat law (of Feb. 28, 1951, *BGBl*, I, 135);

The forty-fourth sphere of jurisprudence is as follows:

44. From firms that produce or trade in mixed feed, additive (thereto), or prepared mixtures, books concerning the production, amounts received, issued, and on hand according to 17, Sec. 3 of the feed law (of July 2, 1975, *BGBl*, I, 1745, compared to 31 of the feed regulation of June 16, 1976, *BGBl*, I, 1497);

The Formation of an Especially Close Connection 167

The Enforcement Regulation concerning the forty-fifth sphere of jurisprudence states:

45. From breeders and dealers of parrots and parakeets, books concerning the type and number of the animals according to the parrot importation regulation (of Mar. 3, 1975, *BGBl*, I, 653); according to 4 of the Psi Hakosis[5] regulation (of July 18, 1975, *BGBl*, I, 1429);

The Enforcement Regulation defines the forty-sixth sphere of jurisprudence as:

46. From pawnbrokers, records of each pawn transaction and its settlement, according to 3, Sec. 1 of the regulation concerning the conduct of business of the pawnbrokers (of June 1, 1976, *BGBl*, 1, 1334);

The books of account that are prescribed by Article 14 of the Pawnshop Business Law in Japan have only a relation to the Police Station concerned (Article 15), and these books have no legal relation with the tax laws.

The Enforcement Regulation concerning the forty-seventh sphere of jurisprudence states:

47. Test centers for the verification of measuring instruments for electricity, gas, water, or heating are to keep verifiable documents concerning the verifications, test results, and special tests according to 17 of the test center regulation (of June 18, 1970, *BGBl*, I, 795);

The forty-eighth sphere of jurisprudence is prescribed as:

48. From travel agencies and hotel brokers, special records, according to state's law (*GVBl*, Rhineland-Palatinate 1958, 173; *GVBl*, Hesse 1958; *GVBl*, Bavaria 1959, 53; *GVBl*, Lower Saxony 1959, 1; *GVBl*, Hamburg, 1964, 99);

The Enforcement Regulation governing the forty-ninth sphere of jurisprudence states:

49. From businesses that produce or distribute certain seeds, records concerning the weight or the number of the seeds issued,

distributed, or used in their own business, according to 13, 19, Sec. 2, and 21, Sec. 2 of seed trade law (of June 23, 1975, *BGBl*, I, 1453);

The Enforcement Regulation concerning the fiftieth sphere of jurisprudence prescribes as follows:

50. From businesses that distribute seeds, or package or process seeds for others for profit, inspection books concerning the receiving and distributing of seed, according to 35, Sec. 2 of the seed trade law (of June 23, 1975, *BGBl*, I, 1453);

At this point, I am reminded of a book published through the Harvard Law School and entitled *Taxation in the Federal Republic of Germany*, the central figures of which are Henry J. Gumpel and Carl Boettcher. Under the heading "The Present Legal System," the book states:

The present German approach is characterized by a striking legalism that permeates all fields of substantive and procedural law. There is a distinct tendency to have the greatest possible variety of situations covered by express statutory regulations. There also is an obvious desire to create a practically complete system of judicial review for every conceivable claim or wrong. In obvious reaction to the utter lawlessness of the Hitler era and an understandable skepticism toward the legislative assemblies and their work, the population turned to the neutral courts of law as the one agency of the state from which dispassionate decisions and fair treatment could be expected.[6]

It may be understandable that present-day legislative activities in the Federal Republic of Germany are intended primarily to remove the weak points that were inherent in the Weimar Constitution under Hitler.

Although I am aware of the courage of the National Assembly of the Federal Republic of Germany, their activities now seem extraordinary. Although both the Weimar Constitution and the Imperial Tax Code went into effect in 1919, the latter has been handed down almost intact, while of the former, only five Articles are included, just as they are, in the current Constitution of the Federal Republic of Germany.[7]

To return to our main subject, the Enforcement Regulation that defines the fifty-first sphere of jurisprudence says:

The Formation of an Especially Close Connection 169

51. From persons who responsibly conduct pest control with highly poisonous substances, records concerning fumigations conducted, as per 12 of the regulation on the implementation of the regulation concerning pest control with higher poisonous substances (of Mar. 25, 1931, *RGBl*, I, 83);

The fifty-second sphere of jurisprudence is as follows:

52. From producers of beef cattle, as well as slaughterhouses, slaughter charts as per 6 and 11 of the regulation concerning producers of beef cattle (of Apr. 28, 1975, *BGBl*, I, 999);

The Enforcement Regulation prescribes the fifty-third sphere of jurisprudence as:

53. From sellers of slaughter livestock and agents at the wholesale cattle markets, market close certificates to be issued for each sale, according to 10, Sec. 1 of the livestock and meat law (of Apr. 25, 1951, *BGBl*, I, 272);

The Enforcement Regulation belonging to the fifty-fourth sphere of jurisprudence has been expressed as follows:

54. From manufacturers of firearms, weapons production books by firms that buy and distribute, or weapons trade books by firms that sell weapons for profit

The Enforcement Regulation concerning the fifty-fifth sphere of jurisprudence states:

55. From any business, which produces ammunition for profit, buys, sells, or distributes ammunition to others, ammunition trade books according to 12, Sec. 1–3 of the weapons law (of Mar. 8, 1976, *BGBl*, I, 432) in connection with 14–18 of the first regulation to enforce the weapons law (of May 24, 1976, *BGBl*, I, 1285);

The Federal Republic of Germany is quite different from Japan. In Article 26 of its Constitution, there are provisions in regard to a war of aggression. Paragraph 1 of Article 26 prescribes the unconstitutionality and punishability of the act of preparing for a war of aggression. Paragraph 2 prescribes as follows: "Weapons de-

170 The Formation of an Especially Close Connection

signed for warfare may not be manufactured, transported, or marketed except with the permission of the federal government. Details shall be regulated by federal law." Hence we have the above-mentioned weapons law. According to the *Brockhaus Encyclopedia:* "Details are regulated by a law of April 20, 1961, concerning the control of weapons of war."[8] Since then, several revisions have been made. As these revisions are not part of the main subject of this study, however, I will not describe progress in this particular matter.

The Enforcement Regulation concerning the fifty-sixth sphere of jurisprudence provides:

56. From businesses in which at least 1,250 swine can be held, inspection books concerning exit and entry of the swine, according to 13, Sec. 1 of the regulation concerning wholesale keeping of animals—swine (of Apr. 9, 1975, *BGBl*, I, 885);

The Enforcement Regulation regarding the fifty-seventh sphere of jurisprudence states:

57. From producers of a serum or vaccine (17c of the Livestock Plague Law, in this case of Dec. 19, 1973, *BGBl*, 1974, I, 1), books concerning—among other things—dates of production, the numbers and amounts of each individual batch, according to 15 of the regulation concerning serum and vaccines (of Feb. 27, 1973, *BGBl*, I, 134);

The Enforcement Regulation regarding the fifty-eighth sphere of jurisprudence prescribes:

58. From businesses that have permits for the use and handling of explosives, listings concerning the amount of the explosives produced, reclaimed, purchased, imported, or otherwise brought into the area of jurisdiction of this law, transferred, used, or destroyed according to 15, Sec. 1 of the explosives law (of Aug. 25, 1969, *BGBl*, I, 1938) in connection with 52 and 53 of the second DV explosive law (of Apr. 24, 1972, *BGBl*, I, 633, amended by the regulation of June 28, 1976, *BGBl*, I, 1713);

The Enforcement Regulation prescribing the fifty-ninth sphere of jurisprudence states:

59. From veterinarians, who have their own in-house pharmacies, records (proof) concerning the purchase, production, storage, and distribution of medicine according to 5, Secs. 2–4 and 13 of the regulation concerning in-house veterinary pharmacies (of July 31, 1975, *BGBl*, I, 2115);

The sixtieth sphere of jurisprudence is prescribed as follows:

60. From owners of establishments for the disposal of animal remains, records ... concerning the amount of material delivered, according to 12 of the regulation of Sept. 1, 1976, *BGBl*, I, 2587;

The Enforcement Regulation prescribing the sixty-first sphere states:

61. From insurance companies, a special presentation of accounts according to the external "RechVUVO" (of July 11, 1973, *BGBl*, I, 1209, amended by the regulation of Aug. 16, 1976, *BGBl*, I, 2388) and according to internal "RechVUVO" (of Oct. 17, 1974, *BGBl*, I, 2453, modified by the regulation of May 11, 1976, *BGBl*, I, 1252);

According to the 1980 edition of *Beck's Concise Commentary: Insurance Policy Law* (Munich: C. H. Beck's Press), although there are only 193 articles in the text of the Insurance Policy Law, in addition to 16 articles in the Introduction to it, there were 36 kinds of laws that should be called additional articles that brought together the provisions of each part of this particular law. In my opinion, this is substantial evidence of how faithfully the National Assembly of the Federal Republic of Germany has thought of the principle of lawful (regular) administration, which has been provided for by Paragraph 3 of Article 20 of the Federal Republic of Germany's Constitution. This particular point may be entirely different in Japan.

The Enforcement Regulation for the sixty-second sphere of jurisprudence is as follows:

172 The Formation of an Especially Close Connection

62. From smaller mutual insurance companies, a special presentation of accounts according to the "RechbkVVO" (of Oct. 18, 1974, *BGBl*, I, 2909, amended by the regulation of Mar. 24, 1975, *BGBl*, I, 847);

The concept of the reciprocal character of a small-scale insurance group is not compatible with the insurance system in Japan. For example, in the Federal Republic of Germany, there is a system "Small . . . People's Insurance," which is similar to Article 189 of the Insurance Policy Law mentioned above. Once again, however, as this has nothing to do with my main subject, I will not go into details here.

The Enforcement Regulation defining the sixty-third sphere of jurisprudence is:

63. From Auctioneers, records concerning the auction contracts, according to 21, Sec. 1 of the regulation concerning auctions for profit (of June 1, 1976, *BGBl*, I, 1345);

Under the Auction Law in Japan, it has been prescribed that in the case of a property auction, the execution organization should be "the execution officer of the District Court controlling the location where the auction is to be held" (Article 3 of the Auction Law). It also states that in the case of a real estate auction, the execution organization should be "the District Court controlling the place where the real estate to be auctioned is located" (Article 22 of the Auction Law). There is no room for intervention, therefore, by the so-called traders concerned. However, the act of an auction sale by auctioneering traders is beyond the scope of the Auction Law in Japan. In my opinion, it is absolutely necessary for us to learn the point at which the records of these auctioneering traders should be looked upon as those under the tax laws. In addition, their completeness, truth, timeliness, clarity, and the completeness with which they satisfy other required conditions should also be demanded as the law in conjunction with penalty laws and regulations.

The Enforcement Regulation regarding the sixty-fourth sphere of jurisprudence states as follows:

64. From administrators of common property of condominium owners, business plans, accounts, and presentations of accounts, according to 28, Secs. 1, 3, and 4 of the condominium law (of Mar. 15, 1951, *BGBl*, I, 175);

The Enforcement Regulation concerning the sixty-fifth sphere of jurisprudence indicates:

65. From animal traders, inspection books concerning the horses, cattle, and swine in their possession, according to 20 of the Bundesrat's implementation instructions to the livestock epidemic law (of Dec. 7, 1911, *RGBl*, 1912, 3);

The year 1911 obviously preceded World War I. The enactment of the Imperial Tax Code occurred after the Weimar constitutional system was established in 1919. Although it is understandable that the Imperial Tax Code adopted laws and regulations that were drafted in 1911, the current Constitution does not include these laws and regulations, except for five articles (Articles 136 to 141) of the Weimar Constitution. Moreover, these articles are concerned only with religious problems. I must wonder whether an enforcement regulation of the Bundesrat from 1911 still has validity.

However, the Constitution of the Federal Republic of Germany, drafted in 1949, has "transitional stipulations," Paragraph 1 of Article 123 of which prescribes that "a law in force before the first meeting of the Bundestag shall remain in force insofar as it does not conflict with the Constitution." Such "transitional stipulations" cannot be found in the Constitution of Japan. This may be due to the fact that the current Constitution of Japan is the outcome of the revolutionary creation and enactment of the whole text of the Constitution of the Empire of Japan. The new Constitution was put in place with the obstinate insistence by Article 73 of the Imperial Constitution of Japan that it was a revision of the Imperial Constitution. Does the reader acknowledge that the Japanese are a people who accept, calmly and constitutionally, a made-up story regarding even the public affairs of the state?

The Enforcement Regulation regarding the sixty-sixth sphere of jurisprudence prescribes:

174 The Formation of an Especially Close Connection

66. From owners of public scales, documents concerning the certified public weighings, according to 8, Sec. 8 of the weighing ordinance (of June 18, 1970, *BGBl*, I, 799);

The sixty-seventh sphere of jurisprudence is defined as follows:

67. From a business, which within the meaning of the wine law (of July 14, 1971, *BGBl*, I, 893) produces, markets, exports, and imports products . . ., winebooks in accordance with 57, Sec. 1, No. 1 of the wine law in conjunction with 1 of the wine supervision regulation (of Mar. 30, 1973, *BGBl*, I, 245); concerning analytical examinations of the products within the meaning of the wine law for other firms, analysis books, as per 57, Sec. 1, No. 3 of the wine law in connection with 2 of the wine supervision regulation;

The Enforcement Regulation concerning the sixty-eighth sphere of jurisprudence dictates:

68. From proprietors of businesses that sell, purchase, exchange, process, or use wild game for profit, game trade books according to 36 of the federal law (in this case, of Mar. 30, 1961, *BGBl*, I, 304);

The Enforcement Regulation governing the sixty-ninth sphere prescribes as follows:

69. From housing entrepreneurs, books (business reports) in accordance with the guidelines of the umbrella organization, according to 23, Secs. 1 and 2 of the regulation of the execution of the equal opportunity housing law (in this case, of Nov. 24, 1969, *BGBl*, I, 2141);

Finally, the Enforcement Regulation defining the seventieth sphere of jurisprudence states:

70. From processing plants and commercial enterprises of sugar production and the storage and transport businesses that store or distribute sugar, books covering all business transactions (especially those concerning purchase, storage, processing, sale, and brokerage), according to 12, Secs. 1 and 3 of the sugar law (of Jan. 1, 1951, *BGBl*, I, 47).

The Formation of an Especially Close Connection 175

The Enforcement Regulation, which is an administrative order to Article 140 of the *AO*, comes to an end here. It concludes with the following sentence: "Infringements of these obligations of keeping non-tax-related books and records, are tantamount to infringements against the regulations concerning keeping tax-related books and records. Refer to 162, Sec. 2 (Estimates), 379, Sec. 1 (Tax Risk)."

In this way, the obligations of entry and records under the tax laws in the Federal Republic of Germany have formed, in as many as seventy spheres of jurisprudence, an especially close connection between Civil Law and Tax Law and have taken root in a broad and diversified way in the citizen's life. The reader may now understand how wide the influence of the principles of regular bookkeeping is. I would hope that those who are concerned with law making in Japan will follow the example of the Federal Republic of Germany and work to break down Japan's unfair tax system.

The Difference between Ordinances and Guidelines and the Legal Injunction

I must now touch on several problems. The first is the dissimilarity between the words "Erlasse" ("ordinances") and "Richtlinien" ("guidelines"). The Enforcement Regulation, the object of which is to create an administrative order of an especially close connection between Civil Law and Tax Law, has been called "Einführungserlaβ zur AO." The word "Erlasse" ("ordinances") is used only in this way in the Enforcement Regulation, and this term is different from "Richtlinien" ("guidelines"), which is a similar administrative order. These two terms differ in that "Richtlinien" ("guidelines") covers all the texts of the tax laws, while "Erlasse" ("ordinances") are to be announced officially only in conjunction with the provision that is particularly recognized as important in each part of the tax law. They are identical, however, in that both only have the character of a "secondary source" of law. That is, they do not restrict a court of justice. Although both are announced officially by the minister of finance, the character of the "primary source" of law is still lacking in both of them.

In this particular respect, the same is also true of "Bundverfügungen" ("circular notices"). Consequently, these three actions are to be pronounced invalid by the Court of Finances, when they are found to deviate from the interpretation of the law. On the other hand, "Durchführungsverordnungen" ("implement orders [regulations concerning execution of a law]"), abbreviated "DVO" or "DV," which have the source of law, are called "Rechtsverordnungen" ("decree laws"). Paragraph 1 of Article 80 of the Constitution of the Federal Republic of Germany has prescribed this particular point, under which the government or the minister has been accorded by law the authority to issue decree laws. What must be attended to, however, is that the content, purpose, and scope of the authorization so conferred must be set forth in such law, and a deviation from this limitation is to be judged invalid by virtue of being an infringement upon the Constitution.

In the light of the philosophy of law, this point, in particular, stands to reason. In my opinion, there is no need for further statement of this particular point. Article 41 of the Constitution of Japan prescribes that "the Diet shall be the highest organ of state power." Therefore, for example, in a case when the authority for enacting the entrusted order is conferred upon outside organs by the Diet, it is logical that the contents, purpose, and extent of this authority should be provided for in the law concerned. When we openly base our actions on this philosophy of law, it may safely be said that both Article 68 of the Income Tax Law and Article 65 of the Corporation Tax Law in Japan are laws that have an unconstitutional character.

Article 68 of the Income Tax Law of Japan prescribes that "outside of those that are specifically prescribed in this clause, necessary matters regarding the scope of various kinds of income and the calculation of the amount of money gained from various kinds of income should be provided for by government ordinance." Article 65 of the Corporation Tax Law, moreover, prescribes that "excepting those items which are specifically provided for in this Section 2 and the prior section [calculation of the amount of money gained from income], necessary matters concerning the calculation of the amount of money gained from income in each business year should be provided for by government ordinance."

It is difficult to say that these two particular provisions prescribe in the law, the contents, purpose, and extent of the authority that was transferred to the government ordinance.

It is recognized that the "ambiguity" of these provisions has brought forth the circular notices in regard to the Income Tax Law and the Corporation Tax Law, both of which have included, in large quantities, "the necessary matters regarding the calculation of the amount of money gained from income." It appears that the Diet in Japan has transferred, without our knowledge, the comprehensive enactment authority of the tax laws to the director general of the National Tax Administration Agency. For the sake of the prestige of Japan's legislation, this should be reformed by mustering the all-out courage of our nation.

Authority for Rectifying the Laws

The next matter to be considered is whether or not the minister of finance or the director general of the National Tax Administration Agency, through their respective administrative orders, can make up for a portion of the tax law that is lacking, or can rectify the defects of the tax law. In regard to this, there once existed, and may currently exist, an opinion that in addition to its function of explaining the text of the tax law, the National Tax Administration Agency in Japan, through a circular notice, can supply a deficient portion in the tax law or rectify a defective portion of the tax law. I suspect that this particular opinion may be nearly identical with that in tax jurisprudence in Germany before World War II.

When the Imperial Tax Code was enacted in 1919, Article 6 prescribed: "When, in the meaning of the law, the officials have to make a decision on their own judgment, it is to be made in consideration of justice and equity."[9] There is no doubt at all that this provision was later replaced by Article 12 of the *AO*, under which the federal minister of finance, through his administrative orders, had the authority to prescribe federal tax law and to rectify it.[10] It is necessary for us to bear in mind, however, that this responsibility was definitely eliminated in the Federal Republic of Germany after World War II.

178 The Formation of an Especially Close Connection

The first paving stone is set down in Article 129 of the Constitution of the Federal Republic of Germany. Under the heading "Continued Validity of Authorizations," Paragraph 3 of Article 129 prescribes as follows: "Insofar as legal provisions within the meaning of paragraphs (1) and (2) of this article authorize their amendment or supplementation or the issue of legal provisions instead of laws, such authorization has expired." What is referred to by "legal provisions within the meaning of paragraphs (1) and (2)" is that Paragraph 1 indicates laws and regulations under the federal laws and Paragraph 2 indicates those in the laws of the individual states. In either case, Article 129 stipulates that henceforth no such actions shall be acknowledged (for example, the laws and regulations that have the character of administrative orders) as taking the place of the law or as changing, rectifying, or newly issuing laws and regulations.

This was further confirmed by a decision of the Federal Finance Court, on November 22, 1951, two years after the enactment of the Constitution of the Federal Republic of Germany.[11] Furthermore, the revised *AO*, which was enacted two years later on July 11, 1953, officially proclaimed the abolition of such authorizations through an express provision under the tax law.[12] We Japanese should reflect on the fact that the authorities of the National Tax Administration Agency in Japan, through the circular notices that are issued by the director general, can not only proclaim customary standards in the interpretation of the law, but can also supply a deficiency in the tax laws and rectify a defect. This practice has been completely wiped out under present-day German tax jurisprudence. In this regard it may safely be said that, when compared with the tax laws of the Federal Republic of Germany, Japan's tax laws and the administration of taxation business lag by more than ten years.

Notes

1. It should be 1919, not 1918—au.
2. Although this book is called a "pocket commentary," it is a major work comprised of two volumes with a total of over 1,600 pages.
3. See Vol. 1, p. 465.

4. See p. 37.
5. This is a contagious disease in birds that also infects human beings.
6. See pp. 74–75.
7. Article 140 of the Constitution.
8. *Brockhaus Enzyklopädie*, Neunzehnter Band, 1974, S. 771.
9. *Die Reichsabgabeordnung vom 13 Dezember 1919 von Enno Becker*, Zweite Auflage, 1922, S. 27.
10. *Taxation in the Federal Republic of Germany* (Harvard Law School, 1963), p. 88; Tipke and Kruse, *Imperial Tax Code: Pocket Commentary* (Cologne: Verlag Dr. Otto Schmidt KG, 1961), S. 58.
11. *BStBl*, 1952, III, S. 6.
12. *BGBl*, 1953, I., S. 511.

13

The Calculation Regulations in the United States and England

The General Situation

The Companies Act of 1948 in England had a total of 462 articles, along with 8 tables. Since the enactment of the Companies Act of 1862, among many companies acts that became indicative of an entire era, the Companies Act of 1948 had the most numerous provisions. As a result of the Companies Act of 1976, Articles 127, 147, 148, 331, and so forth—the provisions regarding calculation—were all abolished and lost their validity.

There are only forty-five articles in the Companies Act of 1976, in addition to "Schedules" 1 through 3. The full text is divided into two parts, as follows: 1) accountants, accounting records, and auditors, and 2) miscellaneous and supplementary. In Section 1, Article 12, "Accounting Records," and the provisions related to auditors in Articles 13 through 20 are considered the most important. As with earlier companies acts, the penalties for not adhering to these articles is imprisonment for less than two years, or a fine, or both.

It is my opinion that this is a splendid piece of legislation. It seems particularly admirable that the term "every company" has been used throughout and that no distinctions between companies —such as the amount of capital, or whether a company is "listed," or "unlisted"—are made. The most important point in Section 2 may be "disclosure of interests in shares," which has been provided for in Articles 24 through 27.

The calculation regulations in the United States are based on the Securities Act of 1933,[1] the Securities and Exchange Act (1934), and the Small Business Act of 1958. Each of the first two laws created a commission, and both commissions have the right to establish regulations. The rules and regulations promulgated by these commissions have become colossal. It is a big job, therefore, to become totally familiar with these rules and regulations, in detail and accurately.

As these American rules and regulations are not necessarily part of my main subject, I will touch on them only peripherally. These laws and regulations are far more thorough in terms of social justice, or in justice in taxation, than those in Japan, especially insofar as these laws make no distinction in calculation regulations in regard to the scale of an enterprise. Special note should also be taken of the fact that as an executive can obtain and review records of transactions, to insure the completeness and truth of accounting records, these laws mandate a prison sentence or a fine to be imposed on those executives who counterfeit or alter records, or make false entries in books of account or on financial statements, and so forth. It is highly admirable that the Securities Act of 1933 had a regulation in regard to a prison sentence of less than five years, or a fine of not more than five thousand dollars, or the imposition of both penalties in the event of unfair accounting.[2]

Article 12 of the British Companies Act of 1976

We must first review Article 12 of the British Companies Act of 1976, which has twelve paragraphs. As a single provision, it is a fairly long article. Paragraph 1 states:

(1) Every company shall keep accounting records in accordance with the provisions of this section.
Paragraph 2 is as follows:
(2) The accounting records shall be sufficient to show and explain the company's transactions.
Paragraph 3 stipulates:

182 The Calculation Regulations

(3) The accounting records shall be such as to
  (a) disclose with reasonable accuracy, at any time, the financial position of the company at that time; and
  (b) enable the directors to insure that any balance sheet or profit and loss account prepared by them under Section (1) above complies with the requirements of Section 149 of the Act of 1948 (the balance sheet to give a true and fair view of the company's state of affairs, and the profit and loss account to give a true and fair view of the company's profit or loss, etc.)

And Paragraph 4 prescribes as follows:

(4) The accounting records shall in particular contain
  (a) entries on a day-to-day basis of all sums of money received and expended by the company and the matters in respect to which the receipt and expenditure took place;
  (b) Ma record of the assets and liabilities of the company; and
  (c) when the company's business involves dealing in goods, the statements mentioned in Section (5) below.

Paragraph 5 states:

(5) The statements referred to in Section (4) (c) above are
  (a) statements of stock held by the company at the end of each financial year of the company;
  (b) all statements of stock takings from which any such statement as is mentioned in paragraph (a) above has been or is to be prepared; and
  (c) except in the case of goods sold by way of ordinary retail trade, statements of all goods sold and purchased showing the goods and the buyers and sellers in sufficient detail to enable the goods and the buyers and sellers to be identified.

In this way, the concept of statements is presented, to say nothing of the statements of inventories at the end of a term, all the statements of the original records that constitute the basis for the statements of the inventories at the end of a term, and even the statements of the identification of the parties concerned with the selling and purchasing of goods—all of which are included in the concept of statements. The above specified statements are presented before the positive laws and regulations of the companies act. This legislation is, in my opinion, admirable indeed.

To continue, Paragraph 6 is written in this way:

> (6) Subject to Section (7) below, the accounting records shall be kept at the registered office of the company or at such other place as the directors of the company think fit and shall at all times be open to inspection by the officers of the company.

In comparison with Japan's current Commercial Code, which prescribes that the location for preserving a company's books of account can be only at the site of the head office (Articles 143 and 429), the British regulations on this matter are more realistic and practical.

Paragraph 7 prescribes:

> (7) If accounting records are kept at a place outside Great Britain, accounts and returns with respect to the business dealt with in the accounting records so kept shall be sent to, and kept at a place in, Great Britain and shall at all times be open to inspection by the officers of the company.

If such a provision existed in Japan, cases such as that of *Ataka* could be prevented in advance.

Paragraph 8 stipulates as follows:

> (8) The accounts and returns to be sent to Great Britain in accordance with Section (7) above shall be such as to
> (a) disclose with reasonable accuracy the financial position of the business in question at intervals not exceeding six months; and
> (b) enable the directors to insure that any balance sheet or profit and loss account prepared by them under Section (1) above complies with the requirements of the said Section 149 of the Act of 1948.

Paragraph 9 states:

184 The Calculation Regulations

(9) Subject to any direction with respect to the disposal of any records kept by a company given under any rules made under Section 365 (1) of the Companies Act of 1948, any accounting records that a company is required by this section to keep shall be preserved by it:
 (a) in the case of a private company, for three years from the date on which they are made; and
 (b) in any other case for six years from the date on which they are made.

Section 365 (1) of the Act of 1948, mentioned above, indicates clearly that, in England, with the agreement of the president of the Board of Trade, the lord chancellor has been granted the authority to establish general rules that are necessary to accomplish the objectives of the Companies Act as far as "winding-up rules" are concerned.[3] The same is true in Scotland under the Act of Sederunt.

Paragraph 10 of Article 12 of the Companies Act of 1976 indicates as follows:

(10) If a company fails to comply with any provision of subsections (1) to (7) above, every officer of the company that is in default shall be guilty of an offense unless he shows that he acted honestly and that in the circumstances in which the business of the company was carried on the default was excusable; and if any officer of the company fails to take all reasonable steps for securing compliance by the company with subsection (9) above or has intentionally caused any default by the company thereunder, he shall be guilty of an offense.

Since the U.S. Securities Act of 1933 was enacted, unlawful accountings made by responsible persons have been dealt with by criminal penalties, a tendency that has taken root among the advanced civilized countries of the world. The reader may recall the fact that, in the past, the Export Committee of the Organization for Economic Cooperation and Development (OECD) has pointed out the lack of originality among the Japanese in the sphere of cultural sciences. I must conclude that those in Japan who obstinately try to restrict their field of vision only to domestic affairs and do not envision Japan's place in the world, will cherish the danger that will make Japan's destiny take a wrong course.

Paragraph 11 follows:

(11) Any person guilty of an offense under this section shall be liable
   (a) on conviction on indictment to imprisonment for a term not exceeding two years, or to a fine, or to both; or
   (b) on summary conviction, to imprisonment for a term not exceeding six months, or to a fine not exceeding 400 pounds, or to both.

Paragraph 12 stipulates:

(12) Section 147 of the Act of 1948 (which is superseded by this section) and Section 331 of that act (regarding the liability provision concerning the responsibility for where proper books of account are to be kept during the period before the "winding-up rules") shall cease to have validity.

Under this provision, Section 147 of the Act of 1948, which had hitherto been considered the provision of the principle of regular bookkeeping under the British Companies Act by some accounting scholars in Japan, was abolished, and superseded by this Section 12.

Section 19 of the British Companies Act of 1976

Sections 13 through 20 contain the rules in regard to auditors. Among these rules, Section 19 is unique, in that there are no similar calculation provisions in the United States or the Federal Republic of Germany. Due to the limits of space, I will touch on only Section 19 and end my examination of the British Companies Act 1976. The title of Section 19 is "False statements, etc., to Auditors," and it is divided into three parts. Part One prescribes as follows:

(1) An officer of a company who knowingly or recklessly makes a statement that:

(a) is misleading, false, or deceptive in a material particular, and
(b) is a statement to which this section applies, shall be guilty of an offense.

Part Two states:

(2) This section applies to any statement made to the auditors of the company (whether orally or in writing) that conveys, or *purports* to convey, any information or explanation that they require, or are entitled to require, as auditors of the company.

Judicial precedent and doctrine in this country acknowledge the concept of *dolus eventualis*. It should be noted, however, that this provision indicates that not only the will but also the intention of the person making the statement is subject to the imposition of penalties, and that this is closely akin to the theory of the Penal Code that maintains that the *dolus eventualis* is the responsible condition for intentional offense as a kind of intention.

Part Three stipulates:

(3) Any person guilty of an offense under this section shall be liable:
    (a) on conviction on indictment to imprisonment for a term not exceeding two years, or to a fine, or to both; or
    (b) on summary conviction to imprisonment for a term not exceeding six months, or to a fine not exceeding 400 pounds, or to both.

I do not know of any other country that has this type of legal provision prescribing that any administrator of a company who makes a false statement to auditors in accounting or in taxation affairs, orally or in writing, will be subject to imprisonment, or a fine, or both. In regard to this, I must express my deep admiration of the truly commendable justice and courage of the members of the British National Assembly and those authorities who are responsible for drafting British laws and regulations.

It seems to me that the elected members of the Japanese Diet, who take an oath to do all they can in the interests of the state and the people, should take a lesson from the British. Our bureaucratic

The Calculation System in the United States

officials, who have a high opinion of themselves shouldering the formation of the destiny of Japan and the people, should make every possible effort to learn a great deal from the drawing up of such a bill and to persuade the Diet.

The Calculation System in the United States

We will now turn to the calculation system in the United States. In America, there is no law similar to the "Lag om bokföring" in Sweden. The U.S. Internal Revenue Code (IRC), Sec. 6001, prescribes that individuals "shall keep such records," and so forth. The nature of the contents and condition of such records, however, and even the period of preservation, have been mandated by regulations. One of the IRC's distinctive features is that the obligation to preserve "permanent books of account or records" has been imposed on all taxpayers (excluding persons engaged in agriculture) and on earners of employment income.[4] This measure is considered to correspond to the point that there is no prescription system in regard to "tax dodging" and "non-filing."[5] Moreover, in regard to the form of accounting records, there is no specified statutory form.[6] As to the method of accounting, as a general rule, any method, such as "cash basis," "incurred basis," "service output method," or the mixed method (the joint use of "cash basis" and "incurred basis") can be freely selected.[7] Under this U.S. legislation, however, once a method of accounting has been selected, an optional change in the method of accounting is not permitted. A change must be approved by the director general of the Tax Administration Bureau or his deputy.[8]

As to this U.S. method of accounting, in Japan some scholars in accounting and the tax laws may have noticed that "the standard of corporate accounting that is recognized as fair and reasonable" (Ministerial Ordinance Regarding Audit Certificates, Paragraph 3 of Article 4) and "the standard of disposition of accounting that is generally considered fair and reasonable" (Paragraph 4 of Article 22 of the Corporation Tax Law) seem to be a Japanese version of the term "generally accepted principles of accounting," which is used in American accounting. They may not realize that no authoritative explanatory rules regarding these concepts have ever been given by laws and ordinances. The concept of the principle of regular bookkeeping (Paragraph 1 of Article 57 of the Enforcement Regulations for the Income Tax Law), namely, the method of accounting in the United States, is in every sense different from the principle of regular bookkeeping, especially in the adoption of the mixed method that is acknowledged in the United States.

In any case, however, in the United States when a taxpayer's method of accounting is considered "not to clearly reflect income," the director general of the Tax Administration or his deputy can order a change in the method of accounting in question.[9] In American tax laws, there are penalty provisions regarding unlawful activities on the part of taxpayers in as many as twelve articles, which follow below.

In the case of an attempt to dodge taxes, there is a provision under which a fine of not more than $10,000, or a prison sentence of less than five years, or both, is to be given (Article 7201). In regard to discontinuing use of books of account, their destruction, damage to them, or counterfeiting or making false entries in them, there is a provision (Article 7206), under which a fine of less than $5,000, or a prison sentence of less than three years, or both, is to be given. Moreover, in the case of nonappearance in a public government office and nonpresentation of books of account, a fine of less than $1,000, or a prison sentence of a term of less than one year is to be given (Article 7210).

This is splendid legislation, however, penalty provisions do not end here. There are also legal provisions that are intended to protect taxpayers. Under the heading "offenses by officers and employees of the United States," Article 7214 of the U.S. Internal Revenue Code lists the offenses in nine items and prescribes a fine of less than $10,000, or a prison sentence of less than five years, or both, in addition to disciplinary dismissal.

Due to space limitations, I cannot introduce the full text of Article 7214 here. After the introductory phrase, "in connection with any revenue law of the United States," the first provision of Article 7214 states "who is guilty of any *extortion* or willful *oppression* under cover of law." Such acts have frequently been observed within the jurisdictions of our local Tax Administration Bureaus in Japan. I regret to say that in Japan, as bills are drawn up by government officials and a statesman can *sponge on* these officials, there is no possibility that such provisions exist.

The second provision continues: "who knowingly demands other or greater sums than are authorized by law, or receives any fee, compensation, or reward, except as prescribed by law, for the performance of any duty." In Japan, such conduct has absolutely not been seen among those persons who are in the so-called career class, however, it has occasionally been seen among those persons who have a sense of their respective defeat in the competition for advancement in life.

In addition, there are various provisions concerning such matters as offering convenience to tax dodgers, or the receipt or presentation of money and articles, however, I cannot describe them all here. What is clear is that in Japan's laws and regulations, including its tax laws, rules for protecting taxpayers have been lacking. For instance, Article 88 of the *AO* enacted in 1977 in the Federal Republic of Germany prescribes the principle of investigation, Paragraph 2 of which states: "The finance office must also take circumstances favorable to the parties into account."[10] In regard to this, Frank Klein and Gern Orlopp have commented: "Der Abs. 2 sagt an sich etwas Selbstverständliches."[11]

In Japan we could not say such a thing even just for fun! In Japan's taxation laws there is not even a trace of such a provision. It should be known that Frank Klein and Gern Orlopp, the coauthors of this book, are high officials in the finance ministry in the Federal Republic of Germany. I feel strongly that a legal provision under which the interests of taxpayers are taken into consideration along with the interest of the national treasury should be introduced to Japan as soon as possible.

Criticism of Professor Earl A. Spiller, Jr.

The reader will, I hope, forgive a digression from my main subject. Professor Earl A. Spiller, Jr., of Indiana University seems to have been in error when he made the following statement in regard to the Securities and Exchange Commission: "Under the securities laws of 1933 and 1934, Congress established this agency in an attempt to regulate the nation's securities markets and to assure that investors had adequate information on which to base their decisions."[12] The truth of this matter, however, is somewhat different. The commission mentioned in Paragraph 5 of Article 2 of the Securities Act of 1933, which was enacted on May 26, 1933, is known as the Federal Trade Commission. This commission was created by the Federal Trade Commission Act, which was enacted by Congress in 1914.

According to Article 2 of the Securities Act of 1933, this commission has an enormously wide sphere of jurisdiction under which its influence is to be exercised not simply over the securities market but also over political parties and the administrative machinery of a state. It is not, therefore, the Securities and Exchange Commission. This commission was created by Article 4(a) of the Securities and Exchange Act of 1934, enacted on June 6, 1934. One law is called the Securities Act, while the other is the Securities Exchange Act; they are completely different laws.

The contents of both laws are quite similar. What each regulates, however, is quite different. Article 4 of the Securities and Exchange Act has various and detailed regulations. For example, Article 4 provides that the fixed number of commissioners serving on the Securities and Exchange Commission is five and that they are to be appointed by the president with the advice and consent of the Senate; no more than three commissioners are to be selected from the same political party; commissioners may not hold other positions simultaneously; the annual salary for a commissioner shall be prescribed; a commissioner's term of office, as a principle, shall be five years, and so forth.

On the other hand, in the Securities Act that was enacted the year before, there are no legal articles that correspond to the items provided for by Article 4 of the Securities and Exchange Act. The reason is that those who drafted it simply tried to make practical use of the commission that had been created by the Federal Trade Commission Act in 1914. Although the Securities Act of 1933 named the Federal Trade Commission, we are apt to think that this commission does not actually function as such. According to John L. Carey, who retired from active service after assuming the post of vice-president of the AICPA, the Securities and Exchange Commission was created to carry out the administration and operations of the Securities Act of 1933.[13]

The Calculation Regulations   191

As both commissions were created by laws, if the administration and operations had been commissioned, we should be able to look up such an article in the law. However, nothing has been actually written regarding this in Spiller's book. I sometimes think that books written by the British or by Americans, unlike those written by Germans, tend to lack the basic bibliographical source material on which facts are based and opinions formed, resulting in a great deal of inconvenience to the unsophisticated.

This is not an unusual example. I was forced to review carefully a 446-page compilation, *Laws Relating to Securities Commission Exchanges and Holding Companies,* which was published in 1976 by the U.S. Government Printing Office in Washington, D.C. I was relieved to find the substantive enactment of Article 210 of the Securities and Exchange Act, which states that "all powers, duties, and functions of the Federal Trade Commission under the Securities Act of 1933 shall be transferred to this Commission."

I am embarrassed by my inattentiveness to my studies thus far and would like to apologize to my readers. The full power for enforcing both the Securities Act of 1933 and the Securities and Exchange Act of 1934 lies with the Securities and Exchange Commission. From the viewpoint of legislation, the scope of the authority of the Securities and Exchange Commission is astounding. In fact, the commission's authority is not restricted to the above-mentioned two laws.

The commission, for example, also has authority under the Public Utility Act of 1935, the Investment Company and Investment Advisers Act of 1940, and the Federal Water Power Act. Furthermore, the scope of the authority of these laws is truly immense and versatile. In this connection, how about the case of Japan's Securities Exchange Council? Article 165 of Japan's Securities and Exchange Act prescribes, as its mission, that "in order to investigate and deliberate on important matters regarding the flotation, sale, and purchase of negotiable securities and other transactions, as an attached organ to the Finance Ministry, the Securities Exchange Council (hereinafter referred to as the 'Council') is hereby established."

Does a serious defect in the governmental structure of Japan exist herein? Japan's Securities Act states that the council only has the authority to investigate and deliberate specified matters.

192 The Calculation Regulations

Whether or not the council's recommendations are adopted is, in reality, entirely at the discretion of the bureaucrats. As the entire national administration is thus in the hands of a group of bureaucrats, I presume that the basis for the supreme well-being of the state and the nation for the coming thousand years may be that groups of bureaucrats will be collective bodies that are just and fair, and that they will possess the "pure insight" that was advocated by Hegel.[14] Hegel defined pure insight as true knowledge. How many persons are there in the world of Japanese bureaucrats, however, who are actually in possession of such "fundamental experience"?

At any rate, it can reasonably be considered that the authority of the U.S. Securities and Exchange Commission has been extended to the administration of all securities. I cannot undertake here to enumerate all of this commission's areas of authority, but a few of its responsibilities are: the authority to establish rules; the authority to give orders; the authority to order books of account and other books to be submitted; the authority to carry out an "on-the-spot inspection"; the authority to make a decision regarding the form of financial statements, the extent to which information must be open to the public, the method of disposition of business matters in accounting; and so forth.

At present, I have at my elbow a book of about a thousand pages entitled *Securities and Exchange Commission Decisions and Reports*, by the U.S. Government Printing Office. When this special commission—whose requests for cooperation and whose initiatives in proposing the principles of accounting, etc., were approved by the AICPA—was created, it was given the opportunity of drawing up and completing the present-day voluminous code of conduct.

Notes

1. Considering the provision of definition in Article 2, the Securities Act of 1933 should be called the "Voucher Law."
2. *Laws Relating to Securities Commission Exchanges and Holding Companies*, comp. Gilman G. Udell, Superintendent of the Document

Room of the House of Representatives (Washington, D.C.: U.S. Government Printing Office, 1976), p. 16, Sec. 24.

3. Generally, it means the law that controls the form of procedure in the Court of Session. The Court of Session has been granted the authority to establish general rules that are necessary to accomplish the objectives of the Companies Act as far as "winding-up rules" are concerned. Like other laws, the British Companies Act also has various regulations and rules.

4. Regs. 1. 6000–1.
5. Regs. 301. 6501(c)-1.
6. Regs. 31. 6001–1.
7. IRC, Sec. 446(c).
8. Regs. 1. 446–1(e).
9. IRC, Sec. 446(b).
10. It means "taxpayers."
11. Frank Klein and Gern Orlopp, *Abgabenordnung Kommentar*, 2d ed. (Munich: Verlag C. H. Beck, 1979), S. 191.
12. Earl A. Spiller, Jr., *Financial Accounting: Basic Concepts*, 3d ed. (Richard D. Irwin, Inc., 1977), p. 11.
13. Refer to John L. Carey, *The Rise of the Accounting Profession*, Vol. 1 (1969), p. 193.
14. G. W. F. Hegel, *Phanomenologie des Geistes*, 6th ed. (Hamburg: Verlag von Felix Meiner, 1952), S. 412 ff.

Part Four

14

The Problems of the Fourth EC Guideline and the Seventh EC Guideline

Several Problems in Relation to the Principles of Regular Bookkeeping

I have repeatedly referred to the threefold structure of the concept of the principles of regular bookkeeping, but I have not yet touched on several problems with the principles of regular bookkeeping that are the result of changing times. The first of these is a problem in regard to the Fourth EC Guideline and the Seventh EC Guideline. A second one relates to the Union Européenne des Experts Comptables, Economiques et Financiers (U.E.C.). The third is the problem of the "declaration of completeness" in auditing. The fourth relates to the principles of regular bookkeeping when using electronic data processing. As I am not a scholar residing in an ivory tower but a businessman whose daily life is run on a tight, minute-by-minute schedule, please allow me to touch on these problems in the remaining four chapters of this study.

The Legal Source of the Fourth EC Guideline and the Main Constituent of the Enterprise to Which It Applies

What is meant by the EC (European Communities)? This is the general name for the ECM (European Common Market), EEC, EGKS (European Community for Coal and Steel, Mining Union), ECSC, and EURATOM (European Atomic Community). According to *Gabler's Business Dictionary* (10th ed., 1979; Vol. 1, p. 1116), "The EC (European Communities) were created during the fifties primarily for political reasons (Mining Union, 1952; ECM and EURATOM, 1958) and to create a united Europe by bringing the European states together in commercial and technological areas."

It is only partially accurate to say that this happened in the 1950s, however. According to the 1965 edition of the *Encyclopaedia Britannica*, the original form of a cooperative organization in Europe was the idea of a customs union, which arose after the Napoleonic Wars (1792–1815), and a customs association in Germany, which was created in 1834. This was the most important customs union prior to World War II, and it was generally considered a model.

The grouping for the formation of a cooperative organization had begun in Europe in the early period of the twentieth century. Between World War I and World War II various kinds of geographically based customs unions were attempted. All such efforts resulted in failure, however, except one. The Benelux Economic Union, organized in London in 1944 by the governments of Belgium, Netherlands, and Luxembourg, was a successful customs union. They had to wait to begin their activities until January 1948, however. Then, negotiations regarding the formation of an alliance between France and Italy resulted in failure. France, Italy, Belgium, the Netherlands, Luxembourg, and the Federal Republic of Germany—these six countries—began to work as the EC (European Communities). After January 1, 1973, Great Britain, Denmark, and Ireland joined. Other members include Portugal and Spain.

It can safely be said that the number of member nations is gradually increasing. The process of establishing the European Communities was initiated in 1950 when Robert Schuman, the then French foreign minister, proposed the creation of this entity. The proposition was further discussed by the so-called Conference of Messina, which met at the old capital city of Messina on the island of Sicily in Italy. On March 25, 1957, the Treaty Concerning EWG and EURATOM was officially signed in Rome; it became effective on January 1, 1958. The treaty is known as the Treaty of Rome.

The European Communities and the European Economic Market have a number of governing bodies in common, namely: the Parliament of the Union, the Council, the Committee, and the Court of Justice. The first two are the main decision-making organizations. *Gabler's Business Dictionary* lists only these four.[1] The 1965 edition of the *Encyclopaedia Britannica*, however, also lists the Economic and Social Committee as a fifth governing body. According to the *Brockhaus Encyclopedia* (1968; Vol. 5, p. 786), the treaty of the European Communities was amended after the EC was officially organized. When I reviewed the preamble to the Fourth EC Guideline, however, I found the following: "according to the opinion of the Economic and Social Committee." Thus, in regard to this matter, the *Encyclopaedia Britannica* appears to be more accurate than *Gabler's Business Dictionary*.

The Fourth EC Guideline has a long preamble, and its full text contains sixty-two articles. In its large-size text edition, it runs a total of twenty pages, the contents of which are quite considerable. The official title of the Fourth EC Guideline, the original of which is in German, is: "Fourth Guideline of the Council of July 25, 1978, based on Article 54, Section 3, Letter g of the treaty concerning the annual financial statement of companies of certain legal form (78/660/EWG)." The Fourth EC Guideline went through several drafts, and the first was made public on November 10, 1971. The second draft was completed in February 1974.

The report of the Inflation Accounting Committee, *Inflation Accounting*, was presented to the Parliament in September 1975 by the Chancellor of the Exchequer and the Secretary of State for Trade by command of Her Majesty. The report contains an explanatory note to the effect that "this second draft has been the basis of our consideration."[2] This report was presented to the Parliament by the Chancellor of the Exchequer and the Secretary of State for Trade for the purpose of requesting from Parliament legislation adopting *Inflation Accounting*.

The object of presenting this report and its limits may be understood by taking a look at the following sentences contained in the "conclusion and a warning," located at the end of the first chapter:

We believe that current cost accounting will indicate more clearly than existing accounting conventions the effect of inflation on a company's affairs and that it is urgent that it should be introduced[3] as soon as possible. However, it should not be assumed that accounting for inflation is in itself a panacea for the difficulties of companies during a time of inflation.[4]

By reading the British government's conclusive assertion in *Inflation Accounting*, which was based on the model of the second draft, the reader may come to understand the angle of the "critical mind," through which the Fourth EC Guideline, and especially the Council, which is one of the EC's organizations, intended to bring about regularity in company accounting among the EC member nations. The Fourth EC Guideline had to decide, first of all, how to define which companies came under the rubric in each member nation, because the legislation in regard to companies in each nation had been drafted in different historical contexts.

In this connection, Paragraph 1 of Article 1 of the Fourth EC Guideline sets the limits of the main constituents of the enterprises to which this guideline can be applied. Because of the legislative differences in the respective countries, the names of the nine countries that were currently members and the kinds of targeted enterprises in each of those countries were listed next to the text of Paragraph 1. For instance, in the case of the Federal Republic of Germany, only three kinds of companies were listed: "die Aktiengesellschaft, die Kommanditgesellschaft auf Aktien, and die Gesellschaft mit beschränkter Haftung." In the case of "im Vereinigten Königreich," the limitation was set at two kinds of companies: "public companies limited by shares or by guarantee" and "private companies limited by shares or by guarantee." I do not plan to introduce and describe here other countries' forms of company laws.

The Problems of the Lowest Capital and the Audit Certificate

The next problem is the Fourth EC Guideline's substantial content and its relation to the principles of regular bookkeeping. Before taking this up, I would like to discuss thoroughly some legislative problems my reader should understand. These problems have no obvious relation to the principles of regular bookkeeping. They should not, however, be overlooked by us, because they have become the essential element that evolves from the reverse side of

The Problems of the Fourth EC Guideline 201

the actual circumstances of company accounting in connection with the principles of regular bookkeeping. They are the problem of "lowest capital" and that of the "audit certificate" by a professional specialist.

The Companies Act of 1980 in Great Britain is a largely revised law. It contains ninety articles along with four "Schedules," and its full text runs 151 pages. Article 2 of this act changed, for the first time in the legislative history of England, the minimum constituent of public companies from seven persons, as prescribed by Article 1 of the Companies Act of 1948, to two persons.[5] According to the Stock Law *(AktG)* of September 6, 1965, Article 2 of which prescribes the number of founders, at least five persons must be involved. Article 165 of Japan's Commercial Code, however, stipulates that "in order to establish a joint-stock company, . . . there must be more than seven initiators." From the viewpoint of the increasing social necessity for making information available to the public in general, it seems to me that the fewer the number of initiators, the more splendid the outcome. I believe, however, that society is not necessarily harmed no matter what the number of initiators is—two, five, or seven persons—and that the point at issue is the amount of capital rather than the number of initiators.

As a result of the revision that was made in 1950, Japan's Commercial Code prescribed the minimum price of a stock as 500 yen. Paragraph 2 of Article 202 of the Japanese Commercial Code and Article 174 of the same code prescribe that "at the time a company is established, if the initiator cannot subscribe the total number of stocks that are to be issued, it is required that he invite stockholders." As the Japanese Commercial Code does not prescribe a statutory number of stockholders, it turns out that even the invitation of only one stockholder is all right. As a result, a joint-stock company with capital of 4,000 yen can be established by eight stockholders, each of whom has to contribute 500 yen. As the registration and license tax that is presently required for the establishment of a joint-stock company is at the lowest 150,000 yen, it turns out that a joint-stock company having capital amounting to approximately one-fortieth of this registration and license tax can be established.

As a result of the revision of the Limited Responsibility Company Law in Japan in 1951, the lowest amount of capital of 10,000 yen, which had been prescribed by Article 9 of the Limited Responsibility Company Law (established as Law No. 74 in 1938), was raised to 100,000 yen. Consequently, at present, a joint-stock company having as capital 1/25 of the lowest amount of capital of the limited responsibility company can be established. Even if the bill entitled "a draft of law concerning partial revision of the Commercial Code and others," which was introduced to the National Diet in May 1981, were passed, a joint-stock company having capital of 400,000 yen could be established, because the bill of revision in the Diet in Paragraph 2 of Article 166 of Japan's Commercial Code prescribes only the lowest amount of stock as 50,000 yen, and this proposed bill does not fix the limit of the lowest amount of capital.

Therefore, this sum of 400,000 yen barely amounts to four times as much as the lowest limit of the amount of capital of a limited responsibility company now. Article 85 of the British Companies Act of 1980 prescribes an "authorized minimum" of capital of "public companies limited by shares or by guarantee" to be 50,000 pounds.[6]

Article 2 of the Implementation Law for the Tax Law, which is the existing law in the Federal Republic of Germany, has a regulation regarding the minimum face amount of basic capital, under which the amount is prescribed to be at least DM 100,000 at the end of 1981. If one deutsche mark is equal to a hundred yen, DM 100,000 can be converted to 10,000,000 yen in Japanese currency.

This Article 2, it seems to me, is full of discernment and courage for the purpose of insuring, essentially, how a joint-stock company should function. I will therefore reproduce it here in full: Stock companies whose capital stock, as a result of the revaluation according to the DM balance law ["D-Markbilianzgesetz"][7] applicable to them, amounts to less than DM 100,000 are dissolved after December 16, 1981, unless by this date the board of managers has registered a resolution concerning raising the capital stock to at least DM 100,000 or an order concerning the organization of the company according to the regulations of the stock company or of the reorganization law for entry in register of companies. If the result concerning the raising of the capital stock or the reorganization is disputed, then the above specified day is replaced by the day three months after the day the decision becomes legally valid.

This article clearly shows both the discernment that what is known as the effectiveness of a joint-stock company organization should be followed by all means and the decisive will of the state, which demands that those companies that do not obey specified reasonable criteria at all should be legally dissolved. The greater part of the joint-stock companies in Japan face circumstances in which the laws and regulations concerning stocks have rarely been observed, a result of the lack of such discernment and courage on the part of those who are responsible for legislation in Japan.

At this point, I would like to review closely the opinions of several of this country's scholars of commercial jurisprudence. Takeo Suzuki is the chairman of the Commercial Law Section Meeting, one of the branch sections of the Legislation Council of the Ministry of Justice, and is also an honorary professor at the University of Tokyo. He has made the following statement:

Furthermore, as to the above-stated amount of capital, there have been no specified restrictions on the maximum amount or on the minimum amount of capital. In view of the present circumstances as a result of the above action, too many joint-stock companies having an extremely small amount of capital have been established so far, and many of them have not followed faithfully the Joint-Stock Company Law in Japan. As an ideal, it is desirable that a joint-stock company be limited only to a large enterprise, while a minor enterprise is a limited liability company. To achieve the above purpose, however, is actually so difficult that I think it will be necessary for us to think out adequate legislation under which joint-stock companies can be divided at least into two kinds: large and small, in accordance with the scope of the business operation of the enterprise.[8]

I must point out that in this statement there has been no trace of an explanation of why it has been difficult to limit joint-stock companies to large enterprises and limited liability companies to minor ones. Moreover, another scholar has stated as follows:

There are many instances in which companies, the substantial forms of which are simply private enterprises, have taken the form of joint-stock companies. No small number, moreover, has not followed the law and the regulations regarding joint-stock companies. In view of this present situation, nowadays legislative theories have been extensively advocated by which the minimum amount of capital for a joint-stock company should be statutory, so that a joint-stock company should be limited to a form of a large type of enterprise, or limited companies should be divided into two kinds—large and small—and the legal control that conforms to each kind of a limited company should be put into actual practice. On the subject of what appropriate standard should be used to divide companies into two kinds (large and small), it is really very difficult to reach an agreement of opinion on this matter. Moreover, because there still remains a problem of how to prescribe the minimum amount of capital for a joint-stock company, it has so far been only in the circumstances in which partial revision has been promoted in the direction of dividing a company into large and small ones.[9]

This argument indicates how poor the philosophy of law is in Japan. Hans Kelsen advocated the establishment of a pure theory of law by differentiating clearly between "positive laws" and "justice," so as to grasp jurisprudence as a pure science. He stated that "what is to be 'just and proper' is the very thing that cannot be found by reasonable recognition," the solution of which can only be accomplished by the regulation of interests.[10] That is, what standard is appropriate in deciding whether a company is large or small, namely, what is "rightful," cannot be based on reasonable recognition—this is a thing that is a matter of course.

Although it has been said that there still exists a problem in regard to how to prescribe the lowest amount of capital for a joint-stock company, I must point out that there are definite legislative examples in the Federal Republic of Germany, Britain, and Switzerland. It may safely be said, therefore, that the real problem in this particular matter lies in whether it is good for us to leave untouched the actual fact that the greater part of our joint-stock companies in Japan do not follow, in any way, the Joint-Stock Company Law, or, paradoxically speaking, that the Commercial Code, which should be the fundamental law for a citizen's life, has brought about, in a sense, the injurious result of publicly encouraging the people in general in disobedience to the law in Japan.

The next problem we must deal with is that of the audit certification to be made by professional experts. Paragraph I of Article 162 f *AktG* of the Federal Republic of Germany has the following provision, which has been stipulated in the law: "Content and scope of the audit: 1) The annual financial statement, including the bookkeeping and business operating report, is to be audited by one or more expert auditors. If an audit has not taken place, the annual financial statement cannot be determined." Furthermore, Paragraph I of Article 164 prescribes the following: "Selection of the examiners: 1) Only (certified) public accountants and public accounting firms can be examiners of the annual financial statement."

The Joint-Stock Company Law is full of provisions regarding full disclosure to the public. From a legislative viewpoint, it should be said that the *AktG* in the Federal Republic of Germany has set forth a clear-cut mandate that puts all joint-stock companies and limited partnerships under the same obligation of going through an audit to be made by certified public accountants, or certified public accountants' companies, and that in a case when such an audit fails to take place, the annual financial statement in a particular business year should not be judged as settled.

Paragraph 1 (a) of Article 51 of the Fourth EC Guideline prescribes as follows: "Die Gesellschaften sind verpflichtet, ihren Jahresabschluß durch eine oder mehrere Personen Prüfen zu lassen, die nach einzelstattlichen Recht zur Prüfung des Jahresabschlusses zugelassen sind." Concerning this point in particular, Dr. Heinrich H. Jonas writes: "A company whose size falls under the provisions of this law is obligated to be audited. In the preliminary draft no use was made of the possibility of granting a five-year extension to those GmbHs that have regulations which have heretofore been exempted from these. Hence, the question of the applicability of this regulation."[11]

I regret to say that as I have not been able to obtain all the drafts of this text, I cannot comment on the explanation I have just quoted. I do think, however, that my Japanese readers need only imagine the foundations of such a structure of law. The quote above implies the existence of the two kinds of limited companies, one of which is under the obligation of being audited, the other being a limited company that has no such obligation at all under the legislative system of the Federal Republic of Germany.

A heavily revised version of the Federal Republic of Germany's Limited Company Law was enacted on July 4, 1980. Article 42a of this law, which was left unrevised at that time, has the following provision: "Annual audit: The Imperial Minister of Justice, with the agreement of the Imperial Minister of Commerce, may specify (require) that the annual financial statement (the annual balance sheet and profit and loss statement) must be audited. He may issue regulations necessary for the execution of, and in conjunction with, the audit." Thus, in the Federal Republic of Germany, with the necessary condition of a consultation between the Minister of Justice and the Minister of Commerce, the Minister of Justice has been granted the authority to the determine which limited companies require auditing and which do not.

Here in Japan "a joint-stock limited partnership"—from the system of such a company itself—was abolished under Law 167 in 1950. In the Federal Republic of Germany, however, the laws and regulations regarding "a joint-stock limited company" were retained in its second Stock Law *(AktG)*. Paragraph 3 of Article 278 of this Stock Law dictates that the regulations governing a joint-stock limited company are "analogous to the regulations of the first law concerning stock companies." It is considered a matter of course that an audit be carried out by a certified public accountant or a company of certified accountants. I firmly believe that the fact that all joint-stock companies and joint-stock limited partnerships, as well as a considerable portion of limited liability companies, are subjected to a compulsory audit by a third party, such as a certified public accountant or a company of certified accountants, should be studied by Japan where the reform of an unfair taxation system has been advocated and the reconstruction of our financial system is currently considered an urgent national problem.

As a businessman who is not in public office, I know that it is considered a mere a drop in the ocean to note the amount of tax evasion and the number of tax dodgers who are made public every year by the National Tax Administration Agency in Japan. There are several statesmen who are foolish enough to maintain, even in the slightest degree, that striving for the realization of justice in taxation leads us to decrease the vigor of our national economy. I believe that such persons should not be elected and sent to the National Diet by the nation, because they do not have the right qualifications for the office. Electing these people is like strangling the neck of our nation with our own hands. At the same time, this particular matter hinges on whether or not those who are responsible for drafting our laws possess both farsightedness in terms of our nation's future and indomitable courage. In Japan almost all the keys for introducing bills into the National Diet are in the hands of bureaucrats. Thus I ardently would like to believe that Japanese bureaucrats are as excellent as those in the Federal Republic of Germany.

When Japan's Commercial Code was revised in 1981, the provision that an auditor is nominated "by a resolution made by the board of directors" was changed so that an auditor is nominated "by a general meeting of stockholders."[12] Paragraph 1 of Article 163 of the 1965 Stock Law in the Federal Republic of Germany already prescribed, under the heading "Appointment of Auditors," that "the annual auditors are to be chosen by the general stockholders meeting." In England, Article 159 of the Companies Act of 1948 made it "the general rule" to nominate auditors at the general meeting of stockholders that was to be held in each business year.[13] This article, however, was replaced by Article 14 of the Companies Act of 1976 with several modifications.

In America, the Securities and Exchange Commission, which was created by Article 4 of the Securities and Exchange Act (1934), has the authority to establish regulations (Article 11). In accordance with Article 6, the "changes in registrant's independent accountant" is provided for in No. 4 of "Form 8–K," and the commission is under the obligation that "the date of the resignation or dismissal, or engagement of the new accountant" and the following matters in five items be given as "periodic reports" that are addressed to this commission.[14] In order to return to our main subject, I will omit additional details.

The Contents of the Fourth EC Guideline

Let us now consider the contents of the Fourth EC Guideline. The previously mentioned *Gabler's Business Dictionary* may deal with this subject most tactfully. Under the heading "Concept of the Fourth EC Guideline," it states as follows:

The fourth guideline (passed on July 25, 1978) is intended to harmonize the regulations concerning annual financial statements, including the regulations concerning the valuation of the assets and the background report, as well as the audit and disclosure for AG, KGaA, and GmbH (with the exception of insurance companies and credit institutions in the member nations of the community). In addition to the continued development of regulations concerning the presentation of accounts, its significance lies primarily in the inclusion of GmbH in the conditions applicable to stock law (though there is a limited disclosure obligation for smaller companies). The companies must apply the amended national regulations by February 1, 1982, at the latest. The obligatory audit for GmbH must be introduced by August 1, 1985.[15]

The explanation above is brief and to the point. Moreover, as I have already mentioned, as a result of the revision made in July 1980, the minimum amount of capital for limited companies in the Federal Republic of Germany was raised to DM 50,000. Article 12 of the Law Amending the Law Concerning GmbH (Limited Companies) also establishes "a period of delay" as a transitional condition. This law established a provision under which those limited responsibility companies who fail to make their lowest amount of capital up to DM 50,000 not later than December 31, 1985, or those limited responsibility companies who do not decide on the change of their respective organizations by December 31, 1985—these companies will be forcibly disorganized. This is the same as in the case of the Stock Law, and both of these laws, it seems to me, are revisions that display an enormous amount of farsightedness and courage.

In regard to the number of employees a limited responsibility company can have at the time it is established, Article 8 of Japan's Limited Responsibility Company Law has provided only the upper limit of the number of company employees by prescribing that "the total number of company employees should not be in excess of fifty persons"; the lowest number, however, has not been provided for. In the Federal Republic of Germany, however, Article 1 of the Law Regarding GmbH Exempt Limited Companies, which was revised in July 1980, prescribes that a company can be established by one or more persons. Thus, the lower limit for the number of company employees can be one person and the greatest number of company employees is not provided for. This is indeed a noteworthy revision.

On the subject of the contents of the Fourth EC Guideline, *Gabler's Business Dictionary* states as follows:

While basically strongly oriented toward German Stock Law, it has, however, significant innovations. a) National legal options: The fourth guideline contains numerous legal options (a total of forty-one) for member states, some of which will be included in the legislation of the Federal Republic. The most important options: (1) organization (grouping) for the balance sheet account form and/or report form permitted similarly for profit and loss statement in which case each form may be kept on the basis of an overall cost methods and/or a turnover cost method (four variations); (2) valuation legal options above all concerning valuations of intangible assets. Activation of "expenditures for the establishment and expansion of the company" and of "research and development expenses," which are to be depreciated within five years and during this time are subject to a distribution ban, unless the reserve available is at least as high as the portion of these expenditures that has not yet been written off. Activation of such intangible assets that have been built by the company itself. On the passive side, permissibility of expenditure dedications; (3) assessment: member nations many permit deviation from the principle of acquisition value until a later coordination. That is, certain positions (e.g., those on the basis of replacement value) may be balanced. The difference between purchase and replacement cost must be allocated to a special revaluation reserve, whose use is carefully regulated.

Article 157 of the Stock Law in the Federal Republic of Germany is different from the Fourth EC Guideline in that the former has specified the form of a statement of profit and loss as a report. Paragraph 4 of Article 153 of the Stock Law also prescribes that "the expenditure for the establishment and raising of capital may not be used as assets," which is clearly opposed to the Fourth EC Guideline provisions.

On the subject of the obligatory regulations of the Fourth EC Guideline, *Gabler's Business Dictionary* states that "among the most important innovations which must be taken into account in application of German law one notes especially the following," and, as the first item, it states:

(1) In addition to the balance sheet and the profit and loss statement, the annual financial report consists of an appendix, which is of equal importance to the other components and which can include data concerning the balance sheet and the profit and loss statement. In addition, it contains supplementary information, for example, the total amount of financial obligations, or the grouping of the sales by sphere of activity and geographically determined markets.

On the subject of the contents of the company report, Article 160 of the Stock Law has detailed provisions, which have been classified into five items. Item 4 prescribes in its first sentence that "the report must conform to the principles of a conscientious and accurate account." Item 4 does not demand, however, the annexing of a supplementary statement, including the grouping of the sales by sphere of activity and geographically determined markets, as the Fourth EC Guideline does. In my opinion, the current progress in regard to demanding the opening of accounting information to the public should be taken into consideration.

The second of the Fourth EC Guideline's obligatory regulations states: "The annual financial statement is supplemented by the situation (background) report, above all, concerning the future foreseeable development of the company and the area of research and development." Paragraph 2 of Article 160 of the Stock Law uses the expression "as certain a view as possible," however, this expression remains a "modifier" to the essential factor that "the valuation and write-off methods are to be specified as completely as. . . ." At this point, I became aware that as a medium for the formation of the Fourth EC Guideline, the philosophy of the German Stock Law and that of the "true and fair view"—which seems to constitute the very nucleus of Anglo-Saxon accounting thought—have collided with each other, have been compounded, and, finally, have reached a compromise.

The third obligatory regulation provides:

The Fourth Guideline refers as well to the principles of regular balancing, but it moreover also requires the annual financial report to give a picture of the state of the property, finances, and profits of the company that matches the actual circumstances [oriented toward the Anglo-Saxon concept of . . .]. In addition to observing the principle of continuity and indicating figures from the previous year, the balance sheet requires a stronger grouping of obligations and accounts receivable according to their deadlines; the profit and loss statement requires the special identification of unusual experiences and unusual profits; taxes on the yields of the normal conduct of business are to be reported separately from taxes on unusual yields.

Concerning "a liability that is not evident from the annual balance statement, including the registration of securities for their own obligations," which has been provided for in No. 7 of Paragraph 3 of Article 160 of the Stock Law, the protective clause has been established by Paragraph 4 of Article 160 of the Stock Law, which provides that "according to reasonable business judgment," failure in stating its details will be allowed. Such articles may be philosophically contradictory to the Fourth EC Guideline.

Lastly, the fourth obligatory regulation, the original text of which appears in *Gabler's Business Dictionary*, is as follows:

The Fourth Guideline places the most important principles of regular balancing of accounts before the valuation regulations. In particular, as regards the corporation law especially, the following modification: the lower included value on the delivery date may now only be applied for investments and shares. In the case of capital (fixed) assets and liquid assets, a lower appraisal may no longer be retained after the reasons no longer exist (offer of restitution of value, compulsory value adjustment, elimination of the option of retention).

Gabler's Business Dictionary's summarized introduction of the Fourth Guideline of the European Communities ends here. In regard to perusing the full text (sixty-two articles) of this Fourth EC Guideline, it seems to me that this summarized introduction is correct, brief, and to the point. Although *Gabler's Business Dictionary* does not touch on the following points, I think further attention should be paid to:

Paragraph 5 of Article 33 of the Fourth EC Guideline has given a right of proposal for the revision of the directed provisions of this guideline, which should be made within seven years after the notice of the Fourth EC Guideline to the committee.

Paragraphs 1 and 2 of Article 55 have established, for each of the member nations, various time limits for the legalization of the directive. Paragraph 3 of Article 55, especially, has imposed on each member nation an obligation to inform the draft at the time when this directive is to be legalized. Furthermore, Paragraph 1 (b) of Article 51 has imposed an obligation on an auditor, regarding "audit," to confirm the consistency between an annual statement of accounts and the accounting made within a business year, and so forth.

According to the August 14, 1978, issue of the *Official Journal of the European Communities*, the English version of Paragraph 1 (b) of Article 51 is as follows: "The person or persons responsible for auditing the accounts must also verify that the annual report is consistent with the annual accounts for the same financial year." The German version of this is: "Die mit der Absehluβprüfung beauftragte Person hat auch zu prüfen, ob der Lagebericht mit dem Jahresabschluβ des betreffenden Geschäftsjahres in Einklang steht." I must admit at this point that I feel there is a delicate difference between the two versions. I take responsibility for translating throughout this work, but I must confess to a feeling of uneasiness elsewhere as well.

"A True and Fair View" Is a Mistranslation

At any rate, the expression "a true and fair view" is found six times in this Fourth EC Guideline. The term "a true and fair view" was originally and widely known as the one that originated in the British Companies Act of 1948. Paragraph 1 of Article 149 of the Companies Act of 1948 prescribes that all balance sheets shall provide "a true and fair view" regarding "the state of affairs of the company" as of the end of the fiscal year. It also prescribes that all the "statements of profit and loss" provide "a true and fair view" concerning the profit and loss of the company in that fiscal year. Thus, the same expression is used twice in one article. In regard to the essential elements for providing "a true and fair view," in Paragraph 2 of the Companies Act of 1948 the detailed regulations were transferred to the "Eighth Schedule." This "Eighth Schedule" became the "Second Schedule" in the Companies Act of 1967, and this state has been extended up to the present. The "Second Schedule" extends from Part I to Part III, and there are thirty-one articles in all.

The contents of the "Second Schedule" are so extremely detailed that there is all the difference in the world between the "Second Schedule" and the Calculation Regulations of Japan's Commercial Code. For example, under the heading "General Provisions as to the Balance Sheet and Profit and Loss Accounting," Part I of the "Second Schedule" prescribes in detail regarding the indication of each item, the condition of its application, and so forth. The contents of Part I are so full that they surpass the articles of the German Commercial Code and the Stock Law in the Federal Republic of Germany. Hitherto in Japan, the expression "a true and fair view" has been translated into Japanese as "Shinjutsu katsu koseina gaikan." As a matter of convenience, I have sometimes succumbed to following the Japanese custom of "equivalent words" in translation. In order to translate the above-mentioned English phrase more correctly into Japanese, however, it should be translated as "Shinjitsu-katsu-koseina-byosha" ("the field of vision" or "visibility"), or "Shinjitsu-katsu-koseina-kenshiki" ("insight," "farsightedness"). On page 737 of Volume I of Palmer's *Company Law*, the following appears: "Thus 'a true and fair view' is a criterion of a higher order than both the requirements of standard accounting practice and the specific requirements of the Companies Act." ("Shikarugayueni-shinjitsu-katsu-koseina-byosha-[kenshiki] narumono-wa-hyojuntekina-kaikei-jitsusen-no-shoyoken-ya-shokaishahojyo-no-tokuteiyoken-no-rosha-yorimo-kojigen-no-handankijun-nanode-aru.")

Since 1971, this particular proposition has been handled by the Accounting Standards Steering Committee, which was formed by five groups related to accounting in England. This committee has taken charge of developing some practical standards of accounting. The members of this committee once admitted that deviations from average accounting practice standards may, in some cases, be consistent with "a true and fair field of vision (farsightedness)," and adhering to average accounting practice standards may actually be injurious to "a true and fair field of vision (farsightedness)." A look at the 1975 edition of *Recommendations on Accounting Principles*, issued by the Institute of Chartered Accountants in England and Wales, may help us understand this paradox. The *Recommendations on Accounting Principles* has touched on the concept of "a true and fair view" in five passages, from pages 77 to 86, and at the end of the first paragraph on page 77, it states that "the need to give a true and fair view is the overriding consideration applicable in all circumstances." I feel that an oversight of the high dimension of this statement may have produced the term "Shinjitsu-katsu-koseina-gaikan" ("the external outline"), which has been the practical "translated term" in this country. I have a proper understanding of the Japanese word "gaikan" as having the meaning "general" and "the outline of a way of looking at things."

The Special Character of the Fourth EC Guideline

Because accounting thought on the European Continent could not but acknowledge this character of a high dimension, Heinrich H. Jonas, in his book *The EC Balance Sheet Guidelines* (1980), might have had to make a statement, especially in his Introduction, that the Fourth EC Guideline is a compromise.[16]

Above all, what is particularly important in Chapter 8 of the Fourth EC Guideline, "Contents of the Notes on the Accounts—Contents of the Appendix," may be the provisions which stipulate that particular consideration should be paid to the protection of an obligee, calling for the indication of "the total amount of any financial commitments that are not included in the balance sheet," which is provided for by Paragraph 7 of Article 43. Another important provision is that of Article 46, Chapter 9 of the Fourth EC Guideline in regard to future estimates, "Contents of the Annual Report—Contents of the Situation Report." Paragraph 1 of Article 46 prescribes as follows: "The annual report must include at least a fair review of the development of the company's business and of its position." And Paragraph 2 states: "The report shall also give an indication of: a) any important events that have occurred since the end of the fiscal year; b) the company's likely future development; c) its activities in the field of research and development; and d) information concerning acquisitions of its own shares prescribed by Article 22 (2) of Directive 77/91/EEC." It seems to me that requirements (a) (b) and (c) in Paragraph 2 are the provisions that introduce, straightforwardly, the thought of "a true and fair field of vision (farsightedness)."

In his *EC Balance Sheet Guidelines* (pages 300 through 306), Heinrich H. Jonas has included a detailed list of comparisons under the heading "A Comparison of the Principles of Valuation According to the Fourth EC Guideline and Corporate Commercial Law." Especially in connection with "the principles of regular bookkeeping," he lists twenty-one items and discusses the presence of a relationship of adaptation to the provisions of the Fourth EC Guideline.

He states, for example, that the provision that fixed assets should be appraised either by purchase price or by cost of production, "which is prescribed in Paragraph 1 of Article 35 of the Fourth EC Guideline, has been adapted to the principles of regular bookkeeping," and the adoption of the "Equity-Method," which is prescribed by Article 59 of the Fourth EC Guideline, is not approved by the "principles of regular bookkeeping," and so forth. There is no point at present (July 1981) in translating the entire list of comparisons, introduce it here, and discuss it in detail. On February 5, 1980, a draft of revisions of many articles of *RefEHGB*, *RefEAktG*, and *RefEGmbHG* was completed and it may already have been made public by the Federal Ministry of Justice in the Federal Republic of Germany.

The Drafts of the Various Laws to Be Revised

An article entitled "A Statement on the Preliminary Draft of the Balance Sheet Guideline Law of February 5, 1980," written by the Commission on Accounting of the Association of University Instructors of Business Administration, appeared on pages 589 through 597 of the December 4, 1980, issue of the magazine *Business Administration*. This magazine is published by C. E. Poeschel Verlag in Stuttgart and its editors are six renowned university professors, headed by Dr. Klaus Chmielewicz, Ruhr-Universität Bochum; its editorial committee is composed of twelve scholars. In that article it is reported that an authoritative "principles of regular bookkeeping" commission has already been established and has already presented various recommendations. The point at issue has been narrowed down to about seventy items. The bills that have been made public by the Federal Ministry of Justice are extremely diversified and lengthy, contrary to previous expectations; the bill to revise the Commercial Code *(RefEHGB)*, for example, is comprised of a hundred articles. I must, therefore, omit entirely a discussion of this statement itself.

Hans Havermann of Düsseldorf, former president of the Institute of Certified Public Accountants in Germany, contributed an article, "The Preliminary Draft of the Transformation Law to the EC Guidelines Is Ready," to the April 1, 1980, issue of *Business Auditing*, which is published by the Institute. In this article, he provides an outline of the bills and his opinion on several fundamental problems and points out that the scope of the revised bills is so massive that they exceed our previous expectations. For example, what Article 1 of the Fourth EC Guideline formerly regulated in the Federal Republic of Germany was limited to a "joint-stock company," a "joint-stock limited partnership," and a "limited company." The revised bills, made public by the Federal Ministry of Justice, include in addition to these three kinds of "business entity" commercial corporations and companies,[17] the enterprises of public bodies, registered cooperatives, enterprises that are obligated to present accounts under the disclosure law,[18] banks and insurance companies, and other companies.

The Federal Ministry of Justice in the Federal Republic of Germany, under instruction of the Fourth EC Guideline, actually announced the draft of the revision of the laws under which all enterprises in the Federal Republic of Germany should be subjected to restriction by law. The magazine *Business Administration* published a special issue on the Fourth EC Guidelines in March 1979, in which recommendations for reform of the presentation of accounts under commercial law were made public in the name of the Commission on Accounting of the Association of University Instructors of Business Administration. At the beginning of this special issue, the commission stated: "The reform of the presentation of accounts under commercial law represents a central problem of the study of business administration."

It is reasonable for professors in business economics to make such a statement, which is full of fighting spirit and excitement. If it were the objective truth, however, how would these professors explain the fact that in none of the three volumes—1570 pages in all—of the important work *Basics of the Study of Business Administration*, by Erich Gutenberg, professor of business administration at the University of Cologne, is there a discussion of the presentation of accounts. Would these professors tacitly maintain that Dr. Gutenburg is not a scholar in business economics in the true sense of the word. At the beginning (page 2) of this recommendation for reform made by the Association of University Instruc-

The Problems of the Fourth EC Guideline   217

tors of Business Administration, it is stated that "the most important recommendations for reform may be summarized in the following theses."

In the first half of the first proposal, it is stated that "today's presentation of accounts, diversified by type of law, should be replaced by a uniform law for the rendering of accounts under commercial law, at least for large companies. This law would supersede the relevant regulations from the *HGB, GmbHG, GenG, PublG,* and *AktG.*" As stated earlier, the first item that had been designated as the most important proposal for revision was denied by the Federal Ministry of Justice. It was divided into *RefEHGB, RefEAktG, RefEGmbHG,* and so forth, and it was finally made public as laws with an enormous number of provisions. Concerning the recommendation of revision made by the Association of University Instructors of Business Administration, most of this proposal has been translated and introduced to Japan by Professor Yasuo Morikawa of Meiji University. I will therefore refrain from further unnecessary discussion of this matter.

The above-mentioned "uniform law for the presentation of accounts under commercial law" had been demanded not only by the Commission on Accounting of the Association of University Instructors of Business Administration, but it was also mentioned as "the formulation of the amendment law," on page 2 of the Introduction of a book entitled *Presentation of Accounts under the New Law* (1980), a work of more than 400 pages. This book was compiled from the *Symposion* and the *Referate und Diskussionen* of the Fourth and Seventh Guidelines that even the Schmalenbach Association participated in, and the work was compiled by Dr. H. C. Marcus Bierich, Dr. Walther Busse von Colbe, Dr. Gert Laβ-mann, and Dr. Marcus Lutter. Although the term is different, scholars on the front line in business economics, it would seen, were also thinking of how to cope with the Fourth EC Guideline.

The Fourth EC Guideline and the Principles of Regular Bookkeeping

As stated in the preamble of the Fourth EC Guideline, almost all of this directive is related to "the coordination of national provisions concerning the presentation and content of annual accounts and annual reports." As a consequence, it may safely be assumed that almost all of the directive will be related to the "principles of regular bookkeeping."

It seems necessary at this point to touch briefly on the fact that the recommendations for revision regarding the law for the presentation of accounts under commercial law, which was made public in March 1979 by the Commission on Accounting of the Association of University Instructors of Business Administration, especially Section 4 of the recommendations for the formulation of the contents of the annual financial statement, have taken up Paragraph 2 of Article 2, Article 3, and Paragraph 1 of Article 31 of the Fourth EC Guideline as of particular concern in regard to the "principles of regular bookkeeping." First of all, Dr. Ulrich Leffson, in *The Principles of Regular Accounting* (5th ed., 1980; pages 143–444), explains each principle in turn, and they are numerous. In *Regularity of Bookkeeping Standards on Bookkeeping and Records* (7th ed., 1978), coauthored by Karl Peter, Kurt Joachim von Bonrhaupt, and Werner Körner, each principle is listed with its source in the law and then each is explained.

For example, the first to be discussed are the "principles of regular bookkeeping according to the bookkeeping guidelines of November 11, 1937," followed by the "general principles of regular bookkeeping according to the decisions of the tax courts," the "principles of regular bookkeeping according to *HGB*," the "principles of regular bookkeeping according to *AktG*," the "principles of regular bookkeeping according to Tax Code 77," the "principles of regular single-entry bookkeeping," the "principles of regular inventory," the principles of "regular cash bookkeeping in ABC form," the principles of "regular cash bookkeeping in current account bookkeeping in ABC form," and the principles of "regular bookkeeping for individual branches of professions and business." The principles of regular bookkeeping are thus far more numerous than the ten principles enumerated in Paragraph 4 of the "recommendations for reform" of the Commission on Accounting of the Association of University Instructors of Business Administration.

The primary objective of this commission was not an all-inclusive enumeration of the principles of regular bookkeeping. After its enumeration of the nucleus of the principles of regular bookkeeping in the Federal Republic of Germany, it stated that a balance must be struck between conformity to these principles and the one principle of "a true and fair view" prescribed by Article 149 of the Companies Act of 1948 in England. As a result, the commission declared that the articles of the Fourth EC Guideline should be followed. It may safely be said that this was an extremely important incident in conventional German accountancy.

Paragraph 1 of Article 2 of the Fourth EC Guideline prescribes that in annual reports, the balance sheet, the statement of profit and loss, and the "schedules," "shall constitute a composite whole." Paragraph 2 of this article prescribes that "they shall be drawn up clearly and in accordance with the provisions of this directive." Paragraph 3 states that "annual reports shall give a true and fair view (field of vision or farsightedness) of the company's assets, liabilities, financial position, and profit and loss."

The professors who served on this committee must have been impressed by the fact that parts of Article 149 of the Companies Act of 1948 in England were substantially and completely adopted just as they stood. Such being the case, in Section 2 of these "recommendations for reform," they state that "the annual statement of accounts should give "a picture consistent with the actual circumstances of the company's assets, financial affairs, and circumstances of profit and loss." They then made a proposal that was in accord with the *main object* of the above-mentioned Article 149. The main object of Article 149 is not necessarily understood by accounting scholars in Japan.[19] The "recommendations for reform" made by the Commission on Accounting of the Association of University Instructors of Business Administration, "Twenty-five Justifications for the Content of Annual Financial Statements" states: "In case of a conflict between the balancing regulations and a view of the actual circumstances regarding the property, finances, and profits of the company, the balancing that is more expressive of that specific firm takes precedence."[20]

This is not an original proposal by this committee of professors; it can be found on page 737 of Palmer's *Company Law*, which I quoted earlier. The central meaning of the expression "a true and fair view" is the following principle. In each individual circumstance, accountants are allowed to ignore laws and regulations, when, in accord with their own insight, field of vision, and discernment, it is necessary to do so in order to adopt a method of preparing a statement of accounts that is a superior presentation.

The Seventh EC Guideline

Finally, *Gabler's Business Dictionary* gives the following description of the Seventh EC Guideline:

The outline (published in 1976) regulates the establishment of statements of account of conglomerates and supplements the Fourth EC Guideline, which applies exclusively to the individual balance sheet. The Seventh EC Guideline requires that multinational groups establish a consolidated statement of accounts that includes all participants located in the territory of the community, even if they have their headquarters outside of the community.

The Seventh EC Guideline is comprised of twenty-six articles. *Gabler's Dictionary*'s description is brief and to the point.

I would like to call the reader's attention to the following: "GoB," the abbreviation of the German term, is usually translated into Japanese as "Sekino-bokino-gensoku" ("the principles of regular bookkeeping"). Article 38 of the existing (as of February 1, 1981) Commercial Code of the Federal Republic of Germany has a provision under the heading "Bookkeeping Obligations" for merchants that prescribes "Bucher zu fuhren . . . nach den Grundsatzen ordnungsmassiger Buchfuhrung" ("books are to be kept . . . according to regular bookkeeping principles"), from which the custom of translating this particular German term "GoB" into Japanese as "Sekino-bokino-gensoku" may have originated.

Paragraph 2a of Article 39 of the German Commercial Code, however, has a provision in regard to "A Statement of the Final Accounts," which prescribes "Das Verfahren muβ den Grundsätzen ordnungsmäβiger Buchführung entsprechen" ("the procedure must conform to the principles of regular bookkeeping"). It seems obvious, therefore, that "GoB" should not be understood as simply "making entries in an account book." Instead, this term also encompasses "the way to make a statement of final account." As Ulrich Leffson has stated: "Under German law, the rules for bookkeeping and balance sheets are designated the 'Principles of Regular Bookkeeping (GoB).' "[21] As the Seventh EC Guideline is comprised of regulations regarding the making of a statement of final account by a conglomerate, the full text of the twenty-six articles of the Seventh EC Guideline should be viewed as concerning the principles of regular bookkeeping.

Thus, the principles of regular bookkeeping as a legal standard continue to go through a process of expansion and progress. Earlier I wrote "a picture consistent with actual circumstances," but I now wish to rectify my use of the Japanese term "eizo" ("an image"), because "byosha" ("depiction") is a much better Japanese translation of the German term "Bild" ("picture"). I must add here, moreover, that it is a matter of common knowledge among international scholars of accounting that the authentic German version of the English term "true and fair view" should be equivalent to the German expression "a picture consistent with actual circumstances."[22]

I am familiar with the following articles in regard to the Fourth and the Seventh EC Guidelines, all of which were published in *Business Auditing*, the bulletin of the Institute of Chartered Accountants in Germany. Describing these articles and criticizing them here, however, will unnecessarily prolong this discussion. Thus I will only indicate the location of these reference materials for your information:

(1) Ulrich Leffson (Munster), "On the General Norm and Certification of the Preliminary Draft of a Balance Guideline Law, As Well As Notes Concerning Other Regulations," June 1, 1980, S. 289 ff.
(2) Wolf Müller (Frankfurt),"Amendment of the GmbH Law and Other Regulations of Commercial Law of January 1, 1981," Aug. 1, 1980, S. 369 ff.
(3) "Joint Statement of the Chamber of Certified Public Accountants and the Institute of Public Accountants Concerning the Preliminary Draft of a Balance Guideline Law," Sept. 15, 1980, S. 501 ff.
(4) Ulrich Leffson (Munster), "Business Audits and the University: A Symposium in Munster (Reports and Summary of the Dis-

cussion: The Influence of a Recognizable Risk of the Company on the Statements in the Auditor's Report and Certification," Dec. 1, 1980, S. 637 ff.
(5) Herbert Biener (Bonn), "Concerning the Transformation of the Fourth EC Guideline," Dec. 15, 1980, S. 689 ff.
(6) R. J. Niehus (Düsseldorf), " 'Materiality'—The Principle of Presentation of Accounts Also in German Commercial Law?" Jan. 1, 1981, S. 1 ff.
(7) Edgard Castan (Hamburg), "The Practice of Annual Financial Statement Disclosures," June 15, 1981, S. 337 ff.

Concerning Marlene Brown's View

As this chapter draws to a close, we must not overlook an article written by Marlene Brown that appeared on February 5, 1981, in issue no. 5528 of *The Accountant*, the journal of the Institute of Chartered Accountants in England and Wales. In "Dramatic Changes, The EC Fourth Guideline," Ms. Brown introduces the Fourth and Seventh EC Guidelines through an examination of the opinions of the directors of the nine big offices of accountants who represent the world. She concludes that these two EC guidelines have a potential impact through which dramatic changes may be brought about throughout the European Continent.

Due to space limitations, it would be difficult to introduce the full text of Ms. Brown's article here. Thus I will quote only what seems essential to her point of view. Above all else, she maintains that Europe is at present making rapid changes in a variety of directions. The Tokyo Resident Office of the EC provided me with the information that the number of EC directives (guidelines) issued each year totals about three thousand. From this number the scale and rapidity of the changes in Europe should be clear. Changes in the sphere of accounting are included in this number. Ms. Brown states:

The Fourth Guideline will directly affect the over one and a half million companies that are located within the European Economic Community. The Fourth Guideline does not accord with United Kingdom practice in all respects. It was perhaps unrealistic to expect member states to be able to bring into law the significant changes required by the Fourth

Guideline within two years of its adoption. Germany has issued a preliminary draft for comment, but reactions have been largely adverse and certain delays are likely. Such being the reason, one of the biggest problems of the Fourth Guideline is that there are a number of options and, if the different countries legislate for some of the options in different ways, the result will be disharmony. Such a rigid framework would not have been acceptable at this stage when there are so many differences in the legal and accounting requirements of member states. Harmonization is not an instant process; it requires a gradual, step-by-step approach.

She adds that "the Fourth Guideline took ten years from its inception to its adoption," but "to suggest amendments is a good practice."

Ms. Brown further states as follows: "In trying to legislate for countries that are as far apart as the United Kingdom and Germany—witness the pragmatic legal system of the British as opposed to Germany's prescriptive legal system (the British system being flexible law backed up with private sector regulations, like accounting standards)—it is very difficult to bring all these into a cohesive document." In regard to the Seventh Guideline, she quotes Mr. Martin Clayton of Price Waterhouse that "it is true that the Seventh Guideline is much more politically sensitive than the Fourth." When Mr. Clayton says "much more politically sensitive," I wonder whether he actually means to imply a strong instability.

Marlene Brown goes on to say that "the Fourth Guideline will undoubtedly get through the United Kingdom's Parliament." In quoting the comments of George Eccles of Deloitte, Haskins, and Sells, Marlene Brown offers the criticism that "one of the deficiencies of the Fourth Guideline is that people are put under tremendous pressure and are dragged one way in trying to comply and another in trying to agree with the fiscal authorities." Ms. Brown deplores that "as an actual problem," most Continental countries, unfortunately, prepare accounts for the taxman.

It seems to me, however, that this lamentation is also Japan's at present. I hope that we Japanese see clearly that the members of the National Diet in Japan are the persons who are responsible for the formation of society through legislative action in Japan. I feel keenly that there are extremely few National Diet members who are aware of this particular problem and that this is Japan's misfortune.

To return to our main subject, Ms. Brown argues by borrowing the opinions of Mr. Andrew Brown of the Ernst and Whinny Accounting Firm:

> One of the major problems is how member states will define "a true and fair view." Touching on the core of the concept of accounting in the Fourth Guideline, he [Andrew Brown] states with a worried air that "if the true and fair view is going to come out in countries such as France and Germany as meaning 'compliance with law' and the countries concerned take up different opinions in different ways, the law will be different from one country to another." This is indeed a pity, because the basic philosophy of "a true and fair view" is much wider than "compliance with law."

It is my opinion, however, that this statement is in error and is due to Ms. Brown's overanxiousness about this particular problem. The proposition was made public earlier by the Commission on Accounting of the Association of University Instructors of Business Administration in the Federal Republic of Germany, and in regard to the principle of "a true and fair view," their statement was identical with what appeared in Volume I of Palmer's *Company Law* in England, as if the commission had copied the original text of this particular debate. At present (August 1981), the legislative bill has not been approved yet in the Federal Republic of Germany, so that it is still unknown how this proposition will be specified in the law. I feel, however, that at least the constitutents of this German Association of University Instructors of Business Administration, who have social influence in one way or another, are not unenlightened.

At the end of her article, in quoting the statement of Mr. Marcel Asselberghs of the Arthur Andersen Office, Marlene Brown states that "in certain countries like Italy, Belgium, and Luxembourg, we are coming out of the Middle Ages!" It is not clear whether she is referring to backwardness in the sphere of accounting or to the tendency to dogmatism in the Middle Ages. Much should be made of the fact that Belgium was the first state among the member states of the EC that enforced the legalization of the Fourth Guideline.

Despite Article 32 of the Fourth Guideline, which clarifies as a valuation principle "acquisition cost theory" or "cost of production theory," Article 33 of the same guideline approves the selection by member states of "valuation by the replacement value method" or another valuation method rather than a valuation method that approves inflationary accounting and the revaluation of "tangible fixed assets" or "financial tangible property," on the condition that the member states concerned prescribe its contents, limit, and applicable regulation by law. Marlene Brown discloses the internal affairs of the progress of establishing the guideline with her statement: "Germany refused absolutely and fought against Article 33, which permitted member states to legislate for inflation-adjusted information to be presented." She concludes her article with the following words: "The battle to permit member states to present current cost information is in effect only an addendum."

The Fourth and Seventh Guidelines, which originated from the Treaty for the Establishment of the European Community and have numerous provisions totaling 248 articles, are based on Article 54, Paragraph 3 (g) of this treaty. As Title 3, Chapter 2 expresses clearly, these two guidelines belong to the category of "the right of establishment," and, I feel, these two guidelines are aimed at settling, through legislation and on a consolidated basis, the conduct in regard to company accounting of each of the member states, which objective will be attended by hardship.

Notes

1. *Gabler's Business Dictionary* (10th ed., 1979), Vol. 1, p. 1118.
2. *Inflation Accounting*, Report of the Inflation Accounting Committee, Chairman F. E. P. Sandilands, Esq., CBE, presented to Parliament by the Chancellor of the Exchequer and the Secretary of State for Trade by Command of Her Majesty, September 1975, p. 230.
3. This means "legislative action."
4. Ibid., p. 7.
5. Companies Act of 1980 (London: Her Majesty's Stationary Office), p. 10.
6. With an exchange rate of 500 yen to a pound, this 50,000 pounds becomes 25,000,000 yen. Refer to the Companies Act of 1980, Sec. 85.

7. This is the abbreviation of "the law enacted on August 21, 1948, concerning a balance sheet of starting a business indicated by German marks, and the law regarding the determination of new capital."

8. *New Edition of the Company Law*, published on February 10, 1981, 1st ed., p. 25.

9. The first edition was published on April 20, 1981, compiled by Masao Takashima, *Basic Lecture on Jurisprudence, the Commercial Code II (The Company Law)* (Hogakushoin ed.), p. 44.

10. Hans Kelsen, *Reine Rechtslehre*, trans. Kisaburo Yokota (Iwanami Shoten ed., 1973), p. 32.

11. Heinrich H. Jonas, *Die EG-Bilanzrichtlinie Grundlagen und Anwendung in der Praxis* (Rudolf Haufe Verlag, 1980), S. 275.

12. Article 3 of the Law Regarding an Exception of the Commercial Code Regarding Auditing of Joint-Stock Companies, etc.

13. Sir Francis Palmer, *Company Law*, 22d ed., England, Vol. 1, p. 762.

14. Lee J. Seidler and D. R. Carmichael, *Accountants' Handbook*, 6th ed., 1981, Vol. 1, pp. 5–13.

15. *Gabler's Business Dictionary*, Vol. II, p. 1987.

16. See p. 3.

17. In accordance with Paragraph 1 (1) of the Corporation Tax Law of 1980 in the Federal Republic of Germany, in addition to these three kinds of business entities—"a joint-stock company," "a joint-stock limited partnership," and "a limited company"—this may indicate such companies as colonial companies and unions under mining law.

18. "Publizitätsgesetz" (Disclosure Law) is an abbreviation; the official name of this law is "Gesetz über die Rechnungslegung von bestimmten Unternehmen und Konzernen" (Law Concerning the Representation of Accounts by Certain Companies and Conglomerates). It is comprised of only twenty-five articles, Article 1 of which, as of February 1, 1981, under the heading "Enterprises Obligated to Present Accounts," states in Paragraph 1: "According to this paragraph, an enterprise must present (render) accounts, if at least two of the three following characteristics apply for the last day of the fiscal year (closing/delivery date) and for the two following closing dates." However eager the people of the Federal Republic of Germany may have been for legislation after World War II, from the standpoint of the Japanese, there is no escaping our feeling of some complicatedness in this matter, even if we understand the following prescriptions of the German laws as the difference of a principle on the limitation of the scope of "bookkeeping obligation," such as is shown below.

Article 141 of the Tax Code has fixed by law the scope of taxpayers who have the obligation to keep books. Article 44 of *HGB* has prescribed the bookkeeping obligation of a merchant in conjunction with its Article 38. Article 5 of the Income Tax Law has equally fixed by law the bookkeeping obligation.

Furthermore, Article 1 of the Disclosure Law has prescribed the obligation to keep books in this way. The first of the three characteristics is: The balance sheet total of the annual balance sheet produced on the delivery/closing date exceeds DM 125,000,000. The second characteristic is as follows: The gross profit on sales of the company in the twelve months prior to the closing date exceeds DM 250,000,000. The third characteristic is: The company has employed on the average more than five thousand employees in the twelve months prior to the closing date.

It follows, therefore, that an enterprise to which two of the above three characteristics apply is an undertaking that is under the obligation to have its accounting records prepared, according to the Law Concerning the Presentation of Accounts by Certain Companies and Conglomerates. These enterprises include even banks and insurance companies and other companies.

19. Accounting Research Section, Kobe University, *Accountancy Dictionary*, 3d ed., p. 677; Chuo-Keizaisha, *Accounting Handbooks*, latest ed., Dec. 1976, p. 829.

20. See Paragraph 3 (Paragraph 3 in this instance indicates Paragraph 3 of Article 2 of the Fourth EC Guideline).

21. *Handwörterbuch der Betriebswirtschaft*, Vierte Auflage, p. 1011.

22. Union Européenne des Experts Comptables, Economiques et Financiers (U.E.C.), *International Accounting Lexicon*, Special ed., 1980, p. 111.

15

Problems Relating to Union Européene des Experts Comptables, Economiques et Financiers (U.E.C.)

Derrick Owles's View and Criticism

A special issue, dated April 3, 1980, of *The Accountant*, the journal for professional accountants in the United Kingdom, is entitled "Annual Review 1979–80." The issue carries an article entitled "Foreign Affairs—International Harmonization" by Derrick Owles, a visiting fellow at the City University Business School. He writes: "The development of standards, national and international, is a comparatively recent activity in the accounting world. Before the 1939–45 war, there was nothing done even on a national scale, and it was only in the aftermath of the war that national standards were developed, but with no idea of any international cooperation."

It is my contention, however, that this conclusion is incorrect. As I indicated earlier, before World War II the United Kingdom and many other countries had no prescribed nationwide standards of their own in regard to accounting. In the Federal Republic of Germany, however, Article 162 of the Imperial Tax Code, which was enacted in 1919, had created detailed accounting standards under the heading "Obligations of Taxpayers and Other Persons." Moreover, when Article 29 *(EStR 29)* was enacted in 1937, a more detailed nationwide standard of accounting went into effect.

In the United States, moreover, before the end of World War II, there were already in effect a number of detailed, nationwide standards in regard to title of account, books of account, accounting, vouchers, and the form and contents of financial statements. The Securities Act (1933), the Securities and Exchange Act (1934), the Holding Company Act (1935), and—based on these acts— Rules 250.27 and 250.28 had been formulated by the Securities and Exchange Commission (SEC). Moreover, Regulation S-X of the Investment Company Act (1940), Accounting Series Release No. 4 (1938), and others were established by the SEC. Thus it is clear that Owles's statement that "there was nothing done even on a national scale" contradicts the facts.

Owles further states that "it was not until 1966 that any steps were taken toward international uniformity." This statement is also in error. Four years prior to 1966, that is, in September 1962, the Eighth International Congress of Public Accountants was held in New York City. Its general assembly took place at the Waldorf-Astoria Hotel, and it was attended by nearly four thousand persons. At this general meeting, to the best my memory, the chief delegate from Holland, speaking from the central rostrum, suggested to all the delegates that there was a pressing need for mapping out internationally unified accounting and auditing standards. I heard this timely proposition from one of the front seats on the second floor of the assembly hall.

Subsequently, in 1966, a conference was held by the three delegations from the United Kingdom, the United States, and Canada, and the Accountants International Study Group was created. In 1972, when the Tenth International Congress of Accountants was held in Sydney, Australia, the representatives of the Accountants International Study Group sent a request for official participation in this meeting to Australia, France, Germany, Japan, Holland, Mexico, and several others. Thus it was that the International Accounting Standards Committee was organized. The first participating groups represented a total of sixteen countries, and its inaugural meeting was held in June 1973.

This newly created International Accounting Standards Committee (IASC) unfortunately had no authority to sanction its constituents, and it also failed to obtain the official participation of the Financial Accounting Standards Board (FASB) of the American Institute of Certified Public Accountants (AICPA). Its problems, however, did not stop there. The IASC's independence was also threatened by the creation of the International Federation of Accountants (IFAC), which was organized in October 1977 in Munich. Sixty-three nations joined this federation.

The IFAC was organized at the Eleventh International Congress of Accountants. It was formed, not as a "standard-setting body," but as "a forum," through which those accountants who have assembled from the four corners of the world can meet and take action. One of the functions of the IFAC is, in fact, to organize various kinds of meetings, and it immediately planned the programs it wanted to hold during the next five years. According to Dr. Owles, the IFAC "is to issue guidelines and a code of ethics, develop programs for training accountants, and report on management accounting techniques."

Owles further points out that at the time of the Sydney International Congress in 1972, the International Coordinating Committee for the Accounting Profession was organized, and that it was through this group that the IFAC came into being in 1977. He also indicates that the IASC was a forerunner of the IFAC, a step in the right direction. He shows that the IASC and the IFAC have mutually independent but closely related spheres of influence, and that when a member of the IASC is also a member of the IFAC, there is a question of whether or not there is any room for the coexistence of these two international organizations whose missions cover the same sphere of influence.

Dr. Owles also asserts that care should be taken that all the members of the international organizations are merely bodies of accountants, and not the governments of the countries, and he points out that in many instances, governments have the right to speak in regard to accounting standards. In the case of the United Kingdom, for instance, he maintains it is the Department of Trade. In France, the Plan Comptable General is under the direct control of the Conseil National de la Comptabilité, and only 15 percent of this Conseil is the responsibility of the Ordre National des Experts Comptable et des Comptables Agrées. In Sweden, the United Kingdom, and Belgium, accounting is subject to those countries' respective legislative organs. He states that "these examples show the difficulties in the way of effective international coordination."

When Owles mentions that the FASB in the United States does not participate in any way in the IASC, he writes that the "FASB is supposed to be the standard-setting authority for the United States." Such an understanding has generally been entertained and many Japanese accounting scholars hold the same opinion. We should be aware, however, of the scholar Homer Kripke, who is currently a professor on the faculty of law at New York University and has been concerned for more than forty-five years with the security administration of the United States government. Indicating that various decisions made by the SEC have been "supercomplicated and overregulation" to those who are not experts, he has publicly questioned the SEC's actions: "By what authority did the SEC franchise its own statutory responsibility to the FASB to make these decisions?" We should remember this scholar's work.[1]

Dr. Owles also states that the United Nations is concerned about accounting and that in May 1978, it organized the Commission of Transnational Corporations, to be headquartered in New York City and operate under the mandate of preparing financial report and accounting standards for multinational corporations. He states that it has been agreed that this commission is to be composed of thirty-four members under the direct control of the United Nations Economic and Social Council. No definite understanding on this matter, however, has been reached so far, particularly in regard to the number of committeemen from each of the constituent states. Recognizing the present state of affairs, Owles clarifies his position saying: "Thus, there are signs that the gulf between developed and developing countries will hinder even the preparation of accounting standards. Any standards that are established will, moreover, be voluntary since the United Nations has no power to order compliance."

Owles refers next to the Fourth EC Guideline and the Seventh EC Guideline. As I have already discussed these guidelines, I will not report Owles's comments. Writing about the Organization for Economic Cooperation and Development (OECD), he states that in 1963 the OECD announced the OECD Draft Double Taxation

Convention and that, in 1976, it published *Guidelines for Multinational Enterprises*. He goes on to say that, in 1978, the OECD established a working committee whose mission it is to study accounting standards and that it circulated a questionnaire regarding accounting practices in the member states. After touching on trends in accounting offices throughout the world, he states that "in the United Kingdom and the United States, the need for continuing professional education after qualification is seen to be part of the price that must be paid for public recognition of the accountant." He writes that "in the future, emphasis will be transferred to professional education after qualification has been obtained." He concludes with an optimistic view that in the 1980s, in the sphere of accounting in particular, many activities, especially international collaboration, will be advanced, and that in twenty years or so, there will be an increase of national pressure directed at accountants.

Just before touching on the subject of the Fourth and the Seventh EC Guidelines, Owles argues the very essence of this chapter.

Concerning the Organization and Achievements of the U.E.C.

Derrick Owles, however, does not touch on when the Union Européene des Experts Comptables, Economiques et Financiers (U.E.C.) was organized. It is said that the U.E.C. was organized at the insistence of Paul Caujolle in France in 1951.[2] As a consequence, its headquarters are located in Paris. The U.E.C. was organized when groups of free professional experts and qualified specialists, representing eleven nations, took part in a meeting. By 1973, the U.E.C. had increased to fifteen member nations. When the Seventh Conference of the U.E.C. met in October 1973, in addition to the affiliated organizations representing fifteen nations, two groups from two additional nations participated as corresponding members.

I must draw the reader's attention to two references. One is the minutes of the proceedings of the Sixth Congress, which was held in Copenhagen, the capital of Denmark, in October 1969. It was published in Düsseldorf in 1970 by the Institute of Chartered Accountants in Germany. The other reference, also published by the

Problems Relating to Union 233

Institute of Chartered Accountants in Germany, is the proceedings of the Seventh Congress, which was held in Madrid, Spain, in 1973. The proceedings were published in 1978. In accordance with the proceedings of the Seventh Congress, the names of the participating groups, classified by country, are as follows:

Belgium: Collège National des Experts Comptables des Belgique, Institut des Réviseurs d'Enterprises.

Denmark: Foreningen of Statsautoriserede Revisor, F.S.R.

England and Wales: The Institute of Chartered Accountants in England and Wales; The Association of Certified Accountants.

Finland: K.H.T. Yhdistys Föreningen C.G.R.

Germany: Institute of Chartered Accountants in Germany, e.V.; Institute of Auditors in Berlin.

Iceland: Félag Löggiltra Endurskodenda.

Ireland: The Institute of Chartered Accountants in Ireland.

Italy: Consiglio Nationale dei Dottori Commercialisti, Federazione Nationale del Collegi dei Ragionieri.

Luxembourg: Ordre des Experts Comptables Luxembourgeois.[3]

The proceedings of each congress carries on its title page "A contribution of Experts Comptables to the development of the European economy." Thus, it is clear that it is professional accountants from each country represented who are making every effort to help the development of the European economy by working toward "regularity" through their deliberations on diverse accounting theories and practices. As the number of experts who attended the two congresses was about fifteen hundred for the Sixth Congress and about two thousand for the Seventh Congress, it can be said that these conferences were quite large.

The official languages to be used in meetings of the U.E.C. are limited to four: French, German, English, and Spanish. In the conference hall, simultaneous translations into these four languages are to be available to all the participants. As is often the case, the language problem seems a major obstacle. The U.E.C., therefore, has published a lexicon of accounting terms for the express purpose of facilitating the knowledge of how to express specific technical accounting terms in each language of the member states.

The books that are readily available to me are *Lexique U.E.C.* (1974) and the *International Accounting Lexicon* (1980). I am interested in the latter *Lexicon* for the following reason. This lexicon reports that based on Article 54 of the so-called Roman Treaty, which established the European Community and became effective in January 1958, the Fourth EC Guideline was issued in July 1978, in which the expression "a true and fair view," which constitutes an important accounting concept under British law, has been frequently referred to. Not only does the *International Accounting Lexicon* contain this phrase, it also indicates the official version of this phrase in the language of each member state, along with an explanation of it. It is indicated clearly in this *Lexicon* that the French version for this specific phrase is "image fidele," and the Danish version is "palideligt billede." The Italian version is "quadro fedele," while the German version is "ein den tatsächlichen Verhältnissen entsprechendes Bild" ("a picture consistent with the actual circumstances").

Earlier I touched on the German version of this British phrase. It is explained in English as:

a concept signifying that the presentation of financial information in the accounts is free from any bias that could be detrimental to the reader's understanding, that it conveys with acceptable accuracy what happened during the period concerned and how matters stood at the end of it, and that such presentation is appropriate to the business transactions it embraces. The concept of a true and fair view, which was introduced in the Fourth EC directive, has been translated in the other languages of the Community (Danish, French, German, Italian) as shown in the table below.

It seems noteworthy that more than ten years elapsed by the time the *International Accounting Lexicon* (Institute of Chartered Accountants in Germany, Düsseldorf, 1980), which was published by the U.E.C., could adopt the British accounting concept "true and fair view" and apply the German expression "a picture consistent with the actual circumstances" as the German translation to the above United Kingdom expression. Details of this matter in particular are sketched out in Dr. Lother Schruff's book *Presentation of Accounts and Audits of AG and GmbH under the New Law (Fourth EC Guideline)*, which was published in 1978 by the Institute of Chartered Accountants in Germany. In accordance with this book, it was on March 9, 1968, that the preliminary draft of the Fourth EC Guideline was first made public. Article 2 of this preliminary draft stated: "It (that is, the annual financial report) must conform to the principles of regular and dependable presentation of accounts." Article 2 was revised, however, according to the Recommendations for the Fourth EC Guideline, which were made public on November 16, 1971: "The annual financial report must conform to the principles of regular bookkeeping." And since then, in accordance with the Revised Recommendations for the Fourth EC Guideline of February 26, 1973, Article 2 was further modified to: "The annual financial report must give an accurate insight into the state of the company's property, finances, and profits." Since then, however, based on the Fourth EC Guideline, which was made public July 25, 1978, the expression in question was further modified to its present form.

In the first preliminary draft, this sentence was the second in the first paragraph of Article 2. In the second draft, however, it was moved to the second paragraph of Article 2. In the third draft, no change was made in regard to the location of the sentence, and, finally, in the fourth and last stage of confirming the full text of the Fourth Guideline, this sentence was transferred to the third paragraph of Article 2.

It seems to me that changing the arrangement of the provisions does not in itself have any significance. The essential point lies in whether the intrinsic nature of the financial report in a specified fiscal year is reviewed from the standpoint of securing strict "relevancy" to the given legal standards or from the stance that it can exceed the given legal standards under certain circumstances. For the past ten years German and British accounting thought have been in severe and continuous conflict. Anglo-Saxon accounting thought has now made a conquest of the European Continent, at least of those member states that are affiliated with the European Community (EC). This is a revolutionary change in European accounting at the end of the twentieth century.

Taking a look at page 1871 and beyond of the *Pocket Dictionary of Accounting* (2d ed.; Stuttgart: C. E. Poeschel Verlag, 1981), edited by H. C. Mult, Erich Kostol, Klaus Chmielewicz, and Marcell Schweitzer, we can find those revised bills mentioned above and others that were made public on May 18, 1981, by the Justice Ministry of the Federal Republic of Germany in compliance with the Fourth EC Guideline in 1978, for example, the revised bills for the Commercial Code, Stock Law, Limited Responsibility Company Law, *PublG*, and so forth. Based on the bills for revision, it is clear that the expression "a picture consistent with the actual circumstances," the German version of the British accounting concept "a true and fair view" in the *International Accounting Lexicon*, published by the U.E.C., is adopted correctly and with changes of not even one word in the above-mentioned revised bills. As far as the form is concerned, this expression is used, just as it is, twice in Paragraph 2 of Article 238, once in No. 2 of Paragraph 2 of Article 239, and once in Paragraph 1 of Article 277 in the German Commercial Code.

In the revised Stock Law, moreover, all of Article 149 was rewritten and the following expression appears: "In drawing up the annual financial statement and the situation report . . . the regulations of the Commercial Law Code . . . in the first and second sections of the third book concerning the annual report and situation report . . . are applicable." It is prescribed that all the articles of the Commercial Code shown above should be applied. This expression also appears in revised Article 42. By using the same phrasing as that used in the revised Stock Law, Paragraph 1 of the revised Article 42 prescribes that the above-mentioned articles of the Commercial Code should also be applied.

In the case of the *PublG*, more correctly speaking, the Law Concerning the Presentation of Accounts by Certain Companies and Conglomerates, Article 5 of this revised law is a fully revised version. Paragraph 5 of the proposed Article 5, by using the same phrasing as that in the revised Stock Law and the Limited Company Law, prescribes that the above-specified various provisions of articles of the Commercial Code should also be applied. Such being the case, the above-stated indication tells us that the stipulations for the preparation of a financial statement that took root before 1937 in the German Commercial Code have thus been changed on a large scale.

As long as the U.E.C. intends to promote "regularity" among the respective theories and practices of each member state affiliated with the U.E.C., and to promote it through the proceedings of congresses and other various publications, thereby making a contribution to the progress of the European economy, the U.E.C.'s problems, it is my belief, will be diverse. *Auditing the Annual Financial Report* (4th ed.) was produced by the Commission for Auditing Books of the U.E.C., headed by W. Dober. Its Appendix gives model sentences for standard auditing reports for each member state. Due to space limitations, I cannot enumerate here all the auditing reports. I will cite, therefore, only the four samples for the United Kingdom, Germany, France, and Switzerland.

I will begin with the United Kingdom. In regard to the "auditing report," there is a provision that states: "A standard auditing report for a limited company without subsidiaries is as follows: In our opinion the accounts set out on pages x to y give a true and fair view of the state of the company's affairs on 31 December 19 —and of its profit (loss) (results) for the year ended on that date and comply with the Companies Acts of 1948 and 1967." Please note that the exact term "a true and fair view" is used.

Auditing the Annual Financial Report, which was published by the Institute of Chartered Accountants in Germany and contained this standard auditing report, was published in January 1977. Thus it is impossible that the Company Act of 1977, which went into effect gradually during the period January 24, 1977, through October 1, 1977, and the Company Act of 1980, enacted on May 1, 1980, were given consideration. It seems to me that this particular auditing report should have been amended later to a certain extent. A book entitled *Guide to the Accounting Requirements of the Companies Acts* (Published for the Institute of Chartered Accountants in England and Wales by Gee & Co., Ltd, 1980) is an important reference.

Next is the example for the Federal Republic of Germany. The standard "auditing report" is as follows: "Bookkeeping, the annual financial report, and the company report conform to laws and statutes according to my (our) conscientious audit." The reader should remember that auditing reports made in the Federal Republic of Germany previously admitted the value in "securing strict conformity to the given legal standards." I suspect that he will also admit that as a result of the expected new revisions of laws like the Stock Law, the Limited Responsibility Company Law, and the *PublG*, to say nothing of the Commercial Code of the Federal Republic of Germany, and the fact that these revised laws introduce, in accordance with the Fourth EC Guideline, the concept of "a true and fair view" from the Companies Acts of the United Kingdom, the contents of the expressions to be used in the Federal Republic of Germany's "auditing report" must be changed, especially in fundamental points.

Next is France's auditing report. The following is the standard form to be submitted to stockholders:

En exécution de la mission que nous a confiée votre assemblée général du . . . , nous avons examiné le bilan et les comptes de l'exercice clos le. . . .
Notre examen, effectué conformément aux mornes de révision comptable, a comporté les contrôles considérés par nous comme necéssaires, eu égard aux regles de diligence normale.
Le compte d'exploitation générale, le compte de pertes et profits et le bilan qui vous sont présentés ont été établir selon. Les mêmes formes et les mêmes méthodes d'evaluation que l'année précédente.
Nous certifions qu'a notre avis l'inventaire et ces documents sont réguliers et sinceres. Nous avons également vérifié la sincérité des informations donnés dans le rapport du conseil d'administration et dans les documents adressés aux actionnaires sur la situation financière et les comptes de la société.

This French auditing report seems to fall between the United Kingdom form and the German form in that it regards not only "regularity" but also "justice" as a final concept of value.

The last example is Switzerland's. It is prescribed that the following should be the standard style of auditing report:

As the auditing agency of your company, I (we) have audited the annual accounts ending on , 19—according to lawful regulations.
I (we) have determined, that:
—the balance and the profit and loss statement agree with the bookkeeping,
—the bookkeeping has been kept in a regular manner,
—in the representation of the financial situation and of the results, the statutes have been observed.
Based on the results of my (our) audit; I (we) submit the present annual accounts for approval. Furthermore, I (we) certify that the recommendation of the managing board concerning the appropriation of profits conforms to the law and statutes.

The Swiss auditing certificate lays special emphasis on the conformity between various tables of closing accounts and the account book, together with the fair and proper custody of the account book.

Some of the other states that require conformity between the financial statement and the account book as an item that must be mentioned in an auditing certificate are Spain, Portugal, and Austria. Other states where the right and proper custody of an account book itself has been designated an item that must be mentioned are Finland, Norway, and so on. What it is necessary for us to remember is that No. (b) of Paragraph 1 of Article 51 of the Fourth EC Guideline prescribes that auditors are held responsible for the confirmation of conformity between financial statements and books of accounts. I would guess that this will be provided for in the law by each member state in the course of time. I doubt there is any thought about this particular issue here in Japan.

At any rate, as T. C. Hartley, a senior lecturer in law at the London School of Economics and Political Science, has stated in *Foundations of European Community Law* (Clarendon Press, Oxford, 1981), this is really the first step toward a European Federation, a United States of Europe.[4] A delicate influence must surely be exerted by the future course of the U.E.C., which has already lasted more than thirty years. The EC and the U.E.C. are different from each other in the scope of their constituting states, however, the idea that the EC's "Roman Treaty" is the Constitution of the Community has already emerged.

Notes

1. Homer Kripke, *The SEC and Corporate Disclosure* (Law & Business, Inc., Harcourt Brace Jovanovich, 1979), p. 152.
2. *Die Prüfung des Jahresabschlusses (Auditing the Annual Financial Report)*, 4 Auflage (Düsseldorf: Institute of Chartered Accountants in Germany, 1977), S. 7.
3. *The Constitutions of the Communist World*, ed. William B. Simons (The Netherlands: Sijthoff & Noordhoff, 1980), pp. 473–74.
4. See p. 6.

16

The Problem of the "Declaration of Completeness"

Why the Problem Is Taken Up

It may be due to poor scholarship on my part, but I have been unable to locate any Japanese accounting dictionary or book that scientifically treats the problem of the "declaration of completeness," which is deeply rooted in the auditing practices of the Federal Republic of Germany. Even before Kotaro Tanaka's *Logic of the Laws Concerning Balance Sheet*, the field of accounting in Japan should have been absorbing the outstanding accounting practices of the Federal Republic of Germany.

I do not understand why the problem of the "declaration of completeness" has been overlooked, or set at naught, so far in Japan. As a man of practical business in accounting and taxation affairs, I can state with conviction that more than 90 percent of Japanese corporations and 99 percent of Japanese private enterprises do not pursue "completeness in accounting records." The great majority of the members of the National Diet, who take an oath to make strenuous efforts and sacrifice even their own bodies and souls for the formation of the destiny of the nation and people, are merchants in one way or another at present in Japan.

I have not been able to detect that the many bureaucrats in Japan—who are considered to belong to the most excellent category of professions and lead their lives thinking only of the protection of their profession and their promotion, and for whom keep-

The Problem of the "Declaration of Completeness" 241

ing these matters to themselves is of the highest value—are now frantically tackling the formation of the destiny of the nation and the people. Well then, who will be responsible for making such efforts in the reestablishment of the national economy of Japan? I really do worry about this matter.

The reference materials I have on hand in regard to the subject of the "declaration of completeness" are as follows:

1. *Auditors Handbook* (1973)
2. *Auditors Handbook* (1977)
3. *Dictionary of Accounting* (1970)
4. *Dictionary of Accounting* (2d ed., 1981)
5. Ulrich Leffson, *Auditing* (1977)
6. K. v. Wysocki, *Foundations of Business Auditing* (2d ed., 1977)
7. Wysocki and Hagest, *The Practice of Auditing* (1976)
8. Wolfgang Lück, *Encyclopedia of Auditing, Rendering of Accounts and Examination* (1980)
9. Fritz Erhard, *Taxation Auditing* (4th ed., 1980)
10. Friedrich W. Selchert, *The Annual Financial Statement under Corporation Law* (1979)

The Evolution of the Basis of the "Declaration of Completeness"

What is meant by the "declaration of completeness" is that which is contained in 44, Sec. 1, No. 1, *KWG* of July 10, 1961 *(BGBl* I, S. 881), according to the *Auditors Handbook* (1977), which was published by the Institute of Chartered Accountants in Germany.[1] The medium of that order is Declaration 3/68 of the Federal Control Board for Credit, Berlin, December 20, 1968 (no. 3/1969).

No. 1 of Paragraph 1 of Article 44 of this Financial System Law states:
The Federal Control Board is empowered: 1.) to require the information concerning all business transactions and the presentation of books and papers from credit institutions and their agencies and to undertake this even without special cause. The employees of the Federal Control Board may enter the place of business of the credit institution for this purpose. The basic right of Article 13 of the Constitution is limited to this extent.

Article 13 of the Constitution of the Federal Republic of Germany is the provision regarding inviolability of residence. Article

13 is limited, however, by Paragraph 1 of Article 44 and is apparently contradictory to Paragraph 3 of Article 1 of the Constitution, which prescribes: "The following basic rights shall bind the legislature, the executive, and the judiciary as directly enforceable law." Paragraph 3 of Article 13, however, admits the infringement, or restriction, on the inviolability of the home in a case based on the law, so that it should be understood that it is in no way contradictory.

The above provision of No. 1 of Paragraph 1 of Article 44 of the Financial System Law provides for the authority of the federal government over banking facilities. I am not satisfied, however, with the reason this provision has been connected to the "declaration of completeness." My inquiries into the expert opinion that was issued in 1933 by the Institute of Chartered Accountants in Germany, has led me to the fact that in 1935, twenty-six years before the enactment of this Financial System Law, the following expert opinion had already been made public: "Filing of a Declaration of Completeness by the Executive Board of the Audited Firm." Furthermore, an opinion with the same title as the above was also published in 1942. In 1958, the experts' opinion, "New Model for the Declaration of Completeness," was made public. That is, the custom of making a demand for the proclamation of completeness has been ripening over a period of twenty-odd years.

Consequently, it can be said that the enactment of the Financial System Law in 1961 was merely an incentive to make this law part of the legal system. In January 1958, the subject of "the declaration of completeness" had already been dealt with in "The Decrees of the Bank Supervisory Authorities of the Federal Territory," and this notification became null and void so that the above-indicated regulations were determined to be applicable only to the annual statement of accounts for the business year to start in and after December 31, 1967.[2]

The Necessity for the Declaration of Completeness

What is the substantive reason for the necessity of the declaration of completeness? According to Professor Ulrich Leffson of Münster University: "The auditor can only audit that which is included in

The Problem of the "Declaration of Completeness" 243

the books. Conversely he cannot or can only more or less randomly check that which they do not include. Thus a gap exists in the possibility of the audit. This gap should be closed insofar as possible by a so-called declaration of completeness."[3]

It seems to me that Leffson's opinion includes a formulation of an important problem in regard to the performance of auditing. Is there any standard among Japanese accounting regulations, the focus of which is on "a gap in the possibility of the audit," as was pointed out by Professor Leffson? Due to my lack of knowledge on this subject, I regret that I have no answer to this question.

Japan's "Working Rules of On-Sight Audits" has adopted the official attitude of "setting a limit to the scope of duty" of an auditor by using the expression "the auditing of the records of transaction." This means that it is all right for an auditor to audit only the records of transactions. On the other hand, Japan's Financial Accounting Principles proclaim, as the first of its "General Principles," the principle of accuracy. The audit to be made by Japan's professional accountants—both certified public accountants and licensed tax practitioners—is regulated by Japan's statutory laws, under which the pursuit of the "principle of truthfulness" shall be conducted. The source of these laws is Article 4 of the Ministerial Ordinance Regarding Audit Certificates, specifically for a Certified Public Accountant, and Article 45 of the Tax Agent Law, which is specifically for a Licensed Tax Practitioner.

That being the case, at least two problems can be identified. One is whether the authorities judge that the pursuit of the principle of truthfulness can be conducted only by the auditing of recorded transactions. In other words, do the authorities believe that the principle of truthfulness can be accomplished with no regard at all to the "gap in the possibility of the audit" that was pointed out by Professor Leffson?

The second problem stems from the state of the statutory laws that exist in Japan. The United States has taken the following statutory action. Under Article 24 of the Securities Act (1933), anyone who violates the law is subject to imprisonment for a term of less than five years, or a fine of not more than $5,000, or both. Under Article 32 of the Securities and Exchange Act (1934), anyone who violates the law is subject to imprisonment for a term of less than two years, or a fine of $10,000, or both; in the case of specialized traders in securities exchange, a fine is not more than $500,000. Article 19 of Britain's Companies Act of 1976 has statutory provisions under which imprisonment for less than two years, or a fine of less than 400 pounds, or both, are imposed on a person who actually submits fraudulent accounting records to an auditor. In the Federal Republic of Germany, Article 283 (b) of the Criminal Law has a statutory provision under which the person who orders the preparation of fraudulent accounting records, or the person who prepares them, shall be punished with imprisonment of less than two years or a fine. In Japan, however, the problem is that whether or not it is judged that the principle of truthfulness in accounting can be accomplished, there are no penalty provisions to induce compliance.

The solution to these two problems is next to impossible, given Japan's current accounting regulations. I firmly believe that herein lies the defect of the current accounting system in Japan and that the Federal Republic of Germany's "declaration of completeness" is a good model for what Japan's accounting system should be.

The Essential Qualities of the Declaration of Completeness

In 1967 the Institute of Chartered Accountants in Germany announced officially "Principles of Regular Conduct for General Audits" as "Expert Opinion, No. 1/1967." It is comprised of three sections: A, B, and C. A is "Introductory Remarks," B is "Assignments of the Final Exam," and C is "Principles for Conducting the Examination." The ninth principle of C is "Obtaining the Declaration of Completeness." In regard to this, the following expert opinion is attached: "The general auditor is to obtain a declaration of completeness from the audited firm; this is not in lieu of auditing procedures but rather a proper supplement to the general audit." And two notes are attached to this. The first note states: "The declaration of completeness is a comprehensive statement by the executive (board) concerning the completeness of the information and records rendered. Thereby it also serves to delineate responsibility (references to expert opinion 1/42)."

I have already pointed out that German laws clearly demand

The Problem of the "Declaration of Completeness" 245

the completeness of accounting records and that both *HGB 43* and *AO 146* require it. What I want to emphasize is that this "declaration of completeness" has made a decisive contribution to the determination of an auditor's limit of responsibility. It seems to me that Japan's accountants should immediately draw a lesson of this particular point from the Federal Republic of Germany.

The second note states: "The Institute of Chartered Accountants has designed models of declarations of completeness. These are based on procedures which occur often in practices and may be modified or supplemented as necessary in individual cases." As I have already mentioned, nearly thirty years have passed since the "declaration of completeness" was made public officially to German society as the expert opinion of the Institute of Chartered Accountants in Germany. It is therefore quite natural that this declaration has been refined by the passage of time and that its expression is more elastic than ever before.

The full text of the expert opinion known as the "Principles of Regular Conduct for General Audits" appears in Appendix 1 (pp. 248–56) of a book entitled *Foundations of Business Auditing* (1977), written by Klaus v. Wysocki, a professor of business administration at the University of Munich. In this connection, Appendix 2 is the full text of "Auditing Electronic Data Processing Bookkeeping," which was made public as Opinion 1/1974 by the Institute of Chartered Accountants in Germany. This is an exceptionally long opinion, extending over twenty-two pages.

In regard to the "declaration of completeness," Fritz Erhard, who was formerly a C.E.O. in the Federal Republic of Germany, also discusses it in his book, *Taxation Auditing* (4th ed., 1980).[4] Quoting from the "contents of activities" prescribed by 33 *StBerG*, and in accordance with the fact that Article 33 actually contains the expression "the preparation of tax statements," he states that a tax practitioner has to clarify the limits of his sincerity and, simultaneously, his responsibility for "true accuracy," and that "as a rule, the tax advisor may rely on the statements made to him, especially when a declaration of completeness has been made by the client." He continues, however, by saying that the tax practitioner "does not owe any special obligation to the FA, so he does not have to verify whether his client has also observed the instructions given to him." I have some different opinions about this matter.

The nonexistence of a "special obligation," as a term of professional registration, at government taxation affairs offices, is as equally applicable to a tax practitioner as to a certified public accountant. In 57 *StBerG*, however, there is a statement to the effect that one should be under the obligation of "conscientiousness." The same expression has also been used in 43 *WPO*. I have already touched on the point that "conscientiousness," as an obligation specifically defined by these two German laws, is more than the "cautious obligation" of an honest administrator under the German Civil Code.

Concerning the obligation to ascertain whether or not the "declaration of completeness" was made cautiously, I am afraid that there are no legal provisions anywhere that define this particular obligation. I must state, however, that simply because a specific provision is not to be found, concluding that there is "no necessity for confirmation" is not compatible with the concept of "conscientiousness."

In Japan there are no penalties for "unfaithful entries," and the Japanese people have learned to be on the lookout for the opportunity to evade taxes. It seems clear to me that we Japanese cannot help but recognize the strong possibility that this "declaration of completeness" may be utilized in an easygoing way. In regard to how the "declaration of completeness," as a supplement to the substantial truthfulness of accounting and financial statements, should be drawn up, the concept of "appropriate cautious obligation," which is provided for by Japan's professional regulations, should perform its expected function.

The Format of the Declaration of Completeness

The model in the *Auditors Handbook* (1977) is an example in three comparatively short sentences. The model printed in Professor Wysocki's book, however, is comparatively long and detailed but simple. A sketchy outline of Professor Wysocki's model follows below.

At the top of this document, the title "Declaration of Complete-

The Problem of the "Declaration of Completeness" 247

ness" is printed in Gothic type, under which appear the address and date and, below them, the name of the auditor, followed by the name of the enterprise to be audited. Below that appears "Business Year of 19—Financial Statement," "Re: Annual Financial Statement and Business Report for the Business Year 19—," and the following statement: "I (we) as member(s) of the executive board/director of the company (in our own name as well as in the name of and by order of all other members of the executive board/director of the company) hereby declare to you as general auditors the following." What follows is divided into four categories: A, B, C, and D. "A" comprises "explanation and proof" and "B" is "bookkeeping and records," which is further broken down into six items. "C" is the "annual financial statement and operating report," the contents of which are classified as fourteen items. "D" is a vacant entry column for "additions and remarks." The lowest portion is reserved for the signature.

In "A," "explanation and proof," the following appears: "I (we) have given you the explanations and proof, which you have asked me (us) for in accordance with 165 *AktG*, to the best of my (our) knowledge and belief. I (we) have named for you the persons listed as follows as informants." Following this are four lines of empty columns and then this concluding sentence: "I (we) have directed these individuals to give you all requested information and records completely and accurately."

My reader may have already perceived the care with which these model sentences try to avoid a "gap in the possibility of the audit," as pointed out by Professor Leffson. I have already explained that the bookkeeping and records in "B" are divided into six items, however, there is no point in quoting all of these. I will quote only the first: "I (we) have given instructions to place the business books and other company documents completely at your disposal." This sentence attempts to discourage any intentions by company officials regarding "window dressing" or the omission of their respective earnings. In the Federal Republic of Germany, "thick and threefold" measures have been taken in order to avoid or to prevent "window-dressing accounting" and tax dodging.

I have mentioned that the annual financial statement and operating report in "C" is divided into fourteen items, however, I would like to introduce here just a sampling of those items. The first states as follows: "In my (our) opinion, in the annual balance sheet audited by you, all assets, obligations, and risks (e.g., losses from pending transactions) required for the balance sheet have been taken into account." The second states: "There are no accounts receivable from loans that are subject to 89 or 115 *AktG* on the delivery date. Only in the amount in which they are identified or noted as such in the annual balance sheet." In this case, there is a square box in which an "X" is to be entered if the situation applies. Among these fourteen items, there are thirty-six columns demanding such selective indication.

I am sure my reader has caught the idea of these items; thus I will omit a discussion of the rest of them. The column for "additions and remarks" in "D" is, needless to say, blank. As stated above, at the lowest portion of this paper, there is a space for the signature(s) of the person(s) responsible for submitting this special report.

It is my hope that a requirement for a "declaration of completeness," like that in Germany, is adopted in the accounting practice of Japan and that it is even more comprehensive, encompassing more than "the auditing of *records* of transaction."[5] I would like to see a system in Japan in which the limit of responsibility of both the auditor and the business is much clearer and through which the incentives of "window dressing" and tax evasion can thus be intercepted. The system in the Federal Republic of Germany, even though it is nonexistent in the accounting practice of the United States, should be introduced to Japan.

It is interesting to note that the British tax return is based on the same idea as this "declaration of completeness." In the United Kingdom's 1981 tax return, at the upper part of the first page, there is a space for the signature of the individual taxpayer. Just above this space, there is a "declaration" in which it is stated that all the items entered on this "return" are, to the best of the preparer's knowledge and belief, "correct and complete." As this statement is printed in large type, just above the space for the signature, no one can claim not to have read it or to have missed it. To the left of this "declaration" is a statement, in parentheses, that a false entry may lead to an "indictment."

The Problem of the "Declaration of Completeness" **249**

As Alexis Carrel, a Nobel-prize winner in medicine, once said in his book *Reflection on Life*, a human being "is free and able to do wrong." The "declaration of completeness" can be said, therefore, to be a necessary tool for auditing so that human beings do not do wrong. The thought of giving an account of this British tax return has been adopted and indicated as a matter of course both in the United States and the Republic of Singapore. Such thought is nonexistent here in Japan.

Notes

1. *Auditors Handbook*, 1977, S. 407.
2. Ibid., S. 409.
3. Ulrich Leffson, *Auditing*, 1977, S. 251.
4. See p. 70.
5. Japan's "Working Rules of Field Audits," No. 2 (2), "General Audit Procedure."

17

Principles of Regular Bookkeeping and Electronic Data Processing

Regarding Reference Materials

I do not know whether there are some legal accounting standards in Japan in regard to this subject. I *am* aware of the statement by the director of the Civil Affairs Bureau of the Ministry of Justice, dated November 18, 1974, regarding "the preservation of books of account and other important business documents via microfilm" and of a referential opinion regarding "the microcopying of books of account and others," which was made public on August 20, 1974, by the Electronic Computer Accounting Committee of Japan's Association of Certified Public Accountants. Both documents are concerned with the preservation, and so forth, by microphotograph of books of account and others. They have no relation at all to the legal standards or theoretical standards that are directly related to electronic computer accounting.

In the Federal Republic of Germany, where legislative activities have been undertaken to a heroic degree, the literature regarding the subject is amazingly abundant. Just a few examples follow.

The three-volume *Electronic Data Processing Law* was written by Wolfgang E. Burhenne and Klaus Perband. This book's subtitle is *Systematic Collection of Legal Regulators, Organizational Fundamentals, and Decisions for Electronic Data Processing*. The first volume contains the following legal standards: forty-nine federal laws (for example, the Federal Data Protection Law) and sixty-one provincial laws. In addition to these, there are also the United States's Data Protection Law, the European Conference's Resolution Concerning Data Protection, the European Community's (EC's) Four-Year Program for the Promotion of Data Processing and the EC's Decision of the European Parliament Concerning Data Protection, the Austria's Government Bill for Data Protection, the full text of the Federal Republic of Germany's notification regarding Principles for the Acquisition of Electronic Data Processing Documents, and the full text of forty-one administrative orders. The second volume contains the full text of ninety-six administrative orders regarding each province of the Federal Republic of Germany and details of federal and provincial electronic computer systems. The third volume is chiefly comprised of commentary on the legal regulations. Viewed from the Japanese perspective, the huge amount of material these volumes contain is overwhelming.

Next is Volume 2 of the *Dictionary of Business* (1980). This book gives a versatile explanation (pages 85–133) in regard to data processing. On pages 1088–1138 of Volume 1 of the *Dictionary of Business Administration* (1974), there are explanations of data bases and data base systems, data collection, data protection and security, data processing, and data processing facilities. Next is the *Dictionary of Accounting* (1981), in which there is an explanation of data bases and accounting on pages 374–83 of Volume III. Volume 1 of the *Dictionary of Tax Law and Tax Studies* (2d ed., 1981) lists the following reference materials in regard to electronic computer-aided accounting:

- *Japanese Data Processing Organizations*, written by the author.
- *Data Base Retrieval* and *Data Base, Taxation*, written by Dr. Joachim Conradi, who completed the data base system in Germany. This is listed with a book entitled *DATEV* (in eight pages), which was written by Heinz Sebiger, the president of the Nuremberg Chamber of Tax Advisors and the chairman of the DATEV Data Processing Organization of the Tax Advisors Profession in the Federal Republic of Germany, e.G. (M.S. rer. Oec.). Also included is a book entitled *Automation in Tax Administration*, written by Dr. Karl Koch, who is Ministerial Director in the Federal Ministry of Finance, Bonn.

252 Principles of Regular Bookkeeping

Furthermore, the literature that directly deals with the problem of electronic computer-aided accounting is as follows:

Werner Kresse, *The New School of the Bookkeeper* (4th ed., 1979), Vol. II.

Siegbert Rudolph, *The DATEV Bookkeeping System* (2d ed., 1978).

Rolf Vieweg, *Bookkeeping with Mechanized and Automatic Data Processing* (5th ed., 1972).

Erhard Reblin, *Electronic Data Processing in Financial Accounting* (2d ed., 1971).

Richard Müller, *Accounting and Electronic Data Processing, Computers, and the Law*, Vol. 5 (1977).

Dieter Gernert, *Introduction to Data Processing for Lawyers* (1974).

Rolf Vieweg, *Comprehensive Applications of Electronic Data Processing for Optimal Direction of a Business* (1980).

Kurt Nagel, *Current Data-Processing Trends: Tables and Help in Decision Making for Data Processing and Computing with Emphasis on Control and Monitoring of Computer Centers* (1979).

Ingo Hafner and Horst Junker, *Electronic Data Processing in Medium-Sized Companies* (1978).

Detler Müller-Böling, *Work Satisfaction with Automatic Data Processing* (1978).

K. F. Peter, *Modern Legal and Tax Advising with Electronic Data Processing*.

In addition to these, I know of ten other books. This list should suffice, however.

The Electronic Computer-Aided Accounting Regulations in the Tax Code in the Federal Republic of Germany

In the Federal Republic of Germany, four legal provisions have been provided for in the Tax Code in regard to the principles of regular bookkeeping and the use of electronic data processing. The

Principles of Regular Bookkeeping 253

first is in Paragraph 5 of Article 146, "Regulations for Bookkeeping and for Records." The second is in Paragraphs 2 and 5 of Article 147, "Regulations for the Keeping of Documents." And the third is in Paragraph 6 of Article 150, "Form and Content of the Tax Declarations." Paragraph 5 of Article 146 prescribes as follows:

> The books and other required records can also consist of the orderly filing of the vouchers or kept insofar as these forms of bookkeeping, as well as the process used, conform to the principles of regular bookkeeping; as concerns records that are only to be kept for tax purposes, the reliability of the method used is determined according to the purpose that the records should serve in taxation. In keeping the books and other required records in data medium one must be especially careful that the data are available during the time period records are to be kept and that they can be made legible within a reasonable period. Sections 1 through 4 apply accordingly.

What is referred to as "data medium" is, undoubtedly, electronic data processing at the present stage. In short, the following in this particular provision deserves our special attention:

(1) This provision acknowledges, right up front, that making an entry in books of account or other necessary records by electronic data processing is found suitable to the principles of regular bookkeeping.
(2) This provision also indicates a standard of judgment regarding the approval of such a processing procedure.
(3) This provision also demands a guarantee of the free use of the data, especially the possibility that these documents will be easily "visible and legible" on computers.

This particular point reminds me that on February 24, 1964, the United States enacted a legislative order in the form of Revenue Procedure 64–12. Article 4 of this legislation prescribes "ADP Record Guidelines," Paragraph 1 of which contains the term "visible and legible records."

To proceed, Paragraph 2 of Article 147 prescribes: Except for the balance sheet, the evidential documents listed in Paragraph 1 can also be stored on a data medium, when this is in accordance with the principles of regular bookkeeping and when it is certain that the copies or data:
1. are identical in appearance with the received business letters and

vouchers and in content with the other documents, when they have been made legible.
2. are available during the period of time they are to be preserved and can be made legible at any time within a reasonable time.

If documents based on 146 Section 5 have been produced on data medium, instead of the data medium, the data can also be stored printed out and the printed documents can also be preserved according to Sentence 1.

In the above special expression, what is referred to as "the evidential documents listed in Paragraph 1" indicates the following items shown below in accordance with Paragraph 1:

1. Books of account and records, an inventory, the balance sheet and job order that is necessary for the understanding of these data, and other materials regarding organization.
2. Various commercial correspondence received and the correspondence on transactions.
3. Commercial correspondence issued and copies of the correspondence on transactions.
4. Written evidence on entries.
5. Other materials that are necessary for taxation.

Such inclusive provisions in regard to the fiscal statement do not exist in Japan. It seems to me that in order for taxation to become just in Japan, it is absolutely necessary that some such definite regulation in regard to the preservation of information should exist. To return to our main subject, Paragraph 5 of Article 147 prescribes:

Anyone who keeps documents only in the form of copies on visual or other data medium, is required to provide, at his own expense, the necessary apparatus and aid required to render the documents legible. At the request of the fiscal authorities he is to print the documents immediately, in full or in part and at his own expense, or to provide reproductions legible without aid.

I firmly believe that this provision, in particular, should be introduced into the taxation laws of Japan. Lastly, Paragraph 6 of Article 150 prescribes as follows:

In order to facilitate and simplify the automated taxation process, the Federal Minister of Finance may specify by decree, with the agreement of the Bundesrat, that tax declarations returns, in the sense of the motor

vehicle tax law or other data required for the taxation process, can be transmitted totally or in part by mechanically usable data medium or teleprocessing. In particular, the following can be regulated:
1. the prerequisites for the use of the process,
2. particulars concerning form, contents, processing, and security of the data to be transmitted,
3. the method by which the data is transmitted,
4. the responsibility for the reception of the transmitted data,
5. the liability of third parties for taxes or tax advantages that may be diminished or obtained due to incorrect processing or transmission of data,
6. the extent and form of the special filing responsibilities of the taxpayer that are received for this process.

Special attention should be paid to the difference between the terms "law" (or "decree") and "general administrative regulation." The former, in this particular instance, is based on Paragraph 1 of Article 80 of *GG*, while the latter is prescribed by Paragraph 2 of Article 84 or by Paragraph 2 of Article 85 of *GG*. In the Federal Republic of Germany, the "guidelines" that are promulgated for the administration of tax affairs belong to the "regulation" category and are, consequently, only a secondary source of law.

A serious view must be taken of the fact that Paragraph 6 of Article 150 of the Tax Code entrusts the federal minister of finance with the authority of enacting legislation that has a wide scope. This legislation can restrict even the Court of Justice in accordance with Paragraph 3 of Article 20 of *GG*, which prescribes that the administration of justice is subject to law and justice. This law was enacted on August 21, 1980, and, since then, it has been inserted in *BGBl*, I, 1617, the title of which is Law Concerning the Filing of Tax Declarations on Machine Usable Data Medium. The preamble states: "Based on 150, Section 6 of the Tax Code of March 16, 1976 (*BGBl*, I, 613), it is enacted with the agreement of the Bundesrat." The order is comprised of five items (eleven articles) in all and is thus quite short. Item 1 of this law has only one principle: "Part 1. General." Item 2 has three articles and its title is "Part 2. Participation in Data Transmission." Article 3 is "Approval of the Data Processing Company." Article 4 is "Revocation of the Permit." The title of Item 3 is "Part 3. Approval of the Data Processing Company," and comprises Articles 5 through 8. Article

5 is "Type, Content, and Set-up of the Data Medium." Article 6 is "Shipping Data Medium." Article 7 is "Data Protection." Article 8 is "Acceptance and Rejection of Data Medium." The title of Item 4 is "Part 4. Liability of the Data Processing Company." It has only one article, Article 9, the title of which is "Liability." Item 5 is "Part 5. Final Regulations." It contains two articles: Article 10, "Berlin Clause," and Article 11, "Effective Date," by which this law is declared to be effective on and after January 1, 1981.

Due to space limitations, I cannot reproduce the full text of this law. In order that it may serve as a reference for future legislation in Japan, however, I will introduce the text of Article 9, which prescribes Item 4, "Part 4. Liability of the Data Processing Company." Article 9 is composed of three paragraphs, the first of which follows:

The data processing firm is liable, due to incorrect processing or transmission, insofar as data medium contain inaccurate or incomplete data concerning facts for paying taxes and thereby taxes are decreased or tax advantages are illegally obtained. The liability does not apply insofar as the data processing firm can show that the incorrect processing or transmission of the data is not due to gross negligence or the intent of the data processing firm or its vicarious agents.

In examining Article 9 we become aware that the Federal Republic of Germany has legislated that data processing traders cooperate with the rightful payment of taxes. Such a national attitude cannot be established, as Heinrich Henkel, a professor at the University of Hamburg, has said, "unless we can fix our eyes on the law as a factor in the formation of the social order and strongly support it as such."[1]

Paragraph 2 of Article 9 states: "The data processing firm may only be held liable for payment, insofar as the foreclosure of the movable goods of the taxpayer is unsuccessful, or if it may be assumed that enforcement will be unsuccessful. Article 219, Sentence 2 of the Tax Code is to remain unaffected." This provision is rather hard for us to understand, because there is no concept similar to the "responsible obligator" in Japan's tax laws. The only clue to our understanding of this particular provision is found in the first sentence of Article 219 of the Tax Code: "If nothing else is specified, a person liable for payment may only be laid claim to insofar as the foreclosure of the movable goods of the one who owes taxes remains unsuccessful, or it is assumed that enforcement is hopeless." That is, the concept of a "secondary debtor," which originates from the tax laws of the Federal Republic of Germany, is similar to the concept of "the secondary taxpayer" for the substantial amount of taxes prescribed by Article 36 of the National Tax Collection Act in Japan.

Paragraph 3 prescribes as follows: "The notification of liability is to be issued by the tax office responsible for the taxpayer." At present in Japan, the concept of "notification of liability" has not yet become popular. Paragraph 1 of Article 191 of the Federal Republic of Germany's Tax Code has the following provision: "Anyone who is liable for a tax (the responsible obligator) by law can be held responsible ... by notification of liability. The notifications are to be made in writing." This helps us understand what the "notification of liability" is. As I have already mentioned, the designation "a person responsible for entry" is made in writing as an administrative action.

I am under the impression that there are people in Japan who believe that the two kinds of administrative actions lack legitimacy and, moreover, have been left unbuttressed under Japanese law. In fact, there is a growing doubt regarding the very conception of the system of income tax returns (Article 1 of the Tax Agent Law in Japan).

In the Federal Republic of Germany, where the same tax return system has been adopted, the situation is entirely different from that in Japan. The same is true in the case of Canada.[2] On the subject of the fair distribution of taxes, it seems unnecessary to discuss which country's tax return system is the better one. I would like to urge the Japanese authorities concerned to do some soul-searching on this particular matter. The title of the above-mentioned Article 150 of the Tax Code is "Form and Content of the Tax Return." A legal provision corresponding to the above-mentioned provision does not exist in Japan. In regard to this point in particular, Japan is conducting the destruction not only of the doctrine of administrative laws but also of the Constitution of Japan.

The Audit Trail and Others

I will now bring my discussion of the Tax Code and computer-assisted accounting to an end. My reader may have noticed the lack of legal provisions regarding an "audit trail," as prescribed by Article 4 of the United States Revenue Procedure 64–12, in the Tax Code of the Federal Republic of Germany. The second item in Paragraph 2 of Article 4 of the United States Revenue Procedure 64–12 prescribes: "(2) Supporting Documents and Audit Trail. The audit trail should be designed so that the details underlying the summary accounting data, such as invoices and vouchers, may be identified and made available to the Internal Revenue Service upon request."

Furthermore, the third item of the same Paragraph 2 stipulates as follows: "(3) Recorded or Reconstructible Data. The records must provide the opportunity to trace any transaction back to the original source or forward to a final total. If printouts are not made of transactions at the time they are processed, then the system must have the ability to reconstruct these transactions."

These United States legal provisions are extremely natural from the point of logical sequence, however, these same provisions cannot be found anywhere in Japan's legislation. I would guess that this is the result of the following. Legislation in Japan has chiefly depended on the preferences of Japanese bureaucrats and the vicissitudes of public opinion. The members of the National Diet, whose main job is legislation, have been preoccupied with their reception by the electorate and by the electorate's requests. As a result, these Diet members have degraded themselves by becoming mere carriers of the lumber that Japanese officialdom has used in constructing Japanese society. It also seems to me that the Japanese journalists who should be shouldering the responsibility for public opinion may be lacking in their scholarship and national consciousness.

In regard to the legislation on this subject in the Federal Republic of Germany, I have repeatedly pointed out that Article 29 of the Enforcement Regulation relating to Article 5 of the Income Tax Law in the Federal Republic of Germany stipulates "regular bookkeeping." No. 2 of Paragraph 2 of Article 29 states:

Principles of Regular Bookkeeping 259

The development of circumstances must be taken into account. To make the work of bookkeeping more efficient and for the business use of data processing facilities in the process of bookkeeping, in practice, business transactions are not continually posted, but rather only periodically. In order not to adversely affect efforts toward efficiency, it will not be objected to if the posting of the credit transactions of one month takes place before the end of the following month, insofar as organizational precautions are taken to insure that the bookkeeping documents do not get lost before their posting in the registers (e.g., by running numbering of the incoming and outgoing bills or by collecting them in special folders or binders); the general requirements of regularity of bookkeeping according to No. 1 must also be fulfilled in this case.

This is the Enforcement Regulation. It seems to me that the legal standard regarding "verifiability" is stated therein.

In his book, Dr. Werner Kresse discusses the "machine readability of vouchers and input data as a requirement for electronic data processing" and concludes that the relationship between voucher and entry must be evident. He does not quote legal provisions in his statement, however.[3] Moreover, I do not know of any documentary regulation regarding programs of computer-assisted accounting in the Federal Republic of Germany. I would welcome information on this matter.

In item 5 of Paragraph 2 of Article 4 of the above-mentioned United States Revenue Procedure 64–12, the following appears:

Program Documentation. A description of the ADP portion of the accounting system should be available. The statements and illustrations as to the scope of operations should be sufficiently detailed to indicate (a) the application being performed, (b) the procedures employed in each application (which, for example, might be supported by flow charts, block diagrams, or other satisfactory descriptions of input or output procedures), and (c) the controls used to insure accurate and reliable processing. Important changes, together with the effective dates, should be noted in order to preserve an accurate chronological record.

Careful attention should be paid to this particular matter, because this is the area that has serious problems insofar as computer-assisted accounting is concerned. It was about twenty years ago that these legal standards were enacted in the United States.

Notes

1. Heinrich Henkel, *Introduction to the Philosophy of Law,* 2d ed., 1977, p. 467.
2. Income Tax Act, Sec. 150 (2).
3. *The New School of the Bookkeeper,* Vol. II, 4th ed., 1979, p. 62, 93.

References

Japanese

Aida, Yoshio (Professor, Keio Gijuku University; Doctor of Economics). *Accounting.* 1976.

Akari, Chotaro (Lecturer, Chuo University). *Tax Accounting by Exemplification.* Reprint, 1964.

Aoki, Shigeo (Professor, Waseda University). *An Outline of Accounting.* 1978.

Arai, Kiyomitsu (Professor, Waseda University; Doctor of Commercial Science). *Theory of Financial Accounting.* 45th enlarged edition, 1979.

Chu, Saichi (Professor, Nihon University; Doctor of Laws). *Tax Laws and Accounting Principles.* Reprint, 1953.

———. *Laws Concerning Accounting for Taxation.* 2d and 6th editions.

Emura, Minoru (Professor, Tokyo University). *An Outline of Corporation Accounting.* 1979.

Hasui, Yoshinori (Professor, Kitakyushu University). *General Rules of the Commercial Code—Commercial Transaction Law.* 1980.

Hasui, Yoshinori (Professor, Kitakyushu University), Toshio Sakamaki (Professor, Waseda University; Doctor of Laws), Harumi Shimura (Professor, Ritsumeikan University). *Lecture on General Rules of the Commercial Code.* 1980.

Hatanaka, Fukuichi. Compiled by Kiyoshi Kurosawa. *Study on Theory for the Title of Account.*

Hattori, Eizo (Professor, Tohoku University; Doctor of Laws). *General Rules of the Commercial Code.* 2d edition, 1975.

Hiraishi, Yuichiro (Professor, Kokushikan University). *Detailed Interpretation of Corporate Income Tax.* Reprint, 1970.

Hoshikawa, Choshichi (Honorary Professor, Waseda University; Doctor of Laws), Kogoro Yamaguchi (Professor, Osaka University; Doctor of Laws),

Wataru Horiguchi (Professor, Hitotsubashi University), Toshio Sakamaki (Professor, Waseda University; Doctor of Laws). *General Rules of the Commercial Code, Commercial Transaction Law.* Revised edition, 1979.

Iino, Toshio (Professor, Chuo University; Doctor of Commercial Science). *Theory of Financial Accounting.* 36th edition, 1979.

Inoue, Kyuya (Professor, Nihon University). *Calculation and Theory on Corporate Income Tax.*

Inoue, Tatsuo (Professor, Chuo University; Doctor of Commercial Science). *New Theory of Financial Statements.* 72d edition, 1978.

Ishii, Teruhisa (Professor, Seikei University). *General Rules of the Commercial Code.* Revised edition, 1979.

Ishikawa, Keiichi (C.P.A.; Tax Accountant). *A Textbook on Corporate Income Tax.* 1978.

Kawahara, Kazuo (C.P.A.; Tax Accountant; Lecturer, Nihon University). *Practice on Income Tax and Accounting Principles.* Revised new edition.

Kimura, Shigeyoshi (Professor, Soka University). *Commentary on Accounting Principles.* 1963.

Kurosawa, Kiyoshi (Honorary Professor, Yokohama National University; Doctor of Business Administration). *Modern Accounting.* 6th revised edition, 1978.

Matsui, Shizuro (formerly of the Ministry of Finance). *Business Practice on Corporate Income Tax Law.* 1965.

Minato, Ryonosuke (formerly of the Japan Tobacco and Salt Public Corporation). *Newly Revised Corporate Income Tax Law.*

Minemura, Shinkichi (Professor, Keio Gijuku University; Doctor of Economics). New Edition of *Accounting.* Reprint, 1976.

Mutaguchi, Minoru (Ex-Revenue Officer; C.P.A.; Tax Accountant; Lecturer, Postgraduate Course, Nihon University). *New Textbook on Individual Income Tax.*

Nakamura, Nobuichiro (Professor, Konan University; Doctor of Commercial Science). *Accounting.* 1st edition, 1979.

Nomizu, Isuruo (Judge of the Court of Appeal for National Tax). *Foundation on Individual Income Tax.*

Numata, Yoshio (Professor, Komazawa University; Doctor of Commercial Science). *A Textbook of Accounting.* 8th revised edition, 1978.

Ohta, Tetsuzo (Doctor of Commercial Science), and Masutaro Arai (Professor, Seikei University). *An Introduction to the New Accounting.* 9th edition, 1978.

Ootori, Tsuneo (Professor, Tokyo University), Ichiro Kawamoto (Professor, Kobe University), Masahiro Kitazawa (Professor, Nagoya University; Doctor of Laws); Yoh Sato (Professor of Seikei University), Shuza Toda (Professor, Chuo University; Doctor of Laws), comps. *Practice, the Commercial Code (General Rules, Commercial Transactions).* Revised edition, 1976.

Ooyama, Takao (Professor, Tax University). *Calculation and Theory of Individual Income Tax.* 1972, 1978.
Osumi, Kenichiro (Honorary Professor, Kyoto University; Doctor of Laws). *General Rules of the Commercial Code.* Revised edition, 1978.
Sakamoto, Yasuichi (Professor, Osaka Gakuin University; Doctor of Economics). *Basic Accounting.* 20th edition, 1979.
Sanekata, Kenji (Professor, Hokkaido University), and Toshiro Shima (Professor of Tsukuba University), comps. *General Rules of the Commercial Code.* 1980.
Sato, Koichi (Professor, Waseda University; Doctor of Commercial Science). *New Accounting.* 21st edition, 1967.
Someya, Kyojiro (Professor, Waseda University; Doctor of Commercial Science). *Modern Financial Accounting.* Completely revised 55th edition, 1979.
Suzuki, Takeo (Honorary Professor, Tokyo University; Doctor of Laws). *New Edition of the Commercial Code.* 1978.
Tajima, Shiro (Professor, Komazawa University; Doctor of Economics). *Revised Accounting.* 4th edition, 1977.
Takamatsu, Kazuo (President and Professor, Soka University; Doctor of Economics). *Theory of Bookkeeping.* New revised edition, 4th printing, 1978.
Takatori, Masao (Professor, Keio Gijuku University; Doctor of Laws). *Basic Lecture on Jurisprudence, the Commercial Code II (The Company Law).* 1971.
———. *General Rules of the Commercial Code—Commercial Transaction Law.* 1976.
Takeda, Masasuke (Professor, Seikei University). *Detailed Interpretation of Taxation of Corporation.* 1962.
Tanaka, Kotaro (Honorary Professor, Tokyo University; Doctor of Laws). *Logic of the Laws Concerning Balance Sheet.* Reprint, 1946.
Tanaka, Seiji (Honorary Professor, Hitotsubashi University; Doctor of Laws). *All-revised Detailed Discussion of General Rules of the Commercial Code.* 1978.
———. *New Edition Commercial Code.* 4th completely revised edition, 1978.
Tanaka, Seiji (Honorary Professor, Hitotsubashi University; Doctor of Laws), and Ryosuke Kita (Professor, Hitotsubashi University; Doctor of Laws). *Commentary, General Rules of the Commercial Code.* Revised edition, 1975
Tatta, Misao (Professor, Kyoto University). *Abbreviated Explanation of the Commercial Code.* 1980.
Toda, Shuzo (Professor, Chuo University; Doctor of Laws). *General Rules of the Commercial Code.* 1980.
Ueno, Michisuke (Honorary Professor, Tokyo University). *New Theory of a Balance Sheet.* 11th edition, 1942.

Ueyanagi, Katsuro (Professor, Kyoto University), Masahiro Kitazawa (Professor, Nagoya University; Doctor of Laws), Tsuneo Ootori (Professor, Tokyo University; Doctor of Laws), Akio Takeuchi (Professor, Tokyo University; Doctor of Laws), comps. *General Rules of the Commercial Code, Commercial Transaction Law.* 1980.

Yamamasu, Tadahiro (Professor, Keio Gijuku University; Doctor of Economics), and Tsuyoo Shimamura (Professor, Meiji University; Doctor of Economics). *Systematic Theory of Financial Statements; Theory Section.* Revised edition, 1978.

Yamashita, Katsuji (Professor, Kobe University). *Theory of Financial Accounting Principles.* Reprint, 1957.

Yoshida, Fujio (formerly of the National Tax Administration Agency). *Individual Income Tax Law.* 1978.

Yoshikuni, Jiro (former chief officer of the National Tax Administration Agency). *Lecture on Corporate Income Tax Law.* 1954.

———. *Corporate Income Tax, Edition for Practice.* 1973.

Yoshikuni, Jiro (former chief officer of the National Tax Administration Agency), and Masasuke Takeda. *Corporate Income Tax Law, Volume of Interpretation of Laws and Ordinances.* 1976.

Accounting (Kaikei). Compiled by The Accounting Institution of Japan.

Accounting (Kigyo-Kaikei). Edition of Chuokeizaisha.

Dictionary of Accounting. Compiled by Institution for Accounting of Kobe University.

Dictionary of Accounting. Edition of Dobunkan; 3d edition.

Dictionary of Accounting. Edition of Seirinshoin-shinsha, 1965.

Handbook of Accounting. Edition of Chuokeizaisha, 1976.

Non-Japanese

Adler, Hans, Walther Düring, and Kurt Schmaltz. *Rechnungslegung und Prüfung der Aktiengesellschaft*, Handkommentar. Vierte Auflage, 1971.

Austin, John. *Lectures on Jurisprudence or the Philosophy of Positive Law.* 1972.

Ballantine, Henry Winthrop. *On Corporations.* Revised edition, 1964.

Barth, Kuno. *Die Entwicklung des deutschen Bilanzrechts.* 1955.

Baumann, Jürgen. *Einführung in die Rechtswissenschaft.* 5 Auflage, 1977.

Baumbach, A., and K. Duden. *Handelsgesetzbuch*, Kurz-Kommentare. 19 Auflage.

Becker, Enno. *Die Reichsabgabenordnung vom 13. Dezember 1919.* 2 Auflage, 1922.

Berger, Klausjürgen. *Kritische Analyse normativer Elemente in der Betriebswirtschaftslehre.* 1979.

Biener, Herbert. "Zur Transformation der 4. EG-Richtlinie." *Die Wirtschaftsprüfung* (1980).

Birkenfeld, Wolfram. *Beweis und Beweiswürdigung in Steuerrecht.* 1973.

References 265

Brönner, Hebert. *Die Bilanz nach Handels- und Steuerrecht.* 8 Auflage, 1971.
Brown, Marlene. "Dramatic Changes: The EEC Fourth Directive." *The Accountant* (1981).
Burhenne, Wolfgang E., and Klaus Perband. *EDV-Recht.*
Buschgen, Hans E. *Bankbetriebslehre.* Wiesbaden, 1972.
Carey, John L. *The Rise of the Accounting Profession.* 1969.
Casey, William J., and Louis H. Rappaport. *SEC Accounting Practice and Procedure.* 3d edition.
Cattien, Hans. *Reichssteuerstrafrecht und Reichssteuerstrafverfahren.* 2 Auflage, 1929.
Christie, George C. *Jurisprudence: Text and Readings on the Philosophy of Law.* St. Paul, Minn.: West Publishing Co., 1973.
Conradi, Joachim. "Datenbankabfrage." In *Handwörterbuch des Steuerrechts und der Steuerwissenschaften.* 2 Auflage, 1981.
Danzer, Jürgen. *Die Steuerumgehung.* 1981.
Dietzen, Nikolaus. *Grundsätze ordnungsmäßiger Bilanzierung für stille Reserven.* 1937.
Dohr, James L. "Materiality—What Does It Mean in Accounting?" *Journal of Accountancy* (1950).
Eckert, Walter Ludwig. *Kompendium Abgabenordnung.* 1980.
Engisch, Karl. *Einführung in das juristische Denken.* 7 Auflage, 1977.
Erhard, Fritz. *Steuerliche Betriebsprüfung.* 4 Auflage, 1980.
Flügel. *Wegweiser.* 1741.
Franzen, Klaus, Brigitte Gast-De Hann, and Erich Samson. *Steuerstrafrecht mit Steuerordnungswidrigkeiten.* 2 Auflage, 1978.
Gastan, Edgar. "Die Praxis der Jahresabschlußpublizität." *Die Wirtschaftsprüfung* (1981).
Gehre, Horst. *Steuerberatungsgesetz Kommentar.* 1981.
Gernert, Dieter. *Einführung in die Datenverarbeitung für Juristen.* 1974.
Godin, Freiherr von, and Hans Wilhelmi. *Aktiegensetz vom 6. September 1965, Kommentar.* 4 Auflage, 1971.
Goessen, Passchier. *Buechhalten fein Kurz zussammengefasset und begriffen nach Art und Weise der Italiener.* 1594.
Gomberg, Leon. *Grundlegung der Verrechnungswissenschaft.* 1908.
Grass, Adolf. *Die Prüfung der steuerberatenden Berufe.* 11 Auflage, 1978.
Gumpel, Henry J., and Carl Boettcher. *Taxation in The Federal Republic of Germany.* Harvard Law School, 1963.
Gutenberg, Erich. *Grundlagen der Betriebswirtschaftslehre.*
Hafner, Ingo, and Horst Junker. *Elektronische Datenverarbeitung in mittleren Unternehmen.* 1978.
Hartley, T. C. *Foundations of European Community Law.* 1981.
Hast, Karl. *Grundsätze ordnungsmäßiger Bilanzierung für Anlagegegenstände.* 1934.
Havermann, Hans. "Vorentwurf eines Transformationsgesetzes zur EG-Richtlinie liegt vor." *Die Wirtschaftsprüfung* (1980).

References

Hegel, G. W. F. *Rechtsphilosophie.* Edition Ilting 2. Stuttgart-Bad Canstatt: Friedrich Frommann Verlag Gunther Holzboog KG, 1974.
———. *Phänomenologie des Geistes,* 1807. 6 Auflage. Verlag von Felix Meiner in Hamburg, 1952.
———. *Grundlinien der Philosophie des Rechts.* Berlin, 1821.
Hein. *Steuerrecht und Handelsrecht.* 1928.
Heisenberg, Werner. *Der Teil und das Ganze.* 4 Auflage, 1972.
Henkel, Heinrich. *Einführung in die Rechtsphilosphie.* 2 Auflage, 1977.
Hübschmann, Hepp, and Spitaler. *Kommentar zur Abgabenordnung und Finanzgerichtsordnung.* 7 Auflage, 1979.
Hüttemann, Ulrich. *Grundsätze ordnungsmäβiger Bilanzierung für Verbindlichkeiten.* 2 Auflage.
Iizuka, Takeshi. "Datenverarbeitungsorganisation, japanische." *Handwörterbuch des Steuerrechts und der Steuerwissenscaften.* 2 Auflage, 1981.
Irwin, Richard D. *Financial Accounting; Basic Concepts.* Third edition, 1977.
Isaac, Alfred. *Die Entwicklung der wissenschaftlichen Betriebswirtschaftslehre.*
Jonas, Heinrich H. *Die EG-Bilanzrichtlinie: Grundlagen und Anwendung in der Praxis.* 1980.
Kant, Immanuel. *Die Metaphysik der Sitten.*
Kehlmann, Gunter. *Steuerstrafrecht.* 3 Auflage, 1982.
Kelsen, Hans. *Allgemeine Staatslehre.* 1925.
———. *Reine Rechtslehre.* 1934.
Klein, Frank, and Gern Orlopp. *Abgabenordnung Kommentar.* 2 Auflage, 1979.
Koch, Karl. "Automation in der Steuerverwaltung." *Handwörterbuch des Steuerrechts und der Steuerwissenschaften.* 2 Auflage, 1981.
Konz, Franz. *Handbuch der Steuerhinterziehung.* 1982.
Kosiol, Erich. *Pagatorische Bilanz.* 1976.
Kottke, Klaus. *Steuerersparung, Steuerumgehung, Steuerhinterziehung.* 2 Auflage, 1962.
Krause, Arnold. *Grundsätze ordnungsmäβiger Bilanierung für Pensionsverpflichtungen.* 1935.
Kresse, Werner. *Die Neue Schule des Bilanzbuchhalters.* Band II. 4 Auflage, 1979.
Kripke, Homer. "The SEC and Corporate Disclosure." *Law and Business.* 1979.
Kruse, Heinrich Wilhelm. *Grundsätze ordnungsmäβiger Buchführung.* 3 Auflage, 1978.
Kühn, Rolf, Heinz Kutter, and Ruth Hormann. *Abgabenordnung, Finanzgerichtsordnung, Nebengesetze.* 12 Auflage, 1977.
Leffson, Ulrich. *Grundsätze ordnungsmäβiger Buchführung.* 4 Auflage, 1976.
———. *Wirtschaftsprüfung.* 1977.
———. "Wirtschaftsprüfung und Universität, Ein Münsteraner Sympo-

sion, Referate und Zusammenfassung der Diskussion. Der Einfluß einer erkennbaren Gefährdung der Unternehmung auf die Aussagen im Prüfungsbericht und Bestätigungsvermerk." *Die Wirschaftsprüfung* (1980).

———. "Zur Generainorm und zum Bestätigungsvermerk des Vorentworfs eines Bilanzrichtliniengesetzes sowie Anmerkungen zu weiteren Vorschriften." *Die Wirtschaftsprüfung* (1980).

Littmann, Eberhard. *Das Einkommensteuerrecht*. 12 Auflage, 1978.

Mautz, R. K. *The Philosophy of Auditing*. American Accounting Association, 1961.

Merz. *Das Recht als soziale Ordnungsmacht*. 1964.

Mittelsteiner, Karl-Heinz, and Horst Gehre. *Steuerberatungsgesetz Handkommentar*. 1975.

Mittelsteiner, Karl-Heinz, and Harald Schaumburg. *Abgabenordnung 1977*. 2 Auflage, 1977.

Müller, Richard. *Buchführung und EDV, Computer und Recht*. Band 5. 1977.

Müller, Welf. "Änderung des GmbH-Gesetzes und andere handelsrechtlicher Vorschriften zum 1. Januar 1981." *Die Wirtschaftsprüfung* (1980).

Müller-Boling, Detler. *Arbeitszufriedenheit bei automatisierter Datenverarbeitung*. 1978.

Nagel, Kurt. *DV AKtuell 1979 Trends, Tabellen, Entscheidungshilfen für Datenverarbeitung und Informatik*. Schwerpunktthema Steuerung und Uberwachung von Rechenzentren, 1979.

Nicklisch, Heinrich. *Die Betriebswirtschaft*. 7 Auflage. Stuttgart, 1932.

Niehus, R. J. "'Materiality' ('Wesentlichkeit')—Ein Grundsatz der Rechnungslegung auch im deutschen Handelsrecht?" *Die Wirtschaftsprüfung* (1981).

Owles, Derrick. "Foreign Affairs—International Harmonization." *The Accountant* (1980).

Palmer, Sir Francis. *Company Law*. Volume 1. 1976.

Paton, George W. *A Textbook of Jurisprudence*. Second edition, 1951.

Peez, Leonhard. *Grundsätze ordnungsmäßiger Datenverarbeitung im Rechnungswesen*. 1975.

Penndorf, B. *Geschichte der Buchhaltung in Deutschland*.

Peter, K. F. *Moderne Rechts- und Steuerberatung mit EDV*. 1973.

Peter, Karl, Kurt Joachim Von Bonrhaupt, and Werner Körner. *Ordnungsmäßigkeit der Buchführung-Anforderungen an Buchführung und Aufzeichnungen*. 7 Auflage, 1978.

Philippson. *Briefe über das kaufmannische Rechnungswesen*. 1813.

Radbruch, Gustav. *Rechtsphilosophie*. 8 Auflage, 1973.

Reblin, Erhard. *Elektronische Datenverarbeitung in der Finanzbuchhaltung*. 2 Auflage, 1971.

Römer. *Reichssteuerstrafrecht und Reichssteuerstrafverfahren von Regierungsrat*. 1927.

Rudolph, Siegbert. *Das DATEV-Buchführungssystem.* 2 Auflage, 1978.
Schmalenbach, Eugen. *Dynamische Bilanz.* 5 Auflage, 1931.
―――. *Grundlagen der Selbstkostenrechnung und Preispolitik.* 3 Auflage. Leipzig, 1926.
Schmidt, Harald. *Buchführung und Steuerbilanz.*
Schopenhauer, Arthur. *Die Welt als Wille und Vorstellung; Parega und Paralipomena.*
Schreiber, Heinrich. *Rechenbuch.* 1518.
Schruff, Lother. *Rechnungslegung und Prüfung der AG und GmbH nach neuem Recht (4. EG-Richtlinie).* 1978.
Sebiger, Heinz. "DATEV." In *Handwörterbuch des Steuerrechts und der Steuerwissenschaften.* 2 Auflage, 1981.
Seckel, Carola. *Die Steuerhinterziehung.* 2 Auflage, 1979.
Seidler, Lee J., and D. R. Carmichael. *Accountants' Handbook.* Volume 1. Sixth edition, 1931.
Selchert, Friedrich W. *Aktienrechtliche Jahresabschlußprüfung.* 1979.
Simons, William B., ed. *The Constitutions of the Communist World.* 1980.
Sombart, Werner. *Der modern Kapitalismus.* 1921.
Spangemacher, Gerd. *Allgemeines Recht.* 5 Auflage, 1978.
Spörlein, Peter. *Der Steuerzahler und das Steuerstrafrecht.* 1979.
Stammler, Rudolf. *Lehrbuch der Rechtsphilosophie.* 3 Auflage, Berlin und Leipzig.
―――. *Die Lehre von dem richtigen Rechte.* 1902.
Streit, Erich. *Grundsätze ordnungsmäßiger Bilanzierung für Rückstellungen.* 1936.
Suhr, Gerhard, and Axel Naumann. *Steuerstrafrecht-Kommentar.* 3 Auflage, 1977.
Tipke, Klaus. *Steuerrecht, Ein systematischer Grundriß.* 6 Auflage, 1978.
Tipke, Klaus, and Heinrich Wilhelm Kruse. *Reichsabgabenordnung, Taschenkommentar.* 1961.
Udell, Gilman G. *Laws Relating to Securities Commission Exchanges and Holding Companies.* 1976.
Vellguth, Hans Karl. *Grundsätze ordnungsmäßiger Bilanzierung für schwebende Geschafte.* 1937.
Vieweg, Rolf. *Buchhaltung mit mechanischen und automatischen Datenverarbeitungsverfahren.* 5 Auflage, 1972.
―――. *Sämtliche Einsatzmöglichkeiten der EDV zur optimalen Unternehmensteuerung.* 1980.
Vinogradoff, Paul Gavrilovich. *Common Sense in Law.* Second edition, 1945.
Welland, Kurt. *Grundsätze ordnungsmäßiger Bilanzierung für Wechsel, Schecks und Akzepte.* 1936.
Wilmowski. *Das preussische Einkommenssteuergesetz vom 24. Juni 1891.* erlautert. 3 Auflage, 1915.
Wittgenstein. *Tractatus logico-philosophicus.* 1922.

References

Wöhe, Günter. *Betriebswirtschaftliche Steuerlehre.* Band I. 5 Auflage, 1978.
Woolsey, S. M. "Objective Base for Making Materiality Decisions." *The Accountant* (1968).
Wysocki, Klaus V. *Grundlagen des betriebswirtschaftlichen Prüfungswesens.* 2 Auflage, 1977.
Wysocki, Klaus V., and Hagest. *Die Praxis des Prüfungswesens.* 1976.

AICPA. *AC Section 1024 Objectives of Financial Accounting and Financial Statements.* 1970.
———. *The CPA Plans for the Future.*
———. *Professional Standards.* 1976.
Beck'sche Kurz-Kommentare, Versicherungsvertragsgesetz. 1980.
Conseil National de la Comptabilité. *Plan Comptable Général 63.*
Deutsches wissenschaftliches Steuerinstitut der Steuerberater und Steuerbevollmächtigten e. V. *AO-Handbuch (AO 1977)/Handbuch der Steuerveranlagungen.* 1979.
Gemeinsame Stellungnahme der Wirtschaftsprüferkammer und des Instituts der Wirtschaftsprüfer zum Vorentwurf eines Bilanzrichtlinie-Gesetzes. Die Wirtschaftsprüfung (1980).
Handelsgesetzbuch, Großkommentar. Berlin: Walter de Gruyter & Co., 1967.
Industrielles Rechnungswesen in programmierter Form. Betriebswirtschaftlicher Verlag Dr. Th. Gabler Wiesbaden.
Institute of Chartered Accountants in England and Wales. *Guide to the Accounting Requirements of the Companies Acts.* 1980.
———. *Recommendations on Accounting Principles.*
Institut der Wirschaftsprüfer in Deutschland. *Wirtschaftsprüfer-Handbuch.* 1973–1977.
Kommission für Buchprüfung der U.E.C. *Die Prüfung des Jahresabschlusses.* 4 Auflage.
Kommission Rechnungswesen—Verband der Hochschullehrer für Betriebswirtschaft e.V. *Stellungnahme zum Vorentwurf eines Bilanzrichtlinie-Gesetzes vom 5. 2. 1980. Die Betriebs-Wirtschaft* (1980).
Report of the Inflation Accounting Committee, Chairman F. E. P. Sandilands, Esq., CBE, Presented to Parliament by the Chancellor of the Exchequer and the Secretary of State for Trade by Command of Her Majesty. *Inflation Accounting.* 1975.
Schmalenbach-Gesellschaft. *Rechnungslegung nach neuem Recht.* 1980.
The Thirteen Principal Upanishads Translated from the Sanskrit. Translated by Robert Ernest Hume. Second revised edition. Oxford University Press, 1981.
Brockhaus Enzyklopädie. 1974.
Encyclopaedia Britannica. 1965.
Gablers Wirtschafts-Lexikon. 10 Auflage, 1979.
Handwörterbuch der Betriebswirtschaft. 1974.
Handwörterbuch der Finanzwirtschaft. 1976.

Handwörterbuch der Wirschaftswissenschaft. Band 2. 1980.
Handwörterbuch des Rechnungswesens. 1970. 2 Auflage, 1981.
Handwörterbuch des Steuerrechts und der Steuerwissenschaft. 1972. 2 Auflage, 1981.
Handwörterbuch zur Deutschen Rechtsgeschichte. Erich Schmidt Verlag, 1971.
International Accounting Lexicon (U.E.C.). 1980.
Lexikon der Wirtschaftsprüfung, Rechnungslegung und Prüfung. von Wolfgang Lück, 1980.
Lexique U.E.C. 1974.

Index

Accounting phrases: "a true and fair view" (England), 144, 210–14, 219; "fair accounting practice" (Japan), 87–91, 96–100; "generally accepted accounting practice," (United States), 91–93, 187
Aida, Yoshio, 79
American Institute of Certified Public Accountants (AICPA), 92, 108, 192, 230
Aoki, Shigeo, 85
Arai, Kiyomitsu, 76
Arai, Masutaro, 61
Association of Certified Public Accountants (Japan), 250
Association of Licensed Tax Practitioners (Germany), 30, 165
Association of University Instructors of Business Administration, 217–18; Commission on Accounting of, 218–20
Auction Law (Japan), 172
Audit trail, 140, 258

Balance sheet, 7, 10–11, 134–37
Ballantine, Henry W., 92
Banba, Kaichiro, 108
Barth, Kuno, 7
Becker, Enno, 10, 16, 42, 105, 116, 152
Berger, Klausjürgen, 21
Bierle, Klaus, 5
Birkenfeld, Wolfram, 113

Boettcher, Carl, 169
Books of account, 8–11, 142
Bossard, Michel, 115
British National Assembly, 186
Brönner, Herbert, 108–11
Brown, Marlene, 222–25
Buddhism, 41
Burhenne, Wolfgang E., 250

Carrel, Alexis, 17, 249
Cashbook, 109–12
CCMC Data Processing Center, 115
Chmielewicz, Klaus, 215, 236
Christe, George C., 26–27
Chu, Saichi, 58
Civil Affairs Bureau of Ministry of Justice (Japan), 96, 250
Civil Law (Germany), 152–53, 157–58, 162, 175
Commercial Code: of France, 100, 114; of Japan, 31, 51–53, 78, 87–91; of 1893 (Japan), 142; of 1897 (Germany), 3–8, 15, 59, 131; of 1900 (Germany), 59
Companies Act: of 1948 (England), 143–44, 180, 212, 219; of 1967, 95; of 1976, 143, 181–87, 244; of 1980, 201
Computer-aided accounting, 119, 139–40, 250–59
Confucius, 41
Conradi, Joachim, 251

271

272 Index

Constitution of Federal Republic of Germany, 173, 176
Constitution of Japan, 173
Corporate Accounting Council. *See* Ministry of Finance
Corporate Accounting Principles: of Japan, 15, 84, 87–91, 93–94; of United Kingdom, 95; of United States, 91–94; principle of "accuracy," 86; principle of "completeness," 5, 99–101, 142, 158; principle of "materiality," 36–46; principle of "timeliness," 29–35, 76–77, 106–8; principle of "truthfulness," 85, 158
Corporate Accounting System Countermeasure Investigation Commission (Japan), 83, 90
Corporation Tax Law: Germany, 15, 31 77, 111; Japan, 176–77, 187
Court of Cessation (Japan), 31

DATEV, 115
Debit ledger, 8
"Declaration of completeness," 240–49
Degrange, Eduard, 9
De la Porte, 9
Deliberative Council for Corporate Accounting. *See* Ministry of Finance
Double-entry bookkeeping, 9, 58, 67, 85

Eckert, Ludwig, 153
Economic Stabilization Board, 90
Eighth International Congress of Public Accountants, 229
Engisch, Karl, 22–24
European Communities (EC), 197–99
External audit, 125, 205–6, 237–39, 242–45

Federal Finance Court (Germany), 6, 16, 30, 34–35, 45, 109, 111–12, 178
Federal Ministry of Justice (Germany), 215–17
Federal Trade Commission Act, 190
Financial Accounting Standards Board. *See* American Institute of Certified Public Accountants
Financial Affairs Court (Germany), 110
Financial System Law (Germany), 242

Flügel, 9
Foreign Laws Research Association of Kobe University, 136
Fugger Company, 9
Fuji Sash Co., 94
Fujitsu, Ltd., 42
Funada, Kyoji, 24
Fundamental Accounting Plan (France), 14
Fundamental Taxation Law (Germany), 10, 15–16, 29, 55–56, 60, 77; Enforcement Regulations of, 33–35

General Commercial Law of 1861 (Germany), 13. *See also* Commercial Code
German National Assembly, 134, 139, 141
Godin, Freiherr von, 38
Grass, Adolf, 32
Guidelines (difference from ordinances), 175–76
Gumpel, Henry, J., 168
Gutenberg, Erich, 216

Hattori, Eizo, 88
Havermann, Hans, 215
Hegel, G. F. W., 40–42
Henkel, Heinrich, 256
Hessian Income Tax Law, 7, 73, 143
Hessian Provincial Government, 7
Hormann, Ruth, 110

Iino, Toshio, 61
Imperial Constitution of Japan, 173
Imperial Tax Code (Germany), 6, 10, 13–14, 42–46, 97, 105–21, 168, 173
Income Tax Law of Germany, 15, 60; of Japan, 176–77, 188
Inoue, Tatsuo, 77
Institute of Certified Public Accountants (Germany), 215
Institute of Chartered Accountants (Germany), 116, 221, 244–45
Institute of Chartered Accountants of England and Wales, 36, 95, 213, 222
International Accounting Standards Committee, 140, 229
International Federation of Accountants, 230

Index **273**

Investment Company and Investment Advisers Act of 1940, 191

Japan Society of Accounting, 143
Japanese National Diet, 186, 202, 206, 223, 240
Jhering, R. V., 100
Jonas, Heinrich H., 214

Kant, Immanuel, 17, 18–19, 22, 25
Kato, Ichiro, 154
Kellenbenz, H., 8, 10
Kelsen, Hans, 24–27, 204
Kimura, Shigeyoshi, 81
Koch, Karl, 251
Kokusai Denshin-Denwa Co., Ltd., 94
Kosiol, Erich, 4, 21, 236
Kresse, Werner, 259
Kripke, Homer, 231
Kruse, Heinrich Wilhelm, 6, 13, 153
Kühn, Rolf, 110
Kuroda, Josui, 137
Kurosawa, Kiyoski, 37, 59, 91
Kusunoki, Masashige, 42
Kutter, Heinz, 110

Leffson, Ulrich, 5, 36, 38, 218, 242–43
Leuchs, Johann Michael, 9
Limited Company Law (Germany), 15
Littmann, Eberhard, 6–7, 30, 69, 117

Medical Practitioners Law (Japan), 162
Meiji era, 144
Mencius, 37
Minemura, Shinkichi, 64
Ministerial Ordinance Regarding Audit Certificates (Japan), 76, 88, 93, 187
Ministry of Finance (Japan), 31–32; Corporate Accounting Council of, 90, 93; Deliberative Council for Corporate Accounting of, 84
Ministry of Justice (Japan), 87
Mittelsteiner, Karl-Heinz, 30, 165

Nakamura, Nobuichiro, 66
National Tax Administration Agency (Japan), 14, 177–78, 206
Nippon Telegraph & Telephone Public Corporation, 94

Numata, Yoshio, 74
Nuremberg Association of Tax Practitioners (Germany), 14

Ohta, Tetsuzo, 61
Ootori, Tsuneo, 88
Organization for Economic Cooperation and Development (OECD), 23, 154, 184, 231–32
Osumi, Kenichiro, 89
Owles, Derrick, 228–32

Pacciolli, Luca, 8
Paton, George W., 21
Pawnshop Business Law (Japan), 162
Peez, Leonhard, 126, 141
Penal Code of Germany, 138, 149–51; of Japan, 32
Perband, Klaus, 250
Plato, 17–18, 25, 130
Principles of positive law, 7, 22–28, 204
Principles of regular accounting. *See* Principles of regular bookkeeping
Principles of regular bookkeeping: concept of, 4–9, 13–28, 51–56, 127; threefold structure of, 4, 86, 136, 144; views of Japanese scholars, 57–86
Prussian General Common Law of 1794, 13, 142
Public Utility Act of 1935, 191

Quarrying Law (Japan), 162

Radbruch, Gustav, 19–20, 26, 38–41

Sakamoto, Yasuichi, 64
Samson, Erich, 123
Samurai. *See* Kusunoki, Masashige
Sato, Koichi, 58
Schmalenbach, Eugen, 11, 42–46, 135
Schmidt, Otto, 109, 116
Schoapp, J. G., 9
Schopenhauer, Arthur, 22, 41
Schreiber, Heinrich, 9
Sebiger, Heinz, 115, 251
Securities Act of 1933, 37, 92, 96, 181, 190–91, 243

274 Index

Securities and Exchange Act of 1934, 89, 92, 181, 190–91, 207
Securities and Exchange Commission, 92, 189–92, 207, 229
Shakespeare, 8
Shimamura, Tsuyoo, 67
Shogun. *See* Tokugawa, Ienari
Shoup, Carl S., 93–94. *See* Shoup Mission
Shoup Mission, 91–94
Single-entry bookkeeping, 9
Small Business Act of 1958, 181
Sombart, Werner, 17
Someya, Kyojiro, 65
Spangemacher, Gerd, 16, 152–53, 157, 165
Spiller, Earl A., Jr., 189–91
Stammler, Rudolf, 18–19
Stock Law (Germany), 15, 37–38, 62, 68, 71, 201, 209–12
Supreme Court of Administrative Litigation (France), 14
Suzuki, Takeo, 203

Tajima, Shiro, 73
Takamatsu, Kazuo, 67
Tanaka, Kotaro, 37, 46, 51–56, 60, 83, 240
Tax Advisors Association of North Baden, 153–54
Tax Advisors Law (Germany), 164–65

Tax evasion, 147–51, 187, 206
Tipke, Klaus, 11, 113, 153
TKC National Federation of Public Accountants, 115
Tokugawa, Ienari, 142

Ueno, Michisuke, 57
Union Européenne des Experts Comptables, Economiques et Financiers (U.E.C), 232–97
Union Law (Germany), 15
United Nations, 231
Upanishad philosophy, 41–42
U.S. Internal Revenue Code, 70, 80, 139, 187

Vinogradoff, Paul G., 20–21

Weimar Constitution, 168
Wilhelmi, Hans, 38
Wysocki, Klaus v., 245–46

Yamamasu, Tadahiro, 67
Yamashita, Katsuji, 58–59
Yokota, Kisaburo, 25

Zen, 57, 61, 63